AF394664

OPEN PEN
ANTHOLOGY: VOLUME TWO

AN OPEN PEN BOOKS PUBLICATION

Edited by Joe Johnston

Cover artwork by Josh Neal

Typeset in Adobe Caslon Pro

First published 14.11.2025

ISBN - 9781838210625

Open Pen Books 25 Crescent Road London, E13 0LU

openpen.uk

OPEN PEN

ANTHOLOGY: VOLUME TWO

EDITED BY JOSEPH JOHNSTON

Contents

Foreword
Sean Preston

For some reason, The Author, that black and white photographed head collapsed into cradling palms, whose name occupies ever-increasing real estate on the front of the books we pick up, and who, in case we forgot, we are reminded of by name every other page within, has maintained a position in society as the cultural vanguard, intellectual provocateur, and even beacon of enlightenment. This is not a little surprising when interrogated a bit. The Author, after all, *reflects*. They are supposed to take the world around us and show it to us in story. They show us what we can already see for ourselves, in a different way. Yet they are celebrated for showing us more.

Recently I gave up meat, which was a much harsher divorce than giving up reading, knowing even that I will probably return to steak one day, maybe even by the time these words are printed. For now I feel like I've eaten enough meat for a lifetime, let alone half of one (God / left ventricle willing), and I had come to feel the same way about The Author. Not necessarily specific people, more the idea of The Author. It hadn't helped that in recent Open Pen projects, I'd brought myself closer to books, fiction and The Author than ever before, such is the nasty habit I have of enmeshing myself with the things I venerate. In removing The Author from my life, books and fiction had gone with them, naturally, and so a great fast on their reflection, incessant opining and intellectual disruption began, replaced by the basic but fast-paced reflection offered by my two young children, whose reveries, whilst often Proustian in length, mainly centre around where poo comes from or where poo goes. I had found the intellectual bullring I was willing to bleed onto. I was sick of The Author, sick of what they had to say.

I rewatched *Sideways* again, in which The Merlot Disparaging Author is accosted in conversation, 'There is so much to know about the world that I think reading a story someone just invented is kind of a waste of time,' and, of course, as funny as I found that, and whilst becoming a full-time philistine is of constant appeal to my tired dadness, I knew I wouldn't ever truly feel that way; that invented stories are a waste of time. Nevertheless, the interest in what The Author had to say was barely perceivable within me, perhaps a predictable end to someone optimistic enough in youth to charter his free short fiction magazine: 'Fiction With Something To Say'.

For no other reason than it is how my bedtimes as a child went, I read to the kids before bed, favouring Hemingwayesque protagonists such as *Grumpy Frog* over pious rhyming slop celebrated with yuletide screen adaptations. In short time, they've grown out of Frog (spoiler: Frog stops being grumpy but, y'know, not altogether), and so I've been able to start reading Tove Jansson's *Moomin* novels to them. I had presented the gateway drug in the TV cartoon series to them on holiday, mitigating their suspicion at starting a book without pictures. This represented change for both me and the children: They were listening to stories without an end before sleep; and I was reading fiction again. I started with 'Moominpappa at Sea', not remembering why, but all the same recalling that it had been my favourite. It began:

> *One afternoon, at the end of August, Moominpappa was walking about in his garden feeling at a loss. He had no idea what to do with himself, because it seemed everything there was to be done had already been done or was being done by somebody else.*

And there it was. There I was. I had become Moominpappa when I'd always fancied I was somewhere between unassuming Snufkin and playfully contemptuous Little My. As the nightly readings proceeded, I found myself smiling, smirking, and warmed by Jansson's reflections through her characters. A master at work, she shows us her world through her characters who manage to be many things at once, to be going through different stages of their lives, to perceive their world and themselves in opposed, divergent modes. Her fiction came to me perfectly, I thought, before seeing that, yes, it had come to me with perfect timing, but not now. Rather when I was a child. Her fiction is dissenting, wry, kind, and reflective, and it shaped or skewed me, my outlook, my reading. She writes with her tongue in her cheek long enough that when she affords us sincerity, it opens her world to us, which is our world, so that we can see it for the first time, in a way we haven't seen it before. The Author is not merely showing us what we've seen before. The Author shows us it anew.

The invented stories of this book, The Open Pen Anthology Vol. Two, hard-won, collated and edited brilliantly by Joe Johnston, are a further much needed reminder to me of that, and hopefully they will be for you, should you need it. There is, always will be, something to be said for fiction, something to revere in The Author, and in fiction with something to say for itself. But I'll be vigilant, reverence shouldn't be without question, you get trapped like that, and need to break loose. Or as Snufkin has it, 'You can't ever be really free if you admire somebody too much, I know.'

The Lapsed Romantic
Joseph Johnston

The literary community is the easiest one to parody. For our modern culture which has largely rejected it at this point, and for writers themselves, the pretensions of literature that make it so mockable count as the biggest mark against it. For something to be parodied there must first be a stereotype. A stereotype points to a cliché, and a cliché is the primary sin in writing. Bad writers are all too readily impressed with themselves and fail to notice their overwrought cliches. It's to be avoided at all costs.

Continuing in this manner, before the literary cliché comes its romantic ideal. I would say this romance is the initial gateway to literature for many young writers, those alienated from their peers and from their own being. These are the people who want to tread deeper so they can discover more. Exactly what this *more* is that literature provides can only be answered by individuals within themselves – an endless discussion, and why it's so hard to monetise.

The romantic ideal is why we're drawn to the label on a wine bottle before we can taste it. This is ok. We have no other recourse really, if we have no one else to speak to on the subject, which most young writers don't. There are many literary caricatures of the Twentieth Century: the hermit poet tending to a private garden, the sawmill worker in a flannel shirt, the journalist in butterfly-rimmed sunglasses observing a doomed youth movement, the dissident with pince-nez and goatee on the frontline, the lousy drunk in a motel room with broken neon flashing in through the window, the grief-stricken sexual awakening of the diarist during a sojourn to Italy, etc. To state the obvious, these images are not the writings themselves.

The idea of being a writer when young is like the idea of drinking in the daytime. It feels like a cultural counterpoint in the beginning, of dropping out for a heightened state of existence. Before long it feels absurd, and rightfully so. We realise that life carries on regardless, and back to reality we are, only now with one step behind the present day. As I've gotten older, I've learnt to appreciate the miracles of holding down a job, of courting friends and maintaining a family. These truths stand upright against the windy myths of literature and remain the immutable pillars of living. I'm often amazed to step outside and see that most people are invested in the world around them, not staging riots or looting their neighbours' houses having murdered the postman. I have this same amazement towards successful authors. The best writers commit themselves to the real-world-ness of their work, the dailiness of sitting behind a desk and getting on with it, 'without hope and without despair' as Isak Dineson described, a quote championed by writers such as Raymond Carver. It's a thankless effort, the same way taking a train back and forth to an office job is thankless. Most office workers commute to their jobs because they want to build a better life for their family. No such luck for a writer, who will never have these sorts of venerable motivations. Writing may even be an obstacle to these ambitions. Even this predicament allows a writer to fall into romantic cliches: the troubled artist who cannot escape the vampiric needs of the ordinary. It's nauseating to behold for anyone on the outside. Writing is a victimless crime and most writers are not heroes either, except for the true outliers like Solzhenitsyn. Dailiness is the maintenance of a tolerable median.

Many writers will notice their pretensions and their overwrought cliches and want to shed themselves of such pantomime costumes in storytelling. Many will perhaps struggle with the frustration of it. Still, a writer will continue because they want to, or feel like they have to – another treacherous state of mind. For good writers, this is where the real work begins, and the writing worth remembering starts to appear. Not long ago I read the lost *Gospel of Thomas*. The second saying goes: 'The one seeking should not cease until he finds. And when he finds, he will be dismayed. And when he is dismayed, he will be astonished.' The saying follows with 'And he will be king over the all.' I don't want to go that far. Literature doesn't make the same grand proclamations as religion, thankfully. Good writing offers more questions through oppositional thinking and the withholding of judgement than it provides answers. This is what gives literature its real diversity.

If not divine, literature is still transcendent, or it aims to be at least. For the writers who trust the process and refuse romantic cliches, keep working and be dismayed. We as readers might become astonished.

The Three Amigos
Wendy Erskine

The plant has a room where, after showering and putting on their suits, the workers can wait for their shift to begin. There's another, similar in size, where they can relax at the end. It opens onto the same locker area. In this second room, they can take off their hairnets, masks and gloves, unzip the first few inches of the suit. There's a kettle in this type of decompression area. Occasionally there's a packet of biscuits. Some pass through without stopping; they go to the lockers and put their suits in the blue bin to be processed for the next day. Their home clothes feel heavy, dirty even, after the sterile lab. They can smell their own houses when they open the lockers. Some people have to pick up kids from a football pitch somewhere, or a music practice. Some put their earrings back in, put on wedding rings, check their phones for likes and messages.

Patrick, at eighteen one of the lowest level workers, tends to stop in the room for a coffee after his shift, to pause going home to his mother. He waves or says bye to those passing through. But then two others begin to join him – first Miriam and then Anna. They also seem in no rush to go anywhere. In the room, there's a line along the wall where the row of plastic chairs has worn away the paint. But Patrick, Miriam and Anna move the seats into a circle in the centre. Someone passing through, sees them, calls them 'the three amigos'.

The name sticks.

The three amigos talk about their shift, the emails they've received from the parent company in China, the mood of the supervisors on a particular day. They talk about their journey to work. They compare the levels of redness at the base of their necks.

The old suits hadn't rubbed people's necks, but the new ones do.

It seems nearly audacious when Anna suggests they go to a café. At the end of the week, they head to the coffee shop in the nearby retail park. And, by the end of the month, they have their own regular table there, the two fake leather sofas either side of it. They begin to diversify into other places: the cinema on occasion, a restaurant now and then. They talk less about work. Sometimes they discuss hypothetical situations, such as would they be prepared to pick up the litter along the railway line from Belfast to Carrickfergus, if, at the end of it they are allowed to spend one evening with the person of their choice, alive or dead? Obviously, if dead, the person would be reanimated for the night.

Miriam comes up with a suggestion. Why don't they go away for a weekend? There's a little house up on the coast that she has seen. It's near enough to the beach to walk, but not far either from the town. Three bedrooms and a big, crazy view. Not too expensive, considering it's the coast. They could get lots of nice food and drink. It wouldn't matter if it rained all the time.

'Why not?' Anna says. 'Sounds good.'

'Depends on the date,' Patrick says.

'Well, you decide the date,' Miriam offers. 'Whatever suits.'

'It's, well, difficult to be away for long.'

'Why?' asks Miriam.

'Just is.'

'Why, what are you up to? What are you up to that you can't go away anywhere?'

'I'm not up to anything. It just doesn't suit to go away for a couple of nights.'

'Why?'

'It just doesn't suit.'

'But why? What's the problem?'

'There's no problem.'

'Well, there obviously is if you can't go away anywhere even for just a night or whatever.'

'Alright, ok, it's my mum. You happy? Gonna shut up and get off my case, Miriam?'

'Why what's wrong with her?'

'Nothing's wrong with her.'

'Well, why the fuck does she need you hanging around then? She could survive a couple of nights without you, surely. I mean, jeez, she's not an old woman. What age is she? About sixty, max. And you can't leave her for a night? I mean fair enough if she was terminally ill.'

'She's not terminally ill.'

'Well then.'

'Well what?'

'Well I don't know,' Miriam says. 'OK, leave it. Your business. End of.'

They end up going to Dublin and back on a day trip.

They have other friends. Miriam sometimes mentions the people she shares a house with. They fight a lot over bills. Anna's close to a couple who run a restaurant. They've two young children and she sometimes babysits for them. Patrick has a friend from school called Glenn. But they never invite any of these others along. They never go to Anna's friends' restaurant. It's through Glenn that the hijack experience comes up. Patrick says that the police are looking for people to take part in a simulation. They need a whole plane full of passengers. It's a training exercise; they do them every so often. Glenn's older brother in the police told them about it. Patrick says it'll probably feel like being in a film. And – even better news – they get paid two hundred quid each for taking part. Each.

'I need a new passport,' Miriam says.

'Fake flight,' Patrick says. 'You don't actually leave the ground.'

'It'll happen early in the morning, four o'clock at the airport. There's an application form they need to fill in. Convictions, health problems and so on.'

'So,' Anna says, 'we just sit and watch? We don't need to do anything other than that? For two hundred quid?'

'Glenn went on one before. It was a police / accident and emergency department exercise. A guy went crazy in a cinema, shooting all around him. They actually got to see about a third of a good film with free popcorn and coke before the guy came in. The people who were injured were all plants. They had fake blood capsules and that kind of thing.'

'Where do they get the hijackers from?' Anna asks.

'Can only imagine they're actors from somewhere,' Patrick says. 'Maybe an MMA fighter looking to make a move into films and getting in a bit of experience.'

'Wonder what they'll wear.'

'Nothing special,' Miriam says. 'North Face. Adidas.'

In the weeks coming up to the hijack, Anna gets some news. She has got funding for the post-grad she wants to do. She is going to be leaving. And then Miriam finds out that she's got a job in the new pharmaceutical plant, opening outside Lisburn.

'But you didn't even say you were applying!' Patrick says.

'Well I didn't think I'd get it. I didn't want to make a fuss over probably nothing.'

It seems to spell the end of the three amigos.

On the day of the hijack, they arrange that Anna will pick them up. She arrives at Miriam's house first. Miriam, when she gets in, asks how Patrick's interview went. 'He didn't text me,' she says. Patrick has applied to the new place where Miriam is heading.

'Don't know if it went too well. There was a problem-solving task and, well, Patrick said he felt the problem was maybe him.'

'Well, sometimes it's hard to judge these things.'

'True. Hard to tell.'

Patrick is waiting outside a neat little house. He has crisps and drinks. He says they might as well make a bit of a night of it. Well, morning. There's non-alcoholic stuff for Anna. He says that they need to go to a church on Templemore Avenue. That's where they've been told to go. 'Try to make your way through a couple of these before we get there,' he says. 'Can't be taking drink into the Child Evangelism Centre or Carmel Pentecostal or whatever the name of the place is.'

'How'd the interview go?' Miriam asks.

'Next question,' he says.

The church hall is dusty. Rows of people sit in front of the stage as though the blue velvet curtains are going to part and a show begin. In the corner there's a big net bag filled with footballs. The three of them sit down behind a man talking about what calibre weapon it's likely that they will have on the plane. He's offering the other two men beside him a history of the Heckler & Koch MP5 and who has used it. He has a small replica of the Heckler & Koch MP5, among others, in the house. Some people have come dressed in vaguely military attire, while others like the four girls in matching short skirts and ankle boots look ready to party. Miriam gets out her make-up bag, opens her compact mirror.

A hush descends when a man gets on the stage. He does a little joke bow. 'Hi folks,' he says. 'Just to let you know what's happening, we're going to be moving from here in about ten minutes' time. That's 0400 hours.

'You will have been allotted a particular seat,' the man says. 'Prior to getting on the bus, you'll get your ticket. That's where you have to sit. Don't be moving around. And could I stress, super crucial you guys don't take any photos during this exercise. Anyone taking photos or filming will be removed from the plane. Like, kicked off. Also, if you haven't returned the personal details forms and bank details, you won't actually be issued with a ticket. Sorry. But yous were told.

'We'll be hoping,' he continues, 'to get yous all back here again by 0700 hours at the latest. But, as I am sure you realise, the nature of the exercise means that we can't be exact.'

The man interested in guns turns round. 'Guys that hit the World Trade, they were pretty precise. Pretty fucking precise. Whereas our lads don't know what time we are returning to a church hall.'

'A bit different,' Anna says.

'Gotta fight fire with fire,' he says, before facing the front again. 'No one looks like a potential hijacker.'

A group of young guys with severe, matching haircuts eat bread rolls that one of the gang produces from a plastic bag.

'Could be women hijackers,' Patrick says.

'Could be,' says Anna. 'Unlikely though.'

'They aren't going to have all of the main guys or girls hanging out here. They'll just blend in when we all get on the plane,' says Miriam. 'That's what I would reckon anyway.'

There's a shout from the back of the hall. 'Time to move. Operation underway. Let's go.'

People form a queue in front of the table to receive their seat numbers. Outside the coach waits for them. Its seats are red plush and reclining. It's quite luxurious. It makes some sorry that they aren't going on a trip further than the airport, less than ten minutes away. If the people look out of the windows, they see a sleepy and dark city. An occasional figure shambles its way along the road, heading home from drinking session or to an early morning shift. Their seat numbers mean that Miriam and Anna are beside each other, whereas Patrick is three rows in front.

The bus doesn't go down the main road to the airport. Instead, it passes through a gate with security guards. Everyone is then told to leave and to walk towards a plane a hundred metres away. It's still dark and the way is by square ground lights and the marshals in reflective jackets, holding torches. It feels almost Christmassy. Air-stewards greet the people as they board the plane.

'Real or fake, what do you think?' asks Miriam, when she and Anna sit down.

'Real maybe? Although I don't think I've ever seen that uniform. Looks like something you'd wear to an interview. Nothing on the side of the plane, did you notice that? No EasyJet or whatever.'

There are no inflight magazines either, although the passengers look in the pockets automatically, expecting them to be there. And even though there's no need, they put their coats and bags in the overhead lockers, same as usual. Seat-belts are fastened even though the plane will never take off. The seat beside Miriam is empty.

'Do you think we should say to Patrick to move back?' she asks Anna.

'Maybe, but that guy earlier seemed to be stressing out about people moving about.'

Anna and Miriam have never been in proximity this close before, side by side, with just the plastic arm between them. Anna can see the couple of spots on the left side of Miriam's chin near her lip. They're covered in concealer just a little too pink. There's the indentation of a crescent-shaped scar. Specks of mascara have gathered in the line beneath each eye. When Miriam talks, her hand keeps going up distractedly to one of the spots, gently touching it. Their arms are touching, both resting on the plastic arm of the seat. No electric zing, just a little warmth. But neither moves an arm away.

Anna looked out of the window. It is starting to get light, the sky streaked pink and yellow. Driving in formation on the tarmac are four dark blue vans. They all turn now at the same angle. On the other side of the plane, soldiers taking position on the roof of the airport.

'Something's happening out there,' she says.

Miriam peers out too.

'Look at them,' she says.

A line of men crouch low as they run across the tarmac, carrying guns.

'Getting ready for a hijack that's not happened yet.'

'All going to kick off soon.'

'Yeah.'

'You think this might actually be frightening?' Miriam asks.

'Nope.'

A gun fires. It comes flat and unimpressive from the front of the plane.

Then another two shots, along with a shout.

Silence.

A further shot, like a cap-gun, amateurish.

And then from the front of the plane come words, shapes of words, guttural, followed by high pitched.

'What's that?' Miriam says. 'French?'

'Dunno. Could be. Shush.'

Out of the window, they see further manoeuvres. Fire engines have arrived, and a couple of ambulances. A cluster of guys stood in riot gear. The sun is rising.

A man is coming down the aisle. His hair's shaved close and he wears chinos and a leather jacket. He walks the full length of the plane, holding a hand-gun in the air.

In a heavily accented voice, he says they need to do exactly what he says. 'I'm in charge now,' he says.

'Think the line is, I'm the captain now,' Miriam whispers. 'Look at me. I'm the captain now.'

Another man comes, one who ambles down the aisle, wearing a black tracksuit of a shiny material. He too has a handgun but it hangs casually by his side. He stares at the passengers in a slow, insolent way. Most look away or out of the window, but a couple return his gaze. One of the young guys who had been eating a roll in the church hall looks back, unblinking. Have a go mate. Come on. It's almost sexual. But then the hijacker, with a quick movement, grabs by the scruff of the neck another passenger, an older guy with a baseball cap. He pulls him to his feet, pushes him in front and sticks the gun in his back. 'Move,' he shouts and the guy starts walking down the aisle, his hands in the air. From behind where Anna and Miriam sit, another man rises to his feet. He moves deliberately, bulky in a black body warmer, oh no, suicide jacket.

Outside Miriam can see that the vans are still in the same position. The soldiers on the ground are poised, waiting for action. She notices Anna's lips and how dry they are. There's a bit of white skin that she could take between her thumb and ring finger and gently pull away. That's painful though. The dead is still attached to the living, and that is pink and tender and exposed when the skin is pulled away. It sometimes bleeds. Miriam considers the little tin of Vaseline in her bag, thinks of having it on her fingertip, then running it over those lips, the top and the bottom, running it over again.

More shouting.

'Right pain not being able to see what's happening,' Anna whispers. 'I'd love to stand up.'

'Shut up, somebody's coming down again. Which one is it?'

'Leather jacket again.'

'OK, shush, he's coming.'

The man in the leather jacket is shaking his head in mock disbelief and looking at the passengers, his gun, then back to the passengers. 'You guys,' he says, his voice high and wheedling, although with noticeably less of a foreign accent than before. 'You aren't doing what I told you to do. Why, why, aren't you doing what I told you to do? You want bad things to happen? Because lemme tell you, bad things will happen.'

'Think he's milking it a bit,' Miriam whispers. 'He's loving the attention.'

Anna nods. The man in the leather jacket is now near.

'You got to listen fucking carefully. You are to fucking do what we say. Any fucking around and –'

'Listen to the language of him,' says a woman in the back row to the person beside her. 'I didn't think there was going to be all of this cursing and swearing. Don't think I would have come along if I knew there was going to be all this cursing and swearing.'

'Think the clue was in "hijack" love,' comes a low voice. 'It ain't a Sunday school excursion.'

The hijacker catches this. 'What did you say? You hear me, what did you say? You people think this is a joke. This is not a joke.'

And then he fires. No bullet comes, just a little smoke, an acrid smell and shattering, reverberating noise. A few of the passengers, one or two, might have heard such a sound before, long ago, might feel now something layered beneath the years stir.

From the front of the plane comes shouting and although it's difficult to see or know for sure, more people seem to have appeared. Is that metallic banging coming from outside the plane? Anna and Miriam can see the soldiers positioned, their weapons trained on the plane, the vans in formation. Yes definitely, more people now seem to be on board. The hijacker in the shiny black tracksuit no longer ambles. He strides down the aisle and they turn to see him spring at a woman in the back row, an older woman with grey hair neatly set. He pulls her from her seat, his arm around her neck. The other holds the gun to her head. Anna and Miriam see her blouse come loose from the waistband of her skirt, revealing a soft roll of white skin. And now a soldier has appeared and he is pointing his weapon at the hijacker, who holds the woman in front of him. 'Drop the gun and get down on the floor,' the soldier shouts.

But still he holds it to the woman's head. She's whimpering in fear. He tightens his grip. There are small, choking noises.

'Drop the gun and get down on the floor.'

He pushes the gun into her temple.

Someone is standing up.

It's Patrick.

'What the fuck you doing?' the hijacker whispers. His accent sounds different. So Belfast. 'Sit down!' He tightens his grip around the woman's neck once more and jerks her backwards quickly, roughly.

'Leave her alone,' Patrick says. 'Let her sit down.'

Anna stares at Miriam. 'What?'

'Mate, will you please mind your own business,' the terrorist says. 'Just sit the fuck down, right now. Seriously.'

'I said, leave her alone. Get off her.'

He pushes past the other two passengers in his row and stands staring at the woman, older than his mother.

The soldier at the other end looks quizzical. Is this part of the operation? He points his gun briefly at Patrick, then returns to the guy in the shiny tracksuit, who releases his grip a little on the woman. For a second, she isn't frightened but instead angry and impatient. Patrick doesn't see this. He doesn't hear her mutter, 'For fuck's sake.'

Patrick's fists had never been any good against Bernard. His mother's boyfriend Bernard.

The hijacker hesitates, and then once more tightens his hold around her neck, places the gun at her temple. A couple of buttons have come undone on her blouse, exposing her bra. Her face is turning red.

'Leave her alone,' Patrick says. 'Please get off her. Let her go,' he says.

Another, older, soldier comes down the aisle and signals to the hijacker who lets go of the woman. She does up her buttons in her blouse and tucks it into her skirt. Her face remains red as she glares at Patrick.

'OK,' the soldier says when he is close to the hijacker. 'Can't legislate for this kind of thing.'

He very quickly points his finger at his head and wiggles it, to signify, screwy guy. He shouts to Patrick who stands, silent, in front of the woman. 'Alright,' he says, 'let's get you off and let's get you off now.'

'Oh, so he's not part of it,' the woman who had commented on the language says. 'I thought he was part of the whole thing. Didn't you?'

'No,' says the man beside her.

Miriam and Anna get to their feet.

'Excuse me,' Miriam says to the hijacker. 'That's our friend that the guy is taking off the plane there, so I think we better go too.'

'Yeah, sorry,' Anna says.

They make their way down the aisle, passengers gawping, towards a cluster standing at the open door. The suicide bomber is there between the two air stewards, and the hijacker with the leather jacket exchanges an exasperated look with the captain. As they come down the steps, the soldiers in position lower their guns. The people in the fire engines and vans and ambulances stare through their windscreens. Anna mouths, 'Sorry.' From the steps they can see Patrick, with someone on either side of him, moving across the runway towards the terminal. A woman in a reflective jacket approaches them. 'Alright,' she says. 'Over there. Quickly please.'

The woman opens the terminal door and there, by the seats, is Patrick with a policeman.

They look like arrivals, three friends arriving home from a holiday abroad, white-faced through partying. They follow the carpet, with its stains and old pieces of chewing gum. They walk through passport control and into the bright white light of the empty airport concourse. Anna gets three drinks from the self-service machine and the amigos sit around a table in the café that isn't due to open for another couple of hours.

'Jeez Patrick, what in the name of god did you think you were doing?' Miriam says.

'Well, no need to go over it now,' Anna says quickly, her hand on his arm. 'Did you see how pink that sky was?'

We All Have Our Uses
B.B. Fitton

Sid arrived home from a business trip to find his wife with her feet propped up on another man.

Alice's footstool was on all fours, emitting a soupy, soapy smell. His hair hung down in strands, a mousey valance obscuring his face.

'Alice, what the?'

'I didn't hear you come in. I must've dozed off.' She glanced at her watch. 'Did you get delayed at Heathrow? Or did Jeremy get you too boozy to fly again?'

'Alice, what's this man doing here?'

'I needed to put my feet up. He seemed happy to oblige.'

'But who the Hell is he?'

Alice stretched her legs and wriggled her toes. 'Don't shout. He's not Christian Grey. He's just a homeless man.'

'And you're... using him as a pouffe?'

'A pouffe, Sidney? Really! No, I'm certainly not.'

'What *are* you doing then?'

'He is temporarily serving as a footrest until his soup is fully digested. You should never lie down after eating. It causes heartburn.'

Sid shook his head. 'I need an aspirin.'

'You shouldn't drink on aeroplanes,' Alice called to her retreating husband. 'It dries you out.'

Sid downed two glasses of water along with four pills. Had he not taken enough malaria tablets? Had he drunk too much on the flight? He slapped his face three times and headed to the bedroom.

'Why is your face all red?' The floral duvet was tucked under Alice's chin. At the end of the bed, the homeless man was curled on the counterpane. Her feet were wedged against his belly, cocooned by his elbows and knees. 'Ah, we're nice and toasty, aren't we, Harry?' She looked at Sid. 'Well, don't stand there staring. Get in. He's much warmer than you'd think.'

Sid blinked. 'Are you using him as a foot-warmer?'

'It's a two-way street, dear. It's freezing outside.'

'I'm not sure I like the idea of a strange man in our bed.'

Harry looked at Sid with wide, shivering eyes.

'He's *on* our bed, not *in* it,' Alice said. 'And he's hardly a stranger. We've passed him dozens of times under the railway bridge.'

'But still...' Sid slid into bed.

'You're never here for me to warm my feet on. You can't object to me improvising. I did ask you for an electric blanket at Christmas, but that must have slipped your mind.'

'But –'

'He's clean, Sidney, if that's what you're worried about. I got Dot to give him a good scrubbing.'

'Who's Dot?'

'Our new cleaner. So, Dot... Well, I can't remember her name – how embarrassing! – but I've nicknamed her Dot... Anyway, she gave him a thorough scouring while she was cleaning the rest of the furniture. She washed all the curtains and the bedsheets, too.' Alice peeked at Sid from under her eyelashes. 'You *know* there's nothing I like more than clean bedsheets.'

'Er... not with him there.'

'But you've been gone for three weeks! He doesn't mind, do you, Harry? I'm sure you've seen all sorts of things in your time. Two old goats fucking isn't going to hurt you, is it? Didn't you say your mother brought you up in a brothel?'

'Really, Alice, I don't think I can.'

'God, Sidney, you're so selfish. You never attend to my needs.' Alice turned over with a loud, protracted sigh, pulling the duvet off Sid.

Sid woke in the night feeling feverish. He crept out of bed and headed to the ensuite.

'Argh!'

Alice switched the bedside lamp on and rubbed her eyes. 'What are you doing?'

'I tripped over something.'

A pale young man lay in the bathroom doorway, a syringe sticking out of his neck. His arms were pocked pink and streaked with scars. A bloody droplet had crept over his shoulder and onto the carpet.

'Alice?'

Harry blinked sleepily.

'Keep your voice down,' Alice hissed, stroking Harry's belly with her big toe. 'Don't make such a fuss. Dot will clean up the stain.'

'What?'

'You know how chilly it gets in here with that bloody bathroom window. You did say you'd fix the crack. I had to do something. Sleeping in a draught provokes my migraines.'

'Do you think he minds being a doorstop?'

'Draught excluder. Just look at him, Sid. He's as happy as a pig in shit.'

The man's eyes were closed, a gurning grin on his gaunt face.

'Alice, this isn't right. He's a drug addict.'

'Where's your community spirit? He'd be getting up to the same thing in some alleyway anyway. Here he's safe and warm.'

Sid leaned over the man and dropped his sodden pyjama shirt into the linen basket. 'You and I have to talk tomorrow, Alice.'

'Turn the light off, Sid. Stop waking everyone up.'

Sid awoke to find the bed empty, bar Harry, who looked at him blankly from the bottom of the duvet. Raised voices came from the living room. Alice would be watching her usual Sunday soap opera marathon.

Sid called 'Hello' to the heroin addict, who glowed green in the late morning light. After no response other than the briefest flutter of an eyelid, Sid stepped over him into the bathroom. The man's body was blocking the door from closing. Sid grabbed his dressing gown and took a piss awkwardly, holding the fabric out to shield himself. His bladder still felt heavy, but he didn't want to push it and risk farting in front of the men. He washed his hands, nodded at Harry, and traipsed downstairs feeling seasick.

In the kitchen, a frosty-faced woman was violently scrubbing the toaster with a toothbrush.

'Er, do you mind if I use the kettle?'

She shrugged at him and returned to the toaster, poking the bristles into the grill. Sid made himself a coffee. As he lifted the cup, a soapy cloth slid under it, wiping away a speckle of spilt grounds.

'Good, good. Very thorough,' Sid said and edged out of the door.

Alice held a handkerchief to her throat, letting luxurious tears spill onto it as they rolled off the tip of her nose. 'Oh Sid, I think Danny wants to leave her...'

Sid rolled his eyes. 'I don't know why you watch this bloody stuff, since it –' He tried to turn the television off, but found his finger not touching the switch, but poking somebody's eyeball.

'Watchit,' a woman snapped. 'I got enough problems without some dickhead nearly blinding me.'

A yellowy woman was slouched against the wall where the widescreen had been. A swollen jawed man sat next to her, rocking. The woman slugged from a Hennessey bottle, the jagged edge of a tooth clinking against the glass. She wiped her lips with her fist.

'Gimme that, Delilah.' The man snatched the bottle. 'Stop running your mouth. I'm fed up of it. You always gotta keep on running your mouth.'

Delilah launched into a slurry song: 'Keep on running, keep on hi-i-i-i-ding. One fine day I'm gonna be the one, to make you undershtan"

'I'm gooooonna be your man,' the man joined in. He grabbed Delilah roughly and pressed her face to his in a slurpy kiss, which only half of her mouth joined in with.

'Aw, they're making up,' Alice dabbed her hanky to her eyes. 'Maybe Danny won't leave her after all.'

'Leave my Delilah? No, ssshe's all I got. We're gonna get married, aren't we shnowball? And have a baby, and we'll call it... Well that depends if it's a boy or a girl.'

'A girl.' Delilah's eyes welled and lit up simultaneously. 'I'd buy her My Little Ponies and –'

'Do they still do My Little Pony?' asked Danny.

'We'd shpoil her, wouldn't we? A little housshe and a Little My Pony. And we'd all be together.'

'Like The Young Ones.'

'Don't be ridiculoush. You're thinking of something else. Hey, do you remember Tamago hees?'

'Tama-who?'

'You had to feed them and pet them or they'd die or go depressed.'

'Tama-what?'

'They were computer monshters, Japanese.'

'Alice!'

'There's no need to panic. No theft has occurred. I *gave* them the Hennessey. Good brandy's much cleaner for their intestines than that syrupy brew they were drinking. Their breath stank as if rats had shat in their stomachs.'

'But, what are they doing here?'

'It's obvious, isn't it? They're having a drink and, y'know, doing what they do.'

'And you're watching.'

'They were doing it anyway. Half the neighbourhood was watching. She punched him in the face, then he was tearing her hair out. It was awful. I approached them and said "Look, I represent a charity. I can help you. You needn't be doing this on the street."'

'You're on the board of T.A.C.K.Y. That's got nothing to do with... alcoholics.' He whispered the word apologetically and nodded to the couple, who were flicking the bottle cap at each other and hiccupping.

'The Amersham Consortium for Kindness to Youths deals with substance misuse all the time. At the last meeting, one of the trustees was weeping. She'd found a baby in a skip sucking on a bottle of beer. That could have been *their* baby. But they're safe and sound here. Anyway, you always turn my soaps off to watch the sport. It's most inconsiderate.'

'Look, Alice, can we go somewhere private?'

'We're at home.'

'But there's other people everywhere.'

'We could go to the garage. No, wait a minute. Skinny's buffing the cars.'

'Dare I ask?'

'He's ever so quick, Sid, gets everything shiny. You should see the silverware. The heroin guy. He won't tell me his name. For legal reasons, I think. He introduced us. He's on an amphetamine trip, has been for years. Apparently, you can get stuck on them.'

'It's called psychosis.'

'You're a timeshare salesman, dear, not a psychiatrist. If you bothered cleaning those beloved bangers of yours, I wouldn't have had to hire him. Anyway, I guess we could go to the shed.'

'No gypsy gardeners around?'

'Don't be silly. We got decking put in months ago. You probably don't remember. The landscapers came when you were playing ping-pong in Barbados with Jeremy.'

Alice stood in the shed doorway, hands on hips, while Sid crouched beneath the shears and shovels that hung from the ceiling.

'This must be the most cramped conference you've ever had, dear,' Alice said. 'I imagine your meetings are usually on breezy beaches, atop majestic mountains, in Patchouli-soaked massage parlours, flying through the sky, strapped to Jeremy while you both drink champagne. Not like the charity meetings, where we drink weak tea and there's barely half a biscuit to go round.'

'Why' – Sid breathed deeply and steadied himself against a pile of paint pots – 'is our home suddenly full of rejects doing your bidding?'

'They're people, Sidney. Don't compare them to poorly-stitched handbags.'

'You're missing my point. You're exploiting them.'

'How? Harry has free rent, food, and warmth from my feet. Dot lives for her job. Without it, she'd be alone, stuck on benefits, surviving on beans, because of her diagnosis.'

'What diagnosis?'

'OCD. Honestly, doesn't the government see that these people have their uses? Why label them and send them to live in a shoebox, where they scrub at the same depressing square foot of lino again and again? It's better for Dot to have a whole house to clean. It's much more engaging for her.'

'Has she told you that?'

'She hasn't left, has she?'

'And the others?'

'Danny and Delilah have a free bar, and –'

'Don't tell me you're buying anyone drugs.'

'I can see how you don't understand, dear. I don't expect you can.'

'You're taking liberties.'

'It's liberation. They have a purpose now. Do you think any one of them would prefer their old life?'

Sid's brain squirmed, desperately trying to find the neural capacity to form a meaningful argument. Of course, he couldn't agree with what his wife was doing, but he couldn't explain why not. Many words came to mind, but none he could slide past his wife. 'It's indecent,' was all he managed.

Alice raised an eyebrow. 'How can it be indecent to make arrangements that suit both parties equally? I wonder if your own selfishness makes it hard to grasp that deals aren't always one-sided. O-o-o-h,' she laughed. 'You're not jealous are you? That I'm getting my needs met elsewhere.'

'How ridiculous. Hang on Alice, are you... using these people to get back at me?'

'How dare you, Sid —'

A groan came from the garden. The heroin addict was stumbling towards the shed. 'I'm sick, man. You gotta call my dealer. I'll die if —' He vomited up the final sentence, luminous slime dripping from his lower lip.

'Sidney, fetch his phone from the bedroom. Call Jake and ask for a balloon. He knows the address.' Alice put her arm around the grey-faced man, who was writhing on the floor like a cut worm. 'There, there. It'll be alright.'

Sid stayed in the shed watching the strangely tender way Alice caressed the sick man's neck.

'Come on! Haven't you a heart? Make the call.'

Sid couldn't move.

'Oh, you're useless! I'll call him myself.' Alice marched across the decking, the addict crawling after her.

The afternoon sun had sunk low, covering the garden in a tarry bleakness. Sid wasn't sure whether he didn't want to move or couldn't.

At dusk, Alice came down to the shed where Sid was still stuck to the spot. 'The heroin guy needs more money,' she said. 'He was very polite about it, but said he could make more on the streets. I told him, I have a set allowance and you wouldn't increase it.'

'Jeremy —'

'Yes, yes, I know it's down to him. I'm not asking you to suck his balls on my behalf. But, we can't stay here. We're moving out.'

'We?'

'Yes, I was quite surprised myself. But they don't seem to mind an old goat like me tagging along.'

'But, where will you go?'

'Harry knows some places. Maybe the railway bridge.'

In a daze, Sid followed Alice back into the house. He watched as she packed a small suitcase, the vagabonds helping, Dot carefully folding her clothes.

'Oh Sid,' she said in the doorway, as Harry helped her on with her coat. 'Please see a doctor. You don't look very well.'

Sid tried calling Alice's mobile. Sometimes the phone would cut off immediately; sometimes it would ring for a while before redirecting him to Alice's chirpy digital greeting. He didn't leave a message, never sure what to say.

Sid called Jeremy, who laughed at his predicament. 'Bloody hell. What a story. You could sell the rights to Warner. Well, life goes on.'

When Sid passed under the railway bridge, he looked for Alice. He thought he'd easily pick her out. Her blunt, breezy voice still rang in his ears every night. But he never saw her. She could have been any one of the dozens; desperate, begging, beckoning. But if she was, she never beckoned to him.

The Sky Salesman
by B. B. Fitton

Once upon a time, I longed to own a piece of the sky. I would stare out of the window for hours, my eyes reflecting the endless blue. When the sky raged grey, slashing with knives of light, I tenderly traced the rumbling clouds with my fingers as they bloomed in the dark.

As my mother passed the playroom door, she tutted. Why did I sit by the window for hours, rather than playing with dolls like a normal little girl? My heart went into hiding as she snapped the curtains shut.

But our priest told me that God listens. And didn't He have some say over the sky? So, I sometimes said, as if to myself, 'I'd give anything to play up there among the clouds.' I hoped He would catch on.

When Spring cartwheeled into town, feet gleefully bruising the air, it brought a funfair to the local park. Dad promised we'd go on Sunday after church.

The sky stretched like a wide, blue tongue that afternoon, coating the Earth with a cool, damp cloak of saliva. Wandering between the rides, I inhaled the mess of music, horns and buzzing.

Beside the spin and flash of the waltzers, my heart dizzily followed the beat of the pulsing, sweaty air. Tangles of teenagers whirled by, bodies bumping together, arms and legs thrashing, hair flipping in the twist. It reminded me of tornado days, when the sky swirled and puffed out a purple stack of smoke. I clambered onto the gangway, the convulsing coloured lights riding up my winter-white legs.

A barker chewing on a cigarette barred my way. 'Too young,' he said. His breath smelled like burnt cherry biscuits.

Deflated, I played the usual games: throwing hoops, hooking ducks. I won a goldfish and a bright red balloon, which dad tied to my wrist. I waved to the fish, which dangled from mum's hand in a bubble of water. It weakly flipped its fin and gawped at me with withered eyes. I imagined it would be happier swimming among the clouds. As dad murdered metal cowboys with tinny pellets and mum jingled her purse for more coins, I slipped behind the shooting range and prayed.

A man overheard my sighed-out wishes meant for God. 'Look up, little one,' he winked. 'The sky is on sale. Choose any piece you like.' He spread a long arm across the cerulean display and wriggled his fingers, presenting his wares.

I peered up between the striped marquees at the beautiful blue sky threaded with candyfloss clouds. I had never dreamed I would meet a sky salesman. 'Really? I can have it? Any bit at all?'

The salesman palmed my hand and trotted me forward. 'Yes, any bit. But consider the entire range before we close the deal.' A little laugh rattled round his final syllables. My balloon jigged up and down, dancing to the tune of his tongue.

I thought for a moment. 'If a cloud floats into my patch of sky, is it mine?'

'Yes, you can capture it if it's on your turf. Those are the rules.'

'Can I choose whether to make it rain?'

'Of course. You can make it as wet as you like.' The man cackled and thrust his hand into the air, wiggling his fingers, mimicking rainfall. He sprinkled his raindrop fingers through my fringe. His fingernails scratched and tickled as they dripped down my nose and over my lips.

I giggled at the tiny storm, then looked back to the sky. 'And will the sky be mine forever?' I paused, solemnly. 'Even when I die?'

'Forever.'

My balloon bobbed happily as I pumped my fist in the air.

The sky was a wonder to me. It played at dressing-up, disguising itself delightfully. Sometimes it was as white and fluffy as a lamb. Or it was warm and streaked with pink – a slab of sizzling bacon. Some nights, it glowed orange – a sassy stripe of fire. It smelled different every season: like grass, like tinsel, like smoke.

Its arms were tender and tireless, holding the blazing sun all day and rocking the moon at night. It never aged, ached, or seemed bored of its duty. I knew if I owned a patch of sky, when I died, I would be reborn as a star, cocooned by its limitless arms.

Overjoyed that a bit of the sky would soon be mine, I forgot my dad and his long, vanilla coat, good for snuggling into. I forgot my mum and her clean, soapy smell. I forgot my promise not to wander away into the fields beyond the fairground. I forgot everything but the sacred sky.

As we crossed the grass, the salesman chattered in colours, music and shapes. I skipped along, imagining my feet already bouncing on the clouds.

When we stopped, we were far from the fair, at the entrance to the woods. 'Have you decided, little one?'

'That bit.'

I pointed to a piece of sky so high, bright and blue that the salesman gasped. 'That bit? Well, I think you've chosen just about the best bit there is. That's a prime piece of sky and no mistake.'

I beamed at him and he smiled back. He had a symmetrical, yellow-toothed grin and pink, clownish lips.

My mouth suddenly drooped. A horrible thought had occurred to me. 'Oh, but I haven't any money.'

The man stopped smiling too. His eyes narrowed and his plump mouth shrivelled into a thin twist. His palm felt rough and hot as it tightened around my hand. 'No money? You've led me all across the field and you haven't any money?'

I looked back at the fairground, now only a glowing red light in the distance. The drop tower, which stood erect and bright above it all, discharged a sudden chorus of faraway screams as the cage of riders fell.

I turned back to the man, whose face seemed to pinch and hollow. My throat was too tight to even squeeze out a 'sorry'. I swallowed a few times. 'M-maybe we could find my mum. Or maybe you'd swap a bit of sky for my balloon? It's r-really big and such a pretty shade.'

'What do I want with a balloon? There are dozens of them over at that fair. If I wanted one, I could take one, any colour or size I liked. But I don't want a balloon.' He grabbed a stick from the ground and poked my precious prize. It banged, leaving red flakes in the grass.

My lips started to tremble.

'Don't cry,' the man said. 'You're a big girl, aren't you? How old are you?'

'I'm six-and-a-half,' I sobbed.

'Okay, tell you what. How about we play a little game? If you win, I'll give you your piece of sky for nothing.'

'Really?' I rubbed my eyes. 'What if I lose?'

'Well, we'll see. What have you got to lose?'

I shrugged, looking at the rubbery remains of my balloon.

'Isn't it kind of me to give you a chance after you've wasted my time like this?' His face was so close to mine that his eyes were one wolfish shadow.

'Ohhyes,' I agreed.

'Okay, kneel down and close your eyes.'

He shoved me down as he let go of my hand. Startled, I got onto my knees and shut my eyes. The position was so familiar from church that I automatically steepled my fingers.

I was transported to the smooth, golden plumes of the altar, soothed by the cinnamon incense, the dusty, velvet cushions nestling at my knees. The quiet chatter of prayers echoed around me as I bowed lower to offer my own.

Every Sunday, I pressed my palms together and asked God for three things: to keep me safe, to make me a grown-up, and to gift me a piece of the sky.

Now I prayed harder than ever. I squinched my eyes so tightly that white shadows crossed my eyelids.

'Okay, this is the game. I'm going to put something in your hand. I want you to give it a rub and try to guess what it is. If you guess right, you win. Are you ready?'

I nodded.

'Put your hand out.'

His voice was stern, like my teacher's when he caught me sneaking my pet rabbit into school. Those were his exact words after he'd snatched her away. He'd spanked my hands with a ruler and told me he'd be calling my parents. I ached for my poor bunny in the dark staffroom locker. My stinging fingers couldn't write in class. I spent the whole day feeling sickly, knowing my real punishment was yet to come. As the familiar dread oozed into my stomach, I felt dizzy, like my head was floating up away from my body. In a daze, I had a strange vision that I was sitting up on a cloud in my favoured swathe of sky looking down at myself in the field, blue and red lights flashing around me, closing in.

A stabbing pain in my chest brought me back to the salesman and his game. I choked on a cry as the sharpness hit me.

'Come on, girl. Stop messing about.' The salesman's tone had stiffened up. 'Concentrate on the game.'

I imagined I was a wooden soldier and tensed my back, standing to attention as best I could while on my knees. Still dizzy, I put one hand out, pressing the other to the ground to steady myself. My fingers felt numb in the damp mud. My mother had never forgiven me for covering my church dress in grass stains when I played in the graveyard last summer. I swept my dress from under my knees, hoping it hadn't been marked.

'Good girl.' His voice was quavery, discordant, like the dying tinkle of a music box.

As I opened up my palm, I felt its cool, pure emptiness. I tried to hold my hand still, but my fingers twitched, unsure what awaited them.

Something warm landed on my skin.

I inhaled sharply, but didn't dare pull my hand away. The object was smooth, but squidgy. It was moist and throbbed in my cupped palm, like something alive.

'Have a good feel of it,' whispered the man. 'See what you think it is.'

I rubbed the thing, which felt both firm and fleshy. It smelled like the butcher's shop. I tried not to breathe in the stale, meaty odour.

As my fingers explored the object, it seemed to change its size and shape. I was sure I'd never felt such a thing before in my life. My hand hesitated as I tried to think what it could possibly be.

'Don't stop,' the salesman said. 'Keep playing. Your dream is at stake.'

So, I fingered the thing desperately, trying to find a clue. I faintly hoped a genie might pop out and deliver me my three wishes rather than having to carry on.

Instead, a gush of warm liquid hit my arm.

I shuddered, fighting to keep my arm straight. The fluid slowed to a weak, gluey trickle. Then the object stopped throbbing and shrivelled until it lay flaccid and dead across my fingers, like my balloon in the grass below.

I stayed perfectly still. Was the game over? Had I done something wrong?

The object in my hand was so still and small, I could barely feel it any longer. The liquid on my arm was starting to cool. Everything was silent.

'Are you still there?' I whispered.

There was no reply.

I opened my eyes.

The sky salesman was gone.

I stared at my outstretched hand.

In the middle of my palm was a tiny, withered heart, all the blood drained away. My arm was splashed with scarlet liquid, which was starting to dry and darken. I looked down at my dress, which was smeared with blood and scratched with green along the hem. My eyes stung and ached, as if they had grown too big for my face.

The noise of the fairground was wailing in the distance. The drop tower was lost in the gathering darkness, but the whoosh of the cage falling and the screaming continued. The blot of red light was now pulsing, and blinking blue between the red. It was coming towards me.

I twisted around. Another set of lights, which howled and screamed as well. From a different direction, yet more were closing in. The fairground had split and scattered around me, chasing me from all sides. I longed for my dad's cosy, vanilla coat and the warm, soapy smell of my mother. It was starting to snow.

I threw the shrivelled heart to the ground. Icy white flakes quickly began to bury it.

I looked up at the sky. How long had I been gone? The sun had vanished, but there was no moon, nor a single star. The sky was bare and bleak, almost colourless, like a milk stain on a glass.

I wrapped my arms around myself, but there was nothing to hold onto. I couldn't even feel the grass beneath my knees. Everything was numb. Everything was gone. There was nothing left except the sky, which continued tossing spiky droplets down.

Then the sky rumbled as if the clouds were stampeding from above.

The quaking sky cracked and dropped.

It smashed itself into a million white crystals, which fell upon each other, until the whole world was only sky.

And the world was stained so white that it looked completely black.

Cantaloupes
Esther Cann

He has a board meeting but I call him anyway, while peeling the butternut squash. He answers just as I negotiate its treacherous bulb.

'You've got thirty seconds,' he says.

The peeler slips and nicks my thumb. I suck it. 'You never look at my breasts anymore.'

'I do!'

'You don't.' I slice the bottom off the squash. 'In the past you always perved on them, whenever I got undressed or came out of the shower.'

'Clare, I'm at work.'

'You won't even say it,' I snarl. 'Tits! Boobs! BREASTS!' I saw away at the trunk. It is resistant.

'Look Clare, you've got great… Mike, yep, the end-of-years. One sec.'

'So you're going now?' I bang the knife down on the roundest part.

'Listen.' He goes kind and husband-like. 'Can I get you anything on the way home? Got any cravings? Or is it too early for all that?'

'Melons,' I say, digging out seeds with the tip of the knife. 'Two of them. Cantaloupes.'

'You're being absurd –'

'No,' I say quietly, the squash's sweet stink rushing my nostrils.

'– Mike, the accounts, absolutely… Listen, we'll talk when I get home, ok?'

'If I haven't bled to death by then.'

'Fuck!' He practically screams. 'Are you having a –'

'From cutting them off,' I continue. 'You wouldn't have to look at them then, would you?'

'Jesus, Clare, stay calm. Don't – just, leave yourself alone, ok?'

'Alone?' I ask. 'And how shall I do that? Leave myself in bed and stay up til 4am watching telly? Or shall I leave myself alone while I go to work early and come home late? I know, I'll leave myself here throwing up all weekend, and go to Jessica fucking Sykes's barbecue!'

'Fine,' I tell the dial tone.

The box of baby things, from the time I made it to thirteen weeks, is still under the stairs. I pull out a nursing bra. Its pristine cups stretch easily, cradling the slimy heap of seeds and peel from the chopping board. I lay the bra over his slippers, one cup each. 'It's not even yours anyway,' I tell the slippers. It sounds wonderful.

BorrowMyBaby
Jacob Parker

At this late stage of life BorrowMyBaby has come as a blessing to Joan. She has two grown-up children, a daughter and a son. She has been divorced for a long time. She is now more or less estranged from her old husband. She's loved having young children and has always secretly hoped for Grandchildren. However, neither Joan's daughter nor her son have ever expressed any intention of having children. They have decided to make lives based around travel and work. Her daughter alternates a couple of years of hard work and saving with long periods away travelling with her boyfriend, seeing the world. Her son works all hours for some large, demanding corporate business. He likes the finer things. Joan's children have their own lives. Exciting lives. She makes no demands. She has her garden, which is a lot of work. And the radio for late at night and the early hours of the morning. Her children phone regularly, and she really does consider herself lucky.

When Joan sees the advert for BorrowMyBaby in the paper it is her body that reacts. This heart of hers gasps open, as if brought back to life. Yes, it says, unmistakably: this. But then – well she suspects she will never actually sign-up, as usual. In fact, she knows she won't. She lets it pass into the periphery of her thoughts, tucks it away safe in the knowledge that it can be something she entertains the idea of every now and then without ever having to commit to.

Then cancer declares itself. The lymph nodes. The doctor estimates Joan has six months. In the doctor's room, when he tells her, Joan feels merely a resigned acceptance. Almost, can she say, a form of relief. To know. The unknown now a date in the diary. To see it coming to meet her. The doctor, he is so young. He seems like a boy to Joan. Her first impulse is to reassure him. She's almost apologetic. Joan says, 'It's okay, I understand.' She says, 'We all have to go at some point, don't we. And I've had a good life.' It appears he hasn't broken this kind of news many times, the poor boy. He finds it hard to look at her. She wants to appease him. She tries to soften this difficult experience she is putting him through. 'I would, if you could, just like to know a bit about the practicalities of the very end,' she offers. 'I'm a little weary of the potential pain, you see.' And the boy-doctor is off; practical, problem-solving, reassuring her. In the car outside Joan momentarily feels utterly cheated. The cancer has been lying there within her; her own body deceiving her. 'You motherfucker,' she says aloud, rather surprisingly.

Back at home Joan makes a cup of tea in her favourite cup and sits out in the garden. She looks around, at the familiar flowers. It is quiet. She had already decided, even before the doctor had given her the news, not to tell the children. What would be the point? The unnecessary worry. Besides, they have their own lives to live. Busy lives. Her instinct is still to protect them. Sitting there in the garden Joan has the uneasy feeling that most of her life she hasn't really said what she meant. Now she goes into the house to find the paper and the advert.

The following Sunday a young couple come over to meet Joan and see her home. They bring their baby, Martha, who really is adorable. All cheeks and these enormous eyes. The parents are professionals: the father is an architect, the mother a doctor. Such difficult jobs, working long hours. And their own parents are too far away in other countries, Ireland and Finland. They are a quietly determined couple. Doers. Joan imagines they have plenty of savings. The father is an open person, naturally trusting, and so he makes jokes, makes light of this situation which is new to them all. Joan can see that he has made a quick decision that she is just the grandparent they are looking for. The mother, she is more reserved. Questioning, withholding judgment. Of course she has every right to be wary; the mother of the baby. It is her that Joan will have to convince. She will have to be nice to her. Nicer to her. It goes without saying that Joan doesn't tell them about the cancer. At the end of the visit they let Joan hold Martha, who is sleeping now. The blanket she is wrapped in is the colour of candy floss.

Joan has Martha for one day a week at the start. Soon it's two. Then it's three days a week, while the parents work. They like Joan. They trust her. And Joan loves Martha, undoubtedly. She has been thinking this recently – would she throw herself on top of a bomb to save Martha? Be blown to smithereens? And the answer has come unequivocally from within her. Yes. Smithereens. Did she love her own children at some point like this? When she thinks about throwing herself on a bomb for her son she feels disgust. He has become a man. Greying, self-assured, receding hair. And getting so fat. She can't stand it, if she's honest. His fatness. It seems so unnecessary; a self-absorbed gluttony. Always eating out, the latest restaurants. This obsession with food and wine. Joan is slightly frightened of her son. He mocks her. He always knows better. He is so quick to be irritated by her. When he phones, Joan can hear his television on in the background, too loud. And when did all this happen? To her boy, who had been a baby, like Martha, in her arms once. Had she loved him too, the way she loves Martha now – this complete surrender of herself. Like she's been blown open. Like she is filled with air.

Joan doesn't die after six months. In fact, in herself she is feeling better than ever. She takes Martha everywhere. She does so much with her. In the park she takes Martha on the swings, they feed the ducks – these things. And Joan tells Martha everything. She talks to her all the time. How she feels about dying. How she's grown to dislike her own children. She talks a lot about her own parents too, long dead now, but who are in her mind so often these days. 'I was scared of my father. An unreachable man.' She pushes Martha on the swing.

'Weeee.'

'I was in love with him, I suppose. I do wonder whether he's been the most significant man in my life.' She is pushing Martha quite hard on the swing. Higher and higher. Martha is carving huge arcs through the air. Joan thinks it must feel wonderful – the rush, the acceleration. Like the body is blurring apart, the self being left behind somewhere, almost separated from the body. Joan becomes aware of some parents turning to look at her. She stops as Martha's squeals of excitement turn to silence.

It is raining outside and Joan and Martha are in the kitchen. They are making animals out of plasticine. Joan is making Friesian cows. Joan says exactly what she means now. She tells Martha how huge patches of her life have felt staid and uneventful. How few and far between were the times she's felt wide awake. 'Like around sixteen, those years. Dating Paul Baker. I don't think I should even tell *you*, sweetheart, those things Paul and I did together. Learning each other's bodies.' Joan drinks her tea. Martha, copying her, sucks juice from her cup and watches Joan, waiting. 'A penis is so exciting at sixteen. Well, not exactly exciting, perhaps – more fascinating. A curiosity – to figure out its secret workings. I used to climb out of my bedroom window darling!' Martha's plasticine animals are a disaster. She's too young. She's been mashing all the plasticine together and eating little bits. The scene is horrific, like something out of Goya. Joan is rather pleased with her Friesian cows, however. They are tiny imitations of life. Almost living. As if waiting for their maker to breathe life into them. Joan picks one up, places it in the palm of her hand. Martha watches, incredulous. Joan says, 'Let's see what happens.' She cups the tiny cow inside both hands, brings it to her mouth, and blows.

In the winter in the park Joan tears up bread for Martha to give to the ducks. The bread is so soft and white – her fingers sink right in. Hard to believe it is really food and not something synthetic. Joan feels so light too, like her feet might leave the ground any minute. She tries telling Martha about when she was young. 'Yes, I see now I'd been wildly free then. When the future wasn't just some drab to-do list. When had satisfaction come from hoovering the house and having food in the fridge?'

'Woof woof!' says Martha.

'No darling, that's doggies. Doggies go woof woof. These are ducks. Quack quack.' Martha squeals with laughter – it ripples through her, buckling her knees and making her squat. 'Woof woof!' she shouts, deliciously.

'I sat in bed once with a girl as well. Janice her name was. Janice Mathers, that was it. A girl who lived up the road. And we took each other's clothes off and touched each other.'

'Woof woof!'

'Yes darling, woof woof. Throw the bread to the ducks.' Martha hits a duck with a piece of bread, thrown rather hard. 'That's right darling, well done. It wasn't that I was a lesbian. I've never felt that. We were young and just experimenting, that's all. If you want to be a lesbian darling that's fine. You should do exactly what you want to do, my love.' Martha begins to stagger forward with one arm stretched out. She wants to touch the ducks. Her hand is reaching out, fingers splayed like a fan. 'Okay, sweetheart.' Joan holds the back of Martha's puffy winter baby suit and lets her totter forward. She lets Martha lean out over the icy water, her little hand still stretching out towards the ducks. 'There you are darling.' Martha's whole body is leaning out over the water now. And Joan, holding a firm fist of her onesie, lowers her. Martha's body is taut with desire, the fingers almost curving backwards, reaching out to the ducks. She has no fear of that cold water. 'That's it darling.'

Joan realises, she is aware, that this is another moment in her own life of weightlessness. She can feel it. Not unlike when she was sixteen. But now she knows it – she can be in it and see it from the outside. She sees it in everything in fact. The trees particularly for some reason, in the wind being blown about the place. All the worries, the years of self-doubt, are gone. She wonders if she has been a kind person all her life or just afraid of people? She has an inexplicable yearning to see the East Coast of America in the Autumn. In the Fall, as the Americans call it. Joan has no idea where this has come from. She's never even been to America, so it can't be nostalgia. But she knows these scenes and feels almost desperate to see them. New England. Maine. New England in the Fall – what a wonderful phrase. All those leaves, burning in colour. Driving on winding roads. Roadside diners. Coffee with cream, slices of apple pie, free refills. Oh America! she thinks. Other places too. Wyoming, North Dakota, Idaho, Michigan.

In the house while Martha naps Joan tries porn. Why not? She wants to see what all this fuss is about. She finds out that she can watch it on her mobile phone. It is so easy. She is lying on the bed scrolling through various videos. 'Baaa,' Martha blurts in her sleep. Joan turns her head to check on Martha, next to her on the bed. Martha hasn't woken up. Her mouth is open, her arms resting either side of her head, as if in surrender. Some dream-robbery. Stick em' up. Martha is fine, she is still fast asleep. Joan turns back to the porn on her mobile. It amuses Joan – the thought of her family looking through her phone when she is dead, this internet history. That will give them something to think about. Do they do that, when you die – go through your phone? Read your messages? Do your loved ones keep your mobile, as a memento? She has the strange sensation that maybe all this she's doing now, this melting feeling of something good, will push back at the cancer in her. Disarm it perhaps. Dissolve it somehow.

Joan has been to Currys to buy a computer-games console. She wants to see what teenagers are so obsessed with. She wants to experience everything. She wants to get the whole world in. She has bought the latest, most expensive console. She gets three games to go with it in a deal. She is not very good initially. She has to learn a lot – about how the games work, what all the buttons on the controller do. But she plays for hours at a time and gradually she improves. The game Joan likes the best is the one where she is a sniper. She has to creep around, stay hidden, lie in wait for the enemy – who are mostly non-descript soldiers. Soviets, Afghans. She finds them in her cross-hairs, zooms in. She can get so close. She can even choose where in the head she wants to shoot them. The forehead, the neck, the mouth. She enjoys it immensely. The detail of the blood is fantastic. It gives her quite a thrill. If she shoots them in the neck they die slowly, their hand over the wound, trying to stop the blood. Eventually in each game Joan is found and killed. There are always too many soldiers in the end, coming for her. She always dies. But she's getting better and she stays alive for longer now. 'Take that you fucker,' Joan says, pulling the trigger. Blood splatters everywhere. 'Bang bang!' says Martha, who is sitting on the floor, watching the screen, captivated. Joan has been trying to teach Martha to say, *Goodnight Vienna*. 'Goo-nigh-na' is as close as Martha can get at the moment. 'Goodnight Vienna time,' Joan says to Martha, as she holds an unwitting Soviet soldier in her sights. Joan steadies the cross-hairs over his forehead. 'Goodnight Vienna?' she asks Martha. 'Goo-nigh-na!' Martha smiles and bounces. 'Go-nigh-na! Go-nigh-na!'

Most of the time Joan had just wanted to feel something. It isn't that she's been unhappy, for so many years, but that maybe she'd compromised too much. She does consider running away with Martha. To America perhaps. New England in the Fall. Apple pie glistening with sugar. To be on the run. But she doesn't really want this. She doesn't want to be running away from anything or towards anything: she just wants movement. To feel the world rushing by her. She has a memory of running in a tunnel. It was cold and wet in there. It was the foot-tunnel that ran under the river in Greenwich when she had been a student at Goldsmiths. She had been with a boy. She can't remember who. She doesn't know what had happened with him. She just remembers the running. The air had been cold in there, wet. She knows this whole memory could be a symbol for death. The cold tunnel, the dark, the journey. But it seems too obvious. Anyway, it really happened. Like a child she'd broken into a run. It was a competition, a kind of offering for him, the boy, to chase her. She had been the most marvellous runner as a child. And in the tunnel she'd run as fast as she could. Her arms slicing the air in front, her long legs opening, scissoring wider. And breaking into a smile. Then laughing, being filled with air, shaking her hair from her face and leaning forward, almost falling, falling into the run as she'd been taught. She remembers the cold air rushing to meet her, the sides of her denim jacket catching it like a sail, and blowing her apart.

Hot
Jacob Parker

They're so fucking hot. They're coming out of the gym, this guy and this girl, and they're shining with sweat from a good workout. And they're so hot. So young and so hot. It's hot anyway, it's like twenty-eight or something. And this heat just makes them hotter. And I bet they're going home straight away to just fuck each other because they're so god damn hot. What else do hot people do? I bet they're just going to fuck in their gym kit, there and then in their sweat. Maybe not even in the bedroom. Then they'll have a shower, and then probably just fuck again when they're clean.

They're so fucking hot. So young and so hot. I bet he's like Australian and she's like Swedish or something. I mean, she's so hot. Oh my god. She's wearing this sports vest and leggings. This sports vest she's wearing, it's like florescent orange. It sounds cheap and shit, I know, but trust me she looks so hot in it. Like she couldn't look hotter in anything else. I'm telling you, florescent orange.

He's so hot too. Maybe hotter than her even, if that's possible. He's wearing this vest, it's like white or something, and it shows off all his arms. Which are massive. And his chest too. Which is massive. His head looks kind of small because his shoulders and neck muscles are also massive – but on second thoughts it just makes him fucking hotter. How does he make a white vest look so hot? I'm telling you, on me it would look like a sack of shit.

And it's so hot, it must be like thirty or something and they're sweating and I wish I was fucking them. I wish I fucking *was* them because they're so hot and young and I bet they don't worry about anything when they fuck – like if they're actually any good at fucking, or if they smell a bit, or if they're a bit ugly. I bet they just fuck. Uninhibited fucking. Ultimate fucking. And I bet he's like Dutch and she's like Indian or something because they're so hot and their skin is glistening with sweat, did I say? But in this really hot way, like a fine mist. The kind of sweat that doesn't smell. I just know it doesn't. It couldn't, no way. Makes their skin look like fruit. Like a peach, like a cherry, like a melon. God it's hot. It's so hot, it must be like thirty-five or something and I bet licking them would taste like mountain spring water. They're so hot I bet they never wonder what on earth they've been doing all this time, all these years, because they're so hot, they're too hot for that. Christ, what I wouldn't give to crawl into her cleavage and just fucking die there. Or to curl up in his massive arms and have him crush me to death. Can you imagine being that hot? I bet they've never felt like any decision they've made, even something so small, like what jumper to buy, or what to order in a restaurant, or what they said to someone, was wrong, was so wrong.

And it's so hot, it's so hot, it must be like forty or something and I'm panting, I'm actually panting, my tongue is lolling out and I can't stop staring at them and they're so young and they're so hot and he must be like Japanese and she must be like Nigerian or something because they're so young and it's just so hot and they're so fucking hot I bet she's Brazilian and she must be Russian or something and they're sweating and they're hot and it's Christ it's hot it must be like forty-five or something and he just must be Tongalese and he must be Korean or something and it's so hot it's so fucking hot and they're so hot and I bet they never have moments when one of them can't for the life of them think of anything to say and I bet they don't have any need of CBT or pray for sleep and they're so young and it's so fucking hot and I bet they're just fucking all the time all of the time and after all their endless fucking I bet that he or she or they do this:

They go to their kitchen, which is large and white and quiet. It looks like nothing has ever been cooked there. Their naked feet are on cool marble. They must be. And they go to the fridge, which is one of those huge double-door fridges, with a little cold-water dispenser on the front. And in the fridge they find, like a melon or something. Yes, a melon. They must do. And they take it, heavy and cold in their hands. And then they take a large sharp knife and cut two slices. Two slices. A slice of melon each. And then they eat. They have to. They must. They eat. They bite and suck and slurp and nibble. They consume. And the sound, when they eat, of their strong white teeth on the flesh of the melon, must have the crunch of ice about it.

Poise
Jacob Parker

It is as I'm breaking up with Paul that I notice them: my keys. They are on the carpet, just under the sofa, tucked-in right by the sofa-leg. They obviously fell out of my coat when I threw it down as we came in. That's so incredibly lucky I've spotted them. How awkward it would have been to break up with Paul, leave, then have to come back, ring on the intercom, ask if I'd left my keys, go back up, and search the flat with him.

At this moment Paul's still in the middle of telling me how in love with me he is, how I can't do this to him, and I feel a sudden rush of good fortune- that I've noticed the keys. Can you imagine how awful it would have been? If I'd had to come back. Someone up there must be smiling down on me. I must remember when I get my coat to pick them up, when this is done. By 'this' I mean the breaking up with Paul bit. It isn't going too badly actually. Well, I don't think it is. Paul on the other hand is taking it rather hard. He's just started crying in fact. Which is very awkward in itself. I mean, how can I be the one to comfort him, really? I wasn't looking forward to this at all. Almost dreading it. And admittedly I've been putting it off for a few weeks. But now I've started and we're underway with the break up I feel a lot better. Like a burden's been lifted. Relief spinning down.

So far he's said the conventional things: how incredible I am; how he'll never meet anyone like me. Now he's on to the I-don't-understand part, why, when did you know. Never lose your dignity, my mother says. Paul however, I'm sorry to say, is well and truly losing his. Kicking it into the long grass in fact. Whatever happens I must remember not to say that awful 'I love you but I'm not in love with you' line. So offensive. I tell him it's not him, it's just I don't think we work. Tricky that one though, because I suppose it fundamentally *is* him. Obviously, it's not his fault. But it's him I don't love. Really, he needs to be someone else. He needs to be not him, if that makes sense.

Of course I can't and would never say this. I do seem to have run out of things *to* say though. Hard to both explain to him, and not destroy him. To say enough, but not too much. I'm just nodding a lot now and saying uh-hu, and, I'm sorry. Paul is still going for it though, talking and talking. You've got to admire his persistence I suppose. I start thinking about what food I've got in the fridge for when I get back home. Have I got milk? I should get some anyway. I think I've got some onions left. Pretty sure I have some broccoli. I'll probably just have a simple broccoli and pasta tonight I think, rather than cook anything fancy. I'm going to be back late anyway…

But that's great, he says, so it could work? I zoned out then for a moment. I was just nodding and saying uh-hu. Must have missed what I agreed to. What did you just say? I ask. I said, is there a chance we could get back together, he says. Jesus no, I think. I've got to put this to bed now. Should I tell him? The way he talks too loudly on the tube so everyone can hear, the way he always *has* to have a dessert when we eat out, how he likes chatting to strangers. He laughs too loudly in the cinema as well, and is just so undiscerning of people. But I don't say any of this. I stay composed. Sympathetic, sure, but also quite firm I think.

Come on Paul, we're going around in circles here, don't do this to yourself. He's just launching in to another round of I-don't-understands. I have a strong urge to check my watch. He looks so utterly different in this moment to when I first met him. Has his face actually physically changed? Is it less angular? It's quite remarkable really, looking at him now, how not a single part of me fancies him. He looked so defined when I first met him, at Hanna's party. I don't mean his face was chiselled – he never had that kind of face. But he was all sharp, in-focus somehow. It's odd, the more I've known him, the more blurred he has become. Like he's all odd parts.

And it doesn't help that his face is all blotchy now, what with the crying. When I leave his flat I will go with grace and dignity, like my mother says. Poise, she calls it. Always carry yourself with poise. Never run for a bus. Be impervious. I like that too – impervious. She says, walk slowly yet purposefully: imagine you are walking down the street carrying a very delicate, very unique and beautiful vase, that is filled with bright flowers, whose smell, as you walk, is like silk over you. And people are watching. You walk slowly yet purposefully: with poise. Paul buys me flowers. Bought me flowers.

A Runner's Guide to Counting Time
Mileva Anastasiadou

He counts time by breaths.

Only he runs, which makes the procedure complicated, for he's often out of breath. He runs to catch time, to break monotony, the silence of dead dreams, he runs fast and everything moves faster beside him, the scenery, feelings, me. The faster he goes, the more he's determined, he's got the eye of the tiger, nothing will stop him, like when we were young, *remember?* he asks and I nod, for he's sad, and thinks he'll be happy if he goes back, only he doesn't know the way, so he runs forward and time is objective and linear, despite his efforts.

He counts time by money.

Only he runs out of money, which makes the procedure complicated, for he feels worthless, as if time doesn't exist, when he's not useful, productive, wealthy enough to buy time, so he runs and runs and runs, like time is after him, an invisible enemy, *I'll make it*, he says, and I nod, for he's tired, for he's weary, and he could die running but he'll never buy back time lost.

He counts time by love.

Only he runs empty on love, which makes the procedure complicated, for he feels aged and old and he blames me, he wants out, we're on that seesaw and he's going up, while I'm heading down, he feeds on my misery, like vultures feed on dead bodies, like billionaires get rich on the poverty of others, and he runs away, but then he comes back, he moves like a pendulum, back and forth, unable to decide, unable to rest.

He counts time.

Only I remind him of the past, back when we walked, the arrogant youth, we walked slow, never hurried, the world at our feet. He says he's too old, but youth is in the eye. Disguised as unbridled hope. That vast indifference to any possible obstacle. That certainty that all will end well and the right path will be found. Funny how time expands, now that we don't care, now that we don't count.

The Jungle
Josephine Bruni

Subhashini lived alone with one hundred and forty-three African violets. She bred them like puppies, fed them like children. Shelves full of pots of every size ran around the walls of her two-bedroom flat, releasing a smell of old-fashioned sweets. Each plant had a name. The mother plant, a florid thing of austere vegetable grandeur, was called Chimera and was particularly loved by Subhashini. Its lilac flowers made her smile like no human being could. She spoke with it, told it how she felt, how the day had been. The plant never replied. It grew well, its foliage thick and shiny but that was it. It showed no affection for its owner.

No one did.

Subhashini's real name was Gladys but she had met a guru in India many years before who, after a complicated ritual, had signed her forehead with red powder and named her 'Subhashini' which in Sanskrit means, 'nice girl'. She had kept that name as a memento of a life lived on a cusp of adventures; a life long gone.

She still dressed like a hippy in longish skirts and tunics but she didn't experiment with colours anymore. Her clothes were mostly brown or grey, sometimes embroidered with a little pink. Her hair was long, mixed black and white and still thick. She wasn't ugly. She was just plain. A nice girl, like the guru had named her all those years ago.

The only person she spoke to was her downstairs neighbour Marion, a gardener by trade who provided her with food for her plants.

'How's your day been?' asked Subhashini as Marion took off her muddy boots.

'Terrible. I have a client with the appetite of a hyena. She has a cake delivered from Harrod's every day and she comes out into the garden with fresh cream at the corners of her mouth. And she dribbles. Disgusting! She pesters me with personal questions I don't want to answer as if I were in need of her or anybody else's help. I am sick of this job.'

Subhashini sat on the edge of the sofa, suspended in a slippery present, like a fish on a rod. She could never relax while she was away from her plants. That day particularly she had a great worry on her mind and Marion's predicament with fat clients didn't interest her at all.

'Chimera has caught Botrytis blight,' she said with tears in her eyes and a wheeze in her voice. 'She has to be isolated from the other plants in case the blight kills the whole collection. It's so painful looking at her, so helpless, so ill.'

'You have tons of the things. What difference does it make if you lose one?' said Marion.

'She's my First Lady, the mother of all my plants. You bought her for me. Remember?'

'*It.* I bought *it* and I regret it. I can feel all those plants growing above my head at night when I try to sleep; they are like a jungle of bad thoughts.'

Subhashini looked dejected. She wished Marion were kinder to her but the gardener was always in a foul mood, always just about to go out or just come in. She was washing her hands in hot water now, vigorously scrubbing her calluses.

'Look at my hands,' she said. 'Red like a monkey's bottom. You are so lucky you don't need to work. And don't look at me like that. Go and get the plant and I'll have a look at it.'

Subhashini shuffled up the stairs of the small council block and carefully removed Chimera from the shelf. It looked like a bad painting with its yellow leaves and wilted flowers. Subhashini stroked it and spoke with tenderness as if it were an ailing relative of hers, the sister she never had.

Outside in the quiet streets of Primrose Hill, young women ran to shape their already perfect bodies. They lived in large white homes with no lace curtains on their long windows. They went on exotic holidays and had husbands with good jobs. Subashini didn't envy them like Marion did. She was beyond that. Her sadness was like a trickle of chlorophyll running through her plant-like existence. It made her sigh sometimes as she groomed her 'babies' but for most of the time she didn't think about it, absorbed as she was with her collection. Now though, with Chimera ill, everything seemed tainted in black.

'Can I put Chimera in your bathroom?' she asked Marion. 'I'll provide the right light for her.'

Marion was heating up some leftovers for her dinner. Her back ached and her feet were swollen. She was no spring chicken and the job, so demanding physically, was wearing her out.

'No, I don't want the thing in my bathroom.'

'Why?'

'Because it might multiply, that's why. I'll put her in the garden.'

'But she's an indoor plant.'

'I know that! I'm a gardener. I'll put it under a bell jar.'

Marion's garden was very small and wild looking. The arched stems of bleeding hearts looked over clusters of tulips shedding their ripe flowers like burlesque dancers.

The strange, phallic flowers of Jack-in-the-Pulpits stood in the shade of weeds grown undetected, with tender, small flowers of different colours on top of long stems. 'mourning widows' scattered their darkness all over the garden, resistant like thoughts of revenge. Now and again between them a cat appeared, looking curious.

'There you go... cosy in a bed of moss,' said Marion putting Chimera in the midst of the crowded stems. 'I'll nurse it for you.'

Subhashini felt as if her baby had been taken into care because she had failed to look after it properly. Her heart ached with unfulfilled motherhood. The vegetable existence of her precious plant overwhelmed her with love. She started crying. Her life, with its failed relationships and childless womb hit her hard as she grieved for Chimera.

Back in her flat her plants seemed full of sorrow too, alone, each in its own vase. She had black curtains to stop the sunlight hitting her plants. Fluorescent lights and an air purifier in the rooms stopped the smoke of her numerous joints harming her precious violets. When evening came, she switched off the lights and moved around with a torch. In a corner a computer lay unused apart from once a week when Subhashini ordered her shopping. If only she had someone to write to, a friend. She sat down and googled 'African violet chat room' and with astonishment she saw a pretty page appear with her favourite flower on display. There were others like her, in America. Subhashini was soon in the forum and spent the night writing, proud of her collection, of her knowledge of AV- so the people of the chat called the particular flower. A typical conversation that she might have, went like this:

Mary45: 'Anyone got ideas on blue African violets anywhere? There are so many different types. It makes me dizzy. How to choose?'

Subha 143: 'If you really want a deep blue- then you have to own Ness Crinkle Blue with its navy blossoms. It's a very floriferous little plant with well-shaped leaves that usually have very good symmetry. You will fall in love with it.'

Mary 45: Subha 143 you are fantastic! We should make you the High

Priestess of our cult. An English rose with the knowledge of an oak.'

Others asked her for technical solutions.

Angela 54: 'I am such a virgin when it comes to lights! Can you help me, Subha143?'

And Subashini did help.

As she devoured a bowl of tepid baked beans she typed and typed, falling into the web-illusion of comradeship. Around her the vegetating beings grew silently, ready to be cloned, to occupy more and more space in the small flat; ready to push Subhashini- or Subha143 as she was now known-into a corner.

She posted photos of Chimera with its spotted, discoloured leaves and its buds dying unopened. Many on the chat room expressed their concern for the sick mother plant and offered leaves to make new plants. Their hybrids were born of months, sometimes years of trials yet they were giving them freely to Subhashini. She felt loved.

The next day she was up at eight, after only three hours sleep. She switched on the fluorescent lights that kept her collection alive and started the exhausting process of grooming her plants. Many had flowered in those last days and their colours brightened Subhashini's soul with satisfaction.

'My darlings, sorry for being such a tired Mummy,' she told her plants. 'But, you see, I have found friends in America. Would you believe it? You are loved beyond the sea. Have you seen the photos I took of you? You haven't? I will show them to you so you can ponder on your own beauty. Don't worry though, I am never going to go to America even if they ask me, and they will. I will stay with you, always, to make sure your green blood flourishes in ever thick foliage and bursting colours. I love you my little ones.'

She couldn't wait to tell Chimera of her new discovery. And Marion too.

'How's my Chimera?' she asked the gardener who was

preparing herself a decent bacon sandwich.

'What about: "how are you, Marion?"' she said. 'Go and look at your plant... go on. Before my neighbour sets fire to the garden.'

'What?'

'She said the wilderness gives her sleepless nights. She said she's going to complain to the council and have a fence put up. And your weird plant with the bell jar, she says, is the hair that broke the camel's back.'

Subhashini wasn't listening. She was in the garden, amazed by what she saw. A flower had bloomed in the heart of Chimera, a black flower with dark purple edges.

'She's reborn,' said Subhashini. 'So Gothic... She looks... like...'

'The mourning widows, I know. You better leave it there for a few days. Its leaves are still a pitiful sight. It's the cramped conditions that made her sick. I've told you before to leave more space between the plants.'

'The Americans would love you,' said Subhashini. 'An English gardener.'

'I am Irish... And who are these Americans?'

Subhashini could hardly speak as she told Marion about her new friends.

'It's amazing how many people are into breeding African violets. There's more than 300 members on our site. With them I can come out of my shell, share the beauty of my plants.' She puffed on her joint, shaking in excitement. 'A lot of members of the site are ex-hippies.'

'So, you talk about other things apart from flowers.'

'Oh no, we don't. I just know. I can feel it in their enthusiasm. Only a hippy can love flowers that way.'

'If I wrote a story about you nobody would believe it. Why do you do it?'

'Breeding African violets is like looking into God's work. Every hair of every root belongs to me and I make it live. It's Creation in a pot. The flowers are like wishes fulfilled. Each hybridization is a new race of colour that speaks of realms beyond this world. I must take a photo of Chimera here in your garden. A speck of order in the maelstrom of life.'

Subashini got up and straightened her tunic, brushing it with her hands. She was maniacally attentive to dust, spending hours cleaning the stuff from her plants' leaves. She washed and changed her clothes twice a day for fear of contaminating the plants. She took a photo then left Marion with a slight movement of her hand in a half-hearted 'goodbye'.

Back in her flat she sat down at the computer waiting for her friends across the Ocean to call in. She was in the middle of a conversation with Pixie 66 when she met Anthony265. He came into the chat room specifically to talk to her. He had heard of her endless knowledge, of the sad portrait of the dying Chimera. He was a great grower of AV, shelved and cared for in his five-bedroom house in Illinois.

'I immediately noticed the notched wavy foliage of Chimera,' he posted. 'She must have been a stunner when she was well. I bet her girl- leaves shook with silky tremors.'

Subha143: 'Yes, she was adorable. I spent years grooming her. Just yesterday a black flower bloomed on her. I was just about to post the photo. Here...'

'OMG! It's fantastic. Thoughts of love and death in that wondrous flower. I would love to cross her with my father plant. Here he is, a pure Chicago Flair.'

Subha143: 'He's a monster!'

Anthony265's plant looked so full of life, its flowers bursting with health, its leaves perfectly heart shaped like a love song. Subhashini fell in love with it and with its owner. It was a sudden thing and in the middle of the night she sighed with pleasure.

'My AV seeds were launched into space,' he posted. 'They orbited the earth for six years. The plants that grow from them are full of mutations, stronger than the ordinary ones and have neat looking flowers with two or more colours. A spark of the universe is in them and I can feel it in the air. They have transformed my life. The leaves root really quickly and I have created two hundred plants in three months. I want to share them with you, Subha 143. No plant is stronger than mine and you deserve strength. You deserve only the best.'

'Dear Anthony265,' wrote Subha. 'I will be very happy to receive your leaves. I will wait from now on with anxious desire.'

The other members cheered the newly made friends. They were all fond of Subha 143.

As another evening descended on Primrose Hill and its privileged inhabitants, Subhashini went downstairs to call on her neighbour Marion.

'I've met a man,' she announced.

'Where? In the corner shop?'

'On the AV chat room. We talk about roots, colours, names for our babies. He delights in pink as much as any woman would and is so generous. He's going to send me some leaves.'

'You are going to make more plants?'

'Only a few,' lied Subhashini. 'Anthony265's plants come from space. Cost him a fortune. I can give you a leaf if you want.'

'I must have an alien plant,' said Marion sarcastically.

'Great! It will change your life.'

'Hurrah... how can I have lived this long without it?'

'Exactly. I'll bring it over tomorrow. Anthony265 is sending them special delivery. Oh Chimera, I almost forgot about you.'

In the garden Subhashini's mother plant had flourished under the bell jar. It had lost some leaves but strangely it looked better that way, like an old woman with her hair cut short years after wearing it shoulder length. More black flowers had bloomed on it, dark as bats. Subhashini went to lift the bell jar but Marion stopped her.

'We better give her some more time. She's alright there.'

There was an anxiety in Marion's voice that made Subhashini shiver. She was a sensitive woman, a bit paranoid and Marion was her only friend. Now she wanted to steal Chimera.

'It's my plant,' said Subhashini.

'You have Anthony265 and the plants from out of space now. You don't need Chimera anymore. I'm taking her back.'

Subhashini left the flat in a state of shock. She felt tears warm her cheeks. She stopped on the landing and leant on the wall as if she found her weight too much to carry.

Chimera was so beautiful now. Subhashini told herself she could pop down and see her plant whenever she wanted but a grief like frozen dew descended on her wavering mind. Never again would she clone a plant from her sweet Chimera. Those days were gone. Now she had Anthony265 and his leaves.

As time went by Subhashini amassed a great collection. The flat was now a labyrinth that led to the microwave, to the bathroom and to an unmade bed in a corner of the living room. Then there was, of course, the narrow path that led to the computer where she met her virtual friends.

As she picked off a dead flower from one of the space plants – a turgid thing of boisterous colours – she started coughing. It shook her body and took her breath away as if she were falling into deep water, going down, down, drowning. The pain in her chest was unbearably intense. The world spun around her, because those rooms were her world, and, for a moment, she saw her plants tower over her, despotic entities of the green realm, taking over her life. But it was only a moment and it brought no fruit. As soon as she caught her breath again Subhashini lit a joint and started the daily grooming of her plants. The space-flowers demanded to be cloned by the earthling that had given up her flat to them. And she cloned, more and more, until she slept in the bath and was reduced to eating cold beans.

Anthony265 continued to send leaves and admiration to his love across the ocean. She had never seen his photo neither had he seen hers but she knew he was the one. At night she would undress and spray her body with the same water she gave her plants, plus a scent of AV which Anthony265 imagined to be irresistible.

'My ruffled pansy,' he wrote. 'It's so nice to imagine you overwhelmed by the pleasure of our flowers. Our offspring is delightful, my bombshell butterfly.'

Subhashini sprayed her hair and arms and wrote back with fervour.

'Seeing all those specks of green makes all the months of waiting worth it. Doesn't it? Soon the flowers will bloom my friend and I will bloom with them.'

'What about our rejects, my Darling? Trashing them must be heart breaking but you can't have inferior plants roaming the world.'

'As you wish Anthony265, my star-eyed Braveheart. I will neglect them and keep them away from the lights. It'll be easier for me than tossing them.'

In her tunnelled vision Subhashini became so obsessed with Anthony265 that her popularity in the chat room declined. The other AV lovers started to question her sanity and when she confessed that she had 449 African violets the president of the association asked her politely to give up her membership.

'Dear Subha449,' wrote the president. 'As hard as this is – you are an excellent grower and much appreciated adviser – we have come to the delicate decision to shun you from the chat; the reason being that the sexual innuendo you express in your dialogues with Anthony265 are offensive to the other members who use our site with innocence and respect. By-Bye Subha 449. Good luck. You need it'

Subhashini sank for a moment into deep shame. She had lost her friends for a passion that was corroding her dignity. But Anthony265 was stronger than any moral attitude Subhashini might have had towards her life. He wrote passionate emails and sent her leaves with names like 'Bedroom Eyes', 'My Wicked Ways', 'Lusty Lilac', and 'Plenty of Pepper'. Subhashini was shocked and delighted. She lost weight and seemed more distracted than usual. Her brown fingers, almost burned by the eternal fire of her smoking habit, were like sticks and her long, black and white hair was thinning.

'I can't breathe,' she told Marion. 'I need to stop smoking.'

'And breeding violets.'

'I can't give up the AV. They're all I've got.'

Subhashini's tunic was filthy and her breath smelt of smoke and hunger. She looked at her Chimera from behind the French windows. Marion had pulled out all the weeds from the garden and the mother plant now looked like a queen.

The mourning widows surrounded it like a retinue of fairies. There had been days, it seemed so long ago, when Chimera was Subhashini's only friend. Now she had Anthony265 and a flat full of flowers. She sighed.

That night she tripped over a fallen plant and fell, bringing with her a tall, very heavy shelf full of pots and earth and colourful, indifferent African violets. They covered her as she lay on the floor, her arm broken, overcome by her passion like an Anna Karenina of the violet world. The pain in her arm was such she couldn't move. She had earth in her mouth and a shelf stuck in her ribs. But, worst of all, she was sober, and a painful overbearing reality tormented her as the hours went by. Subhashini, Subha 449, was now simply Gladys and in the middle of the night, on the floor, she thought about life, about Anthony265 and his leaves; about the seeds of the universe that had broken her bones. George, Jeffrey, Penelope and Louis had fallen out of their pots and were going to die with her. She couldn't bear it. She screamed with all her strength but her voice was overcome by a fit of coughing. She drifted in and out of a semi-comatose state and every breath made her whine in pain. The computer's alerts rang ten times that night as Anthony265 sent ever urgent emails but Subhashini couldn't hear him anymore.

Marion cried when she found her with George in her hands. Then she called for help as another day rose on Primrose Hill.

Dogs and Shakespeare
Josephine Bruni

Florence ate two boiled eggs and a buttered slice of bread before changing into a Laura Ashley dress and a pair of white plimsoles. Then she went up a flight of steep and narrow stairs to Mrs Lewinsky's flat and pressed the bell. She could hear Gorky barking and the shuffle of Mrs Lewinsky's steps.

'Oh, it's you,' the neighbour said. 'You look a bit pale. Are you alright?'

'I have a plan. May I come in?'

'Sure.'

Florence stepped in and followed Mrs Lewinsky to the living room where a few paintings of value hung, recovered from Germany after years of lawyers and pain. A pale-yellow wallpaper gave the room a solar feeling. Mrs Lewinsky was old, very old even, but her mind had a sharpness which often surprised Florence.

'Please do sit down,' she said. 'Come on Gorky… come and say hello to Florence.'

Gorky wagged his bony tail, where tufts of hair were missing, showing black patches of skin. He was so old he looked like a wooden horse and a persistent movement in his left eye made him seem as if he were winking.

Florence grew excited. Her plan was perfect. She had conceived it while she tossed and turned in her single bed, her mind faltering now and then under the pressure of an imagined success.

'I wonder if I could borrow Gorky,' she asked Mrs Lewinsky.

Mrs Lewinsky hadn't put her teeth in yet and there was something endearing about her the way she spoke. 'What on earth would you do with this old dog?'

'I believe my walks on the Heath would be more… meaningful… complete.'

'And slow. Gorky can pee up to a hundred times before you get to Parliament Hill.'

'I'm in no rush.'

Florence hadn't worked since she had frozen on stage while reciting as Lady Macbeth. It had been such an emotional upheaval that she had given up altogether on acting. Until now. Sitting in Mrs Lewinsky's flat she thought of Shakespeare and a warmth not unlike love grew inside her. Gorky, probably sensing the complicated thoughts of his friend, put his drooling mouth on her lap and winked. Florence thought he was the perfect dog for her plan. She drank the coffee that Mrs Lewinsky made and took tiny bites on a 'custard cream'. Outside the trees swung a little, hitting the window. In the flower box weeds had strangely found their ground, sprouting yellow flowers. Florence could see the sky with its puffy little clouds.

'Are you going to Camden Town later?' asked Mrs Lewinsky, as she did almost every day. And Florence had to make the same, demoralizing decision.

'I might go tomorrow.'

Mrs Lewinsky shook her head slightly. She had silver hair and blue eyes, sparkling like the small diamond that hung from her neck onto a light blue frock. She sat in her rocking chair with her hands crossed over her stomach. 'You always say that. You haven't been out of Hampstead for years.'

Florence brushed away a strand of strawberry-blonde hair from her eyes. She had freckles on her nose, a roundish face, a bit childish, and eyes with a look of bewilderment in them, as if she were in the woods and had lost her path.

'I will go. I will go,' she said getting up. 'Now I'm going to the Heath. Can I take Gorky?'

'For the plan?'

'Yes.'

'I don't know what you are up to, Florence, but I do have to say that these stairs bother me and a walk would be good for Gorky. So, you're welcome. Let me get the lead.'

Gorky proved difficult. He didn't want to leave the house and placed his forelegs firmly on the ground growling slightly, one eye full of determination, the other half closed in the effort to stay put. He wasn't a small dog but Florence picked him up nevertheless and carried him away, leaving Mrs Lewinsky puzzled at the top of the stairs.

Gorky walked once he was out of the squealing old gate by the entrance to the house and Florence felt on top of the world. Hampstead was alight with sunshine. Women, with jogger-friendly buggies, walked in pairs, talking about children and husbands and working from home. A group of Eastern European builders shouted from scaffoldings and laughed with such vigour it made Florence shut her eyes for a moment. A man with soft shoes and a hand-free phone walked, seemingly talking to himself.

The park was a piece of the old London fields, a 'garden for the gardenless', a call of the wild, as wild as you could find in a place like Hampstead. The sun, through the leaves of tall trees, cut shapes on the tarred ground. Gorky showed so much interest in bushes, tree trunks and blades of grass that Florence slowed down, taking in the breeze moving through her hair. She left the paths, walking through meadows dashed with daisies and bluebells. She passed Boudicca's Mound thinking, about the Celtic Queen and her fight for freedom.

She reached Kenwood House at one o'clock on the dot. In the café's garden, under a huge tree spraying white flowers on the ground, Letitia Banshea was giving her speech to a group of women looking like nymphs around their Diana. With them, three legged dogs, dogs without tails and teeth, funny dogs with faces like wise old men wagged their tails and drank noisily from a large bowl. Florence, hiding behind a holly bush, looked on with her breath shaken by apprehension.

'And we know, dear friends, that our work is never ending,' Letitia was saying. 'From Romania to Afghanistan; from Spain to Morocco, our net will grow and cover the earth, to be where dogs are neglected and beaten, let me say, yes beaten,' here her voice cracked. 'We shall want our charity to fly with large and powerful wings to free all dogs, caged and tied, poor and sick. Shout with me sisters: *Posh Dogs Don't Matter*.

The women clapped their hands, repeating, as one: *Posh-Dogs Don't-Matter*.

At ninety-one, Letitia Banshea was a queen of charity, white as chalk, with plum lipstick. She wore a long white coat no matter what the weather was and a baseball cap with a paw embroidered on the front. She was mighty and frightening, but Florence found the strength to walk up to her.

'Hello,' she said. 'Lovely day. Isn't it?'

The alpha woman looked at her with an expressionless face shadowed by the cap. 'Do I know you?'

'Well no. But I know you. I hear you speaking when I come here and was wondering if I can join you for the next charity do. It's in a week's time. Isn't it? I can help.'

Letitia lifted one eyebrow. 'It's an important event. People are coming from as far as Peckham to bring their dogs to our competition. Last year we collected five thousand pounds. Your dog looks thirsty.

'What's his name?'

'Gorky.'

'You're a socialist?'

'Ehm… maybe.'

'I like socialists.'

Gorky was not happy. The dogs were sniffing him and barking into his ears. He lifted a corner of his black lip, showed a yellow canine and winked. A whippet with a bony back growled.

'My dog is a bit temperamental,' said Florence. 'He's a rescue … from Saudi Arabia. They really don't like dogs down there.'

Letitia screwed up her eyes and looked at Florence as if she wanted to get into her very heart. 'Our dogs are all rescues, but we have no dog from Saudi Arabia. That is very original of you…'

'Florence.'

'Yes, Florence. What is it that you do?'

'I'm a Shakespearean actress. I work for the Royal Shakespeare Company.'

A sense of deep relief came over Florence as she waited for the words to have their effect. The dice were thrown, the slimy Rubicon of her fear was crossed. White flowers fell on her head and on Gorky's back as he looked at her with his philosophical eyes then bit the air chasing a fly.

Letitia Banshea lifted her eyebrows.

'Really? An actress with the RSC? Well, we must have you on stage for our competition. We need someone with manner. Do you think you could maybe recite something? About dogs?'

'Oh yes. I can, definitely.'

'So: Dogs and Shakespeare. That's sorted. Let's move. I walk four times across the Heath every day fundraising for my charity *Posh Dogs Don't Matter*. It keeps me fit. Come along ladies, come along.

'Move your fat bottoms and walk with me!'

'Can I come?' asked Florence.

'I suppose so. You're part of the team. On probation.'

Letitia turned her back on Florence and, holding her ebony stick, made for the stairs that led out of the café area and into the tidy meadows of Kenwood House. The other women followed her, taking the international company of dogs with them.

They walked by the 'Bridge of Fairies', past the beds of daffodils, towards pastures green. Florence could hardly contain her satisfaction. She was going to break the mental chains that crippled her, finally and forever, leaving a blue sky and the hope of Shakespeare. She was going back on stage.

Gorky walked slowly, his joints stiff like tree knots, his winking eye looking at Florence as if for approval, or maybe it was just surprise.

He seemed to gain some life as he walked with the other dogs, accepting them like a hermit might accept the inevitable world around him. Florence was going to bring him fame. Mrs Lewinsky would be happy. Florence was going to tell her all about it.

She was tempted to go to Camden and have a Thai lunch in 'The Stables' after the walk, but when she finally made it out of the woods, she was tired and needed to go home. She walked up different streets in what might have appeared as a short cut but was actually a longer way, curving around tall houses with strict red bricks and high doorways. She crossed the road, where slow traffic climbed Hampstead hill, and in few minutes reached Mrs Lewinsky's flat.

'Him in a play?' asked a bewildered Mrs Lewinsky.

'Yes, there is a part for a dog. He doesn't have to do much. Just sit there really.'

'Well, he does that very well. Don't you, old chap?'

Gorky lapped his water loudly and made a choking sound before settling in his bed, his face white with age. Florence put her hand in front of his wet nose. He sniffed and smiled.

In the following days, in her flat on the ground floor, as the sun broke through the tall, bay windows, Florence spent time rehearsing the part she had chosen for herself. She was going to be a servant, a clever servant, who would steal the show with a cantankerous dog. She went to the wardrobe and threw everything on the bed until she found the short dress, full of silver beads, that she had worn when she had been given a prize, yes, for the interpretation of Lady Macbeth. The dress draped her hips so softly, so elegantly. She felt completely at ease in it. She found a pair of thick tights, a pair of ankle-high boots and a red, large-brimmed hat. She was going to shine. The most handsome servant in town.

On the day of the show Florence felt taller than usual, as she walked alongside the Heath's ponds with Gorky. In the light of Spring, she felt like a bird coming home after crossing two oceans. She stopped on the top of Parliament Hill to look across at London, at its skyscrapers and cathedrals. She felt so lucky to be living in a place of such great opportunity. Gorky, next to her, scratched his ear, with the thumping sound of his frail legs hitting the path. Florence held his lead as if her life depended on him.

The competition was in the fields, next to the old bandstand. Letitia Banshea was by the stage, ordering her women about. Her face was whiter than usual, and she tightened her ancient lips when she saw Florence.

'You're a bit overdressed,' she said. 'I wouldn't want you attracting too much attention to yourself. After all the dogs are the real stars.'

'I know. I know, Gorky is going to be "Crab" the dog.'

'Never heard of it. Come on lazy buggers, push that pile of chairs over there... and you... yes Priscilla you... take that table away from there. No, we don't need any more glasses, we need more wine. Look at Stephanie with her Toy Pomeranian. It cost her three thousand pounds you know…'

'Florence.'

'Florence, yes. She loves showing it off. Well, she isn't going to win anything here. Melanie… sit at your table. You're a judge for Pete's sake. Florence, take off your coat. It doesn't go with the dress.'

'Yes, sure,' said Florence who was beside herself with excitement. Gorky though seemed baffled by all the movement around him and was probably dreaming about his bed. Florence stroked his head and promised him a bone.

Soon the presenter, a man with a face like a sour plum, was inviting the audience to listen and 'look at the wonderful dogs we have with us today.' The audience, standing around the stage, tried and failed to be silent. It was the wine and the kids and the warm sunshine that got everyone free and fresh on Hampstead Heath.

The first dog walked on stage with an uncertain pace. It was a small dog, with a tuft of fur on the top of his naked tail and ears sticking out like aerials. His owner walked beside him, sporting a patchwork skirt and a large shawl.

'And this is?' asked the presenter.

'This is Berry. She's blind.'

'Oh, is she? Poor thing. I bet she's the best thing that has ever happened to you.'

'Not really. The best thing that's ever happened to me is becoming a grandmother. The baby is so cute, her name is…'

'Well done, Berry. Go over there and good luck. And next?'

Other dogs strolled on stage, all maimed, emotionally some, physically others but all loved. Lucky dogs.

Gorky looked on, with his ears flopping, his nose trembling, full of new scents. Letitia Banshea was talking to the judges, waving her ebony stick as if it were a part of her arm.

'Do not be fooled by breed and beauty,' she was saying. 'Remember: *Posh Dogs Don't Matter*.'

And the dogs kept coming. Letitia applauded and Florence waited. Then she was called.

'So, what's the name of this golden oldie?' asked the presenter planting his face an inch from Florence's.

'His name is Gorky. He's going to recite Shakespeare today.'

The presenter laughed. 'Oh yeah? Who's he going to be, Romeo? No, he's too old for that. Well Gorky go and get yourself some water. You look like you need it. Is he alright? He's got his tongue hanging out between his teeth.'

'He's fine but…'

The presenter pushed Florence aside a little but Letitia walked up to him and whispered into his ear.

'Sorry everyone,' the presenter said. 'Florence and Gorky are actually going to recite from Shakespeare. She has a beautiful dress I must say. Costly, was it?'

'A bit,' started Florence.

'Ladies and Gentlemen: Florence and Gorky.'

Florence felt a wave of stage fright take over her as her determination crumbled. She looked at the audience, sitting on the grass and on white plastic chairs, some chatting, some drinking wine or beer. They didn't know her but she knew them. They were the ones who could make her or destroy her. She heard the sound of children playing in the nearby playground and the dogs yelping and barking. She felt dizzy and lost. Letitia and her entourage were looking on with enquiring faces. Without thinking Florence started to speak.

'I'm here today to talk about dogs. Especially about one dog: "Crab", made famous by Shakespeare who couldn't resist putting him in his early play, *The two gentlemen of Verona*. He was a bad-mannered dog, a bit like Gorky who loves nothing better but to growl at his peers and show his bottom at those who want to stroke him. Crab pissed under dukes' table and on ladies' petticoats, as Shakespeare would have probably wanted to do in those early days of his craft. Crab doesn't give a toss about other people's pains or delights as long as he's got something to fill his ample belly with.'

Florence was sweating but the words now came easily, memories of a different life pouring into her brain like honey from a hive. It was not the stage of the *Old Vic* but it was a start.

Gorky sat with his forelegs straight and his paws turned outwards, looking at the audience with lazy eyes, barking once at a dog nearby. One of his ears was floppy at the end as if he couldn't be bothered to keep it straight. People laughed and clapped their hands while Florence continued.

'There is only one dog in Shakespeare's plays but it's there, reminding us that our greatest friend is worth a show of great poetry.'

The audience, now attentive, applauded. Letitia stood nearby, solemn and watchful.

'I think Crab, my dog, be the sourest-natured dog that lives,' Florence started. *'My mother weeping, my father wailing, my sister crying, our maid howling, our cat wringing her hands, and all our house in a great perplexity, yet did not this cruel-hearted cur shed one tear. He is a stone, a very pebble stone, and has no more pity in him than a dog.'*

She could do it. She could recite again the precious words of the Bard. She asked Letitia for her stick and took off her own hat. *'Now, sir, this staff is my sister, for, look you, she is as white as a lily and as small as a wand. This hat is Nan, our maid. I am the dog. No, the dog is himself, and I am the dog – O, the dog is me, and I am myself. Ay, so, so.'*

Gorky got up on his unsteady legs and barked. The audience laughed but Letitia intervened to spoil the moment.

'Well thank you, Florence. Very good. Now back to our competition.'

There was a murmur in the audience and cries of 'let her go on' but Letitia was determined to take over the show.

It was then that Gorky made the decision to fulfil his doggy mission and his place in the play. He sniffed Letitia's ankle and, with a nonchalance more apt to a younger dog, he lifted his leg, relieving his bladder on her boot. The audience was in uproar. The applause came down like rain on thirsty ground. Florence bowed. Around her the Heath burst with green as a rainbow graced the building of the hospital in the distance. Birds brushed the air with their tiny wings. Crows jumped, eating crumbs. Florence waved and bowed to the audience then left the stage.

'Where are you going?' asked a furious Letitia.

Florence looked blissfully happy. 'I'm going to Camden Town,' she said and left with Gorky. She could already smell a great Thai.

The Death of Margaret Thorne
Katharine Orton

Margaret Thorne. If I hadn't sworn to protect life I'd kill her. She's our first job of the shift and I know it's going to be bad today because whenever I close my eyes I see the boy.

'Well, Margaret,' says Abs. 'Blood pressure's fine, as usual. Oxygen levels, Ems?' He glances over. I nod, mouth drawn tight.

'Fine.'

'Which means you're the picture of health, my darling.'

I could be calm with her once too. Now, something like rage stoppers my throat.

'Margaret,' Abs continues softly. 'Why do you always call us and say you're dying?'

Margaret whimpers. I watch her lip quiver and push down ugly thoughts. 'Because I am,' comes her shaky reply. 'I am, aren't I.'

Every day I bandage people up and blue light them to hospital. At night I dream of Margaret. *I'm dying*, she says. She goes limp and pale. I try everything but nothing works. Afterwards I'm a child, slapping wet sand on to my dissolving dam as the tide spills through.

Other nights it's the boy I couldn't save. I replay his fall, and sometimes even catch him just in time. But, when I peer over the cliff edge, he's there just the same. Face down. Perfectly still. Arms out like a dancer.

Abs and I go about our day. Broken leg. Overdose. Stabbing.

Margaret.

Car crash. Head injury. Burn.

Margaret again. Only this time she's too distraught even to listen to Abs.

'I can't breathe!' *Blink.*
'You *are* breathing.' *Boy.*
'Am I dying?' *Blink.*
'No, Margaret.' *Boy.*
'I'm dying!' *Blink.*
'No!' I snap. 'You're just wasting our time!'

Flushed and shaking, I wait outside. When Abs finishes up, we head to the ambulance in silence. But our monitor is still in Margaret's flat, so I dash back. She startles me by being in her hallway. Perhaps it's the surprise that sets me off – or her strange, sudden calm. Because I crack. Finally. Saltwater spills.

Margaret holds out her arms with balletic grace and I fold into them.

'I'm dying. Aren't I.'

Yes. Yes. Yes.

Molar
Olivia R Dunnett

This morning, as I examined my teeth in the bathroom mirror, I found myself thinking of my skull. In teeth, I suppose we get a first look at our skeletons. The Americans, with all their whitening and straightening, must have the most beautiful dead of any nation.

These considerations, along with some pain in an upper molar, have persuaded me to make an appointment at my dentist's. It is near Christmas and just over a week since Matthew's funeral. From the first floor waiting room I can see a wintry triangle of Upper Street, the semi-tropical plants outside the florist's a dull, bewildered green. Myself and the blonde woman across from me are the only patients.

I am sweating from the change in temperature and my nose prickles with the scent of mouthwash. I cross and uncross my legs. As a younger man, I was always fond of medical settings: the complacent scale of the buildings, the soft, fragrant bustling of experts along bright corridors. But since poor, dear Matthew, and of course my own issues with my prostate, hospitals have begun to be less of a novelty.

Though I have discarded my outer layers I am still too hot. I realize I feel a little faint. I have never been afraid of the dentist before. On a poster by the door a couple embrace, their smiles brandished like engagements rings. The packaged toothbrushes in a bowl on the table remind me of keys at a swingers' party.

My tongue begins to explore the upper molar, prodding at it, eliciting reproachful tweaks. I can feel the iceberg root, plunged deep into my gums. Surely, whatever is wrong, it cannot be so very bad? I do not floss, but then Matthew counts that amongst the signs that one has given up on life.

The blonde woman is applying pink lipstick, overdrawing her mouth as though providing the dentist with a target. I picture his instruments smeared with the dazzling pigment. She catches my eye and I look away, blinking. Am I seeing things? And now suddenly, I know that there is something seriously wrong behind the clamped portcullis of my lips. My upper molar is a plug. If it is loosened, gunk will fill my mouth, run down my chin, drip onto the floor.

By the time the receptionist calls me it is ten minutes past the time of my appointment. I have been dithering on the point of exit.

'Listen,' I say as I enter. 'I've been waiting outside for twenty minutes.'

Two figures are posed either side of the dental chair. They turn to me, my breath catches. Both are pale and blonde, the woman's white plastic gloves are somehow bridal. The man is older, the lines of his face like structural beams.

'We are sorry to hear this.' His voice is faintly accented. 'Today, we are a little behind the schedule.' They both smile at me, but I don't get a good look at their teeth. 'I am Finn, and this is Maria,' he says. 'Please put down your coat. Be seated.'

They turn back to the counter, and after some hesitation I manoeuvre myself onto the chair. Lying prone in another's presence forces intimacy, in a way not dissimilar from a chaise longue at a psychoanalyst's office. I avert my eyes from the tray of tools.

A stereo on the shelves behind me is playing soft choral music, the voices seeming to waft down from a height. I know there was a choir of sorts at the funeral. Libby, my ex-wife, arranged it for him. We three knew each other at Oxford, though I suppose she was always closer to him than I. She thinks I ought to have put in appearance at the church, in fact we had a row over it. But it cannot be such an unusual choice, to keep away.

The singing has distracted me and I flinch as Maria fixes a bib about my neck. I remember an old colleague, ashamed of her adult braces, and the way she smiled, close lipped, peculiar, unable to forget her embarrassment. She did it even as she laughed. It is beginning to seem horrible that I should open my mouth to them.

'All right then,' says Finn, the circular stool creaking as he sits. 'We will do first the evaluations of the hard and the soft tissue. The hard is being the teeth, the soft is being the gums. So, I will lean you back and shine in the light.'

My heart beats faster. I imagine their serene faces contorting as they find something worse than expected. Maggots perhaps, seething in bloody gums, exposing white roots.

Maria is reaching up for an operational light above me. It unbends like the arm of a great mantis, eight lightbulbs forming a ring on the flat, round head. Maria has slipped protective glasses over my eyes, and the world is dimmed. Finn has pulled a mask up over his face, shielding his mouth, and I am reminded of the screen between priest and confessor. From the corner of my eye I catch the twinkle of the first tool. I jerk away.

'To be nervous is OK,' he says. 'Dental anxiety is very common. It is something coming close to your face, I understand.' I picture the tilting mirror, the puppet moon, as it sinks into my mouth. And then, before I am fully aware, I am sitting upright.

'Wait!' I say. 'Hold on. Wait a minute.'

'Relax,' he says. 'Have trust in me.'

The choir seems somehow louder now. They sing in Latin, and I imagine what the words must be, euphoric and merciless. I am breathing heavily. 'I'm afraid I may have to postpone.' I clear my throat. 'Is it absolutely necessary for you to look inside?'

Finn and Maria exchange a glance, and start to nod. 'Yes,' says Finn, 'I am afraid I will need to see inside your mouth. Otherwise how will I know if there is anything that is wrong?'

I stare at him. 'Well, I'm sure nothing is,' I say finally. 'I've had no pain.' I am reddening, my face hot.

'None at all?' Finn is still wearing his mask, but I think beneath it he is smiling.

'Robert, is there perhaps something which you are hiding from me? A little pain?'

My palms are leaving wet marks on the leather of the chair, and I lift them up, breaking eye contact. Finn gestures for me to lie back down, he is still holding the silver tool.

'No,' I say. 'They looked fine in the mirror this morning.'

He sighs and leans back on his stool. Maria watches from the counter, her eyes wide.

'Well, that may be,' he says. 'And possibly there is nothing amiss. But you should know that a tooth can die, and still there will be no pain. There will be no marks on the enamel, it is pristine. But the dentine is decayed, the elasticity lost. Toxicity pools in the gum.'

I am silent. My upper molar is throbbing, like a gagged captive trying to call out.

'Also,' says Finn, 'We find the pain will not always occur in the problematic tooth. In some patients, the discontented tooth is one on the other side from the decay. In some cases, the pain is on the lower jaw when the unhappy tooth is on the upper.'

My heart beat is slowing and I am embarrassed. My eyes scan the posters of teeth on the walls, pink and white rosettes like nursery wallpaper. In this clean, bright room with the choral music, with these people in their fresh white gloves, I begin to compose myself.

'To leave a troubled tooth,' Finn is saying, 'is not wise. And for us to fix the problem, we must first take a little look at it, no?' I lower myself down, back into the chair. I feel weak, as though I have been running. A child, cajoled easily into submission. I listen to the singing and I think of Matthew, decrepit and confused.

'Do not be too sorrowful if we do find something,' Finn is saying, 'nowadays, there is very little that can go seriously wrong. It used to be that many people were dying from infection, but now the procedures are far more dependable.'

'My tooth has been hurting,' I say in a rush, looking up at the ceiling, up at the hovering light. 'My upper molar.'

'Oh yes?' He raises his eyebrows. Very gradually, I open my mouth. His hands move towards me, I feel the brush of the rubber gloves against my face. And then in goes the probing light, illuminating a stage I cannot see, a submarine in the opening to a cave system. My toes curl inside my shoes, my feet twisting on the chair.

'You smoke,' he says after a few minutes, tools in hand, my mouth cold from the spraying water. Then, 'You do not floss.' I can make no response.

My suit is crisply tailored, and lying on the chair I feel wrapped tight beneath a blanket. The voices of the choir are filling the small room, building to a crescendo, and I think of stone effigies basking in music. Above me the eight light bulbs form a ring. My vision is hazy, they merge, split and then merge again. I think of Libby, head in hands. I think of a group outside a church, their heads bowed, and the rain of earth on wood. How widespread is my rot? My mouth gapes in an artificial scream. I see the blinding 'O' of light, the halo above me. It is all that I see. It gets brighter.

Finn extricates his hands from my mouth.

'OK then,' he says. 'You have good teeth, Robert.' Incredibly, I have been on the verge of sleep. I blink, push up my glasses. On the screen in front of me is an X-Ray of a set of teeth. They are mine, I realize. They curve up into my gums, tightly packed, strong looking.

'I am thinking,' Finn continues, 'that you may be needing root canal on this tooth here.' He taps one of the teeth. I cannot tell if it is the same upper molar.

He looks at me for a reaction and when he gets none reaches behind him onto the shelves. 'Let me show you,' he says, placing a plastic model of a tooth on the tool tray. It is about the size of my fist, standing on a little podium. 'Here you see,' he says, prising one half of the tooth away. Inside is a dark festering core, in the pit of the white bone, sloping down into the soft pink tendrils within the tooth.

'The decay has made contact with the canals, the infection is collecting at the base.' He indicates a yellow swelling. I blink, cough, look away. Finn glances up at me and then clears his throat. I notice a bald patch is forming at his crown.

'Excuse me for being so emotional,' I say. 'It's just that a close friend of mine died recently.'

Finn nods seriously. 'Ah yes. This is happening sometimes.'

I glance at the other half of the tooth. It rests in his hand like a single white lung, a smudge of brown rot visible even there. It is grotesque, but the pink prongs against the porcelain white, the black flapping bird of decay, are somehow exquisite.

Reservations
Katie Harrison

Back

He slipped his freshly washed fingers inside the soft pink flesh. Warm. Soft. Bony. It reminded him of Jessica. The day he'd taken her to the river and they floated in a canopy of flies. She was a brag. A brag about the shag by the river with the flies who came to watch. And then Jessica was gone. And he was here. With his hand inside a chicken.

'Shove a lemon up it,' the gruff voice broke through his squidgy thoughts like a garlic crusher.

'Yes chef,' he cried, getting into a rhythm only years of practice could perfect. Keeping pace, the pots began to bang. Cha, cha, cha the cheese grater sang. The head chef blasted up the gas. Hiss, hiss, whoosh went the flame. Spat went the oil. Sob went the sous chef wiping a tear for the onions. Now it was time to prepare the opening act. In the cacophony of cutlery, he noticed how sharp the knives looked tonight. Chop, chop. The great food theatre was warming up and his part ready to play. He couldn't hide behind the curtains for much longer, it was getting too hot. All they needed was the Front of House to announce, *'IT'S SHOWTIME!'*

Front

It was unheard of. In the history of the restaurant he could not recall a thing as catastrophic as this. The occasional empty table, but an empty house? Never. For years this had been the foodies' favourite. Awarded. Adored. People begged, pleaded, sobbed for a table. But if you had not booked up to six months in advance? Impossible. Yet tonight? Tonight, no one. He looked down and saw despair curve in the reflection of a spoon. Behind him the kitchen roared. For hours it had been whipping itself into a hot, bubbling frenzy. Soon it would be ready to spit out its creations, but there was no one here to soothe it with satisfied oohs and ahhs. He gulped, straightened a chair and tried to think, but all he could hear was the kitchen sharpening its knives.

Day Off
Ian M Macdonald

I

As she placed a balled, snotty tissue down onto the floor he moved his hand slowly towards it.

'No. Don't do that,' she said. 'You will get sick.'

'But it is… *dirty.*' he said, his voice slightly muffled and plum-like, affected by the latex pressing against his lips.

'No; leave it alone.'

She had her feet up on the sofa and the tartan blanket draped across her legs. Her hair, usually neatly pulled up into a tight, matron-like bun, fell loose in curls over hair face. There was a property show on the television about a British couple moving into a soviet looking tower block East of Berlin, which was more interesting than the usual places (Costa Brava, the Italian Riviera etc.), but she still could not keep her eyes from drifting over to Dag, who was on the floor on his hands and knees now, like a dog begging for food. His blue latex one-piece, which covered the entirety of his body bare a couple of small eyeholes, nostril holes, and a zip-up mouth hole, shone as if just waxed, but she knew by now that he must smell, and perhaps actually the snotty tissue she had dropped was cleaner than the latex. He was staring at her. She tried to concentrate on the television again.

'Mistress,' she thought she heard him whisper.

She looked at him again as he began to whimper like a dog needing to go out. A high pitched, emasculated noise vaguely resembling '*mama*'. He shuffled closer towards her, or at least tried to. The chain rattled on its fixing; a small metal hoop drilled into the wall by the fireplace.

'*Mistress…*' his voice strained from where the choke-chain pressed against his windpipe.

'Look!' she snapped, her phlegm-laden voice breaking. 'I just need… a couple of days off…. go to sleep.' She pointed to the large dog bed next to the fireplace. 'Or go and make yourself busy elsewhere for a while. Don't you have anything else you… want to do?'

He smiled and then stood up on his knees and presented himself to her. Beneath the latex over his crotch his pathetic erection was clearly visible. He stuck his wet tongue out between his lips as best he could, and he waggled it quickly up and down rapidly.

The emigres on the TV had just entered one of the apartments. It was spacious and minimalist in a way she imagined to be typical of East Berlin. She found herself mumble in approval and then she pulled a tissue from the box and blew her nose hard.

'Mistress, do you forget I am welded to the wall?'

He strained against the chain again and it jingled. It was typical that only the day before she had taken the sole key for the padlock to the shop to have a couple of spares cut; a wise safety precaution she thought, as they had already lost the previous duplicate somewhere (potentially in an orifice).

She had, in her initial excitement, agreed to the arrangement not only for the sexual pleasure, the *power,* and the *ethical* and arguably feminist sex, but also for the vastness of the standing order he had offered to set up, and she had perhaps not properly thought the whole scenario through. There was the bedpan, for a start. She did consider the installation of a chemical toilet in the corner of the room, perhaps behind an attractive Japanese paper screen, but then decided it had the ring of a prison or a private hospital room about it; most un-erotic. And then there was this whole matter; people get ill. People are generally not sex-fanatics uninterruptedly, completely devoted to a life of pleasure and pain, even with the money to have the freedom to be able to do so. Sometimes people get sick, sometimes people just want to let their hair down and sit on the sofa in their big, ugly pants and fart and snot. Sometimes people just want to watch Escape to the Sun.

'Ok. Build a fire,' she said, pointing to the fireplace, but he stayed-put on his hind legs, staring at her, and he smiled in the way that meant he wanted to play a game.

He laughed quietly in anticipation until she turned her attention back to the television, and then he began to make a pathetic moaning sound again. Summoning up all the energy she could muster, she picked up the riding cane resting on the coffee table and whacked him hard across the face with it. He cried out in genuine pain and he slumped to the side, clutching his cheek. He trembled all over.

'BUILD. A. FIRE,' she said, all croak and nasal-slurring.

Her voice like this lacked authority – like a sobbing child – but still he turned and crawled over to the fire place, his arse waggling in the air as he moved the logs from the steel box and into the hearth. Now, *there* was a hole in the latex which never failed to catch her off guard. Hairy and brown, it was well and truly the arsehole of an aged gentleman.

It took him barely ten minutes to construct the fire and get it lit so that she could feel the heat intensely even from eight-feet away on the sofa.

'Good boy,' she said and she settled back down to watch the television, and it wasn't long before she had to remove her cardigan and the blanket draped across her.

She turned up the television to drown out Dag's squeaking and shuffling, but it soon turned into rattling and moaning, and when she found herself unable to feign ignorance any longer, she looked over at Dag. He had one hand behind him – the finger of which was obviously penetrating his anus – and he was moving the digit back and forth rapidly so his whole body wobbled with the action. His tongue hung out of his mouth as the chain garrotted him, apparently to his delight.

'Dag! No! Naughty! You're being naughty!' She knew this was what he wanted and the more she berated him the more pleasure she seemed to detect in his eyes, and the faster the hand shuffled behind his back.

'Uuughhh.' he went, rasping and spitting against the collar. 'MMMM…'

She took the cane again and smacked him twice quickly in the ribs and then once, harder, on his right thigh. He yelped and twitched but didn't stop what he was doing so she whacked him once more around the face and he took his left hand from his arse – the forefinger of which was visibly shitty and she grimaced – and he pressed his palm against his cheek and then sank back a little, sated for the time being.

II

It wasn't long before Dag was at it again, whimpering and panting, begging, and presenting his childish-erection to her, thrusting it in her general direction as she sniffed wetly and swallowed the recurring painful lump in her throat. It was 12.30pm and, therefore, a civilised enough time for a medicinal brandy. She left Dag in the living room (well, she had no choice) and she found the bottle in the dining room. She poured herself a large glass as the chain continued to rattle out of sight, and she sighed. Her face felt swollen with fluid around her eyes and her sinuses throbbed painfully, she could only hear out of one ear. She gulped down the brandy, poured another, and then she made her way into the bedroom.

They were discrete enough, the hired mistress and her slave, and the bedroom's decor was your average *rich-person-living-in-the-past-chic*; all polished mahogany, thick, heavy curtains and luxurious wallpaper. It looked clean, but was it really? There was certainly no dust; Dag liked her to walk him around the room like a dog on a leash as he licked the floors and furniture clean, but she couldn't help feel that it now smelled of his musky saliva gone stale, like old drool on a pillow.

She pulled open Pandora's Wardrobe, as she had coined it proudly. It was neatly organised and contained various sizes and varieties of whips and clubs, stilettos, latex garments, the odd leather item (natural and therefore harder to clean), and racks of ominous looking, dildo-type objects. She reached into a small box on one of the shelves and pulled out a couple of bottles of amyl nitrate and then, for appearance's sake, she grasped hold of an enormous, bulbous dildo. It was not of the realist variety but instead a shiny, smooth, black thing shaped very much like a baseball bat and of a similar size. Which way it was to be inserted was you would assume at first glance, obvious, but the addition of a textured grip-taped handle at the thin end suggested otherwise. She tied up her hair and gave her nose a monstrous, wet blow before returning to the living room.

Dag's eyes lit up, he whimpered, and then he began to clap his hands excitedly like a seal. She hit him on the top of the head with the dildo and he groaned and held his head, before he sank down on to all-fours and turned his arse around towards her. Again, she grimaced. Occasionally – *occasionally* – the idea of this act genuinely turned her on, but this was certainly one of the jobs in which most of the time she felt she was really working for the money.

'Oh mistress! Oh mistress! Oh please! Please…' he said, and she reached over and zipped up the mouthpiece.

He nodded frantically and scrunched his eyes up, and she could see by the change in the shape of the latex at the cheeks that he was grinning manically. She could hear the air rushing in and out of the latex nose-holes over the soundtrack to Come Dine with Me.

'Mm mmtruh! Mm mmtruh! UUng ngnee nn nn nnaa!'

She got down on her knees next to him and put the plastic sandwich bag that she had filled with the poppers over his nose and secured it with a piece of string, like a feed bag for a horse. As he inhaled his eyes opened wide and his whole body seemed to mellow and she heard him chuckling under the mask.

As he began to wobble and his eyes grew more and more blood shot, she left the bag in place but unzipped his mouth piece and an old limp, swollen lip poked out. He sucked in oxygen through the stoma she had created and the swelling around his mouth and eyes began to subside a little as oxygen mixed in with the poppers. She zipped him up again, and as it looked like his eyes were about to shoot from his head – he could only exhale painfully slowly through the zipped mouthpiece – she unzipped him slightly, and air rasped from his lips like a geriatric's unconscious fart. He took a deep breath and then began to chuckle wildly.

'Now mistress now!' he seemed to say as he waggled his behind, and then she did the zip up again.

But rather than performing the deed she simply watched him as he sucked in the amyl nitrate and blew awkwardly out through the tiny gaps between the zipper's teeth. He was still giggling manically, but his eyes slowly began to gain a sleepy look and then he began to go limp. She guided him slowly towards the dog-bed beside the fireplace with gentle nudges, and when he had collapsed almost entirely to the floor she used a hefty tipping action, like rolling a whale back into the ocean. He bowled onto the dog bed and then almost over again into the fire, but she managed to grab him and pull him back. She let him take a few more deep breaths of the substance and then removed the bag and threw it into the waste-paper basket. Relieved, she took another huge slug of brandy and then refilled her glass before chucking a couple of logs onto the fire and settling down onto the sofa. Dag had completely passed out but his head and left leg twitched gently, perhaps in a dream of sexual deviance or child-like pleasure, who could ever know?

III

She *was* aware of a smell, as she came-to, despite her heavily blocked nose, but the thing which roused her fully was that David Dickinson seemed to be in the room, screaming questions about various antique objects to her. She had fallen asleep on the television remote, most notably the volume-up button, and as she scrabbled around for it and turned it down, she became aware of Dag screaming from beneath his mask. She was sweating profusely; it was very hot in the room, the fire roared violently.

The chain attaching Dag to the wall had been pulled taught as he strained against it and he had his hands around the collar on his neck to stop it cutting off his air completely. She noticed a funny haze, a kind of blue, slow smoke, which drifted upwards from behind him. His eyes were wild with desperation and then, even with her blocked nose, she recognised the smell as that of burning plastic or rubber, mixed with cooked meat like roast chicken.

'…*ag?*' she said, unable to pronounce the sounds efficiently what with the swelling in her sinuses.

Behind Dag she noticed the scorched remains of the dog bed, still smouldering, and a charcoal log resting beside it on the fireproof rug (*health and safety, health and safety…*). She leapt up in a panic suddenly and ran out of the room before re-emerging after a minute or so with a bucket of water, which she tipped over the dog bed and the crackling log and they sizzled and smoked heavily, extinguished. Dag was still screaming and when she turned around she could see that the latex on his back looked strange, like it had been shredded, and in-between the gaps there were strips of raw, red skin and milky-white blisters, huge wobbling things, and the ripped latex seemed to have fused with the scalded flesh on his back as if it was trying to consume him. Blue smoke billowed up from the awful mess.

'Oh god!' she cried, and stepped around in front of him.

She unzipped the mouthpiece and his gums were bleeding, it seemed he had gritted his teeth so hard that a couple of teeth had given in and split under the pressure.

'Set me free! Help me!' he screamed.

She stood up and covered her mouth with both hands as a violent nausea all of a sudden consumed her. She gagged but managed to swallow it, then she tried to speak but couldn't. *Call an ambulance,* her brain told her, but it was as if the passage between thought and action was constipated. She just stood there, frozen, her mouth aghast, somehow unable to take her eyes from the horror. *I'll have to ask them to bring bolt-cutters…*

'Sorry!' Dag gasped. 'Sorry! I mean, set me free please, *Mistress.*' He clawed at the collar, his whole body shaking and steaming. 'Help me, *MISTRESS!*'

Rats Lay Down Flat
Ian M Macdonald

He was not going to drink this week. He was sure of that. He was as sure of that as he was of the fact last week he had drank most of his waking hours. He was not going to drink this week as he was sick. He could keep nothing down. Was it a result of the drinking last week that he could this week not keep anything down? This morning he had tried to eat an egg, and it had wobbled at the very top of his throat and then with a gag and a cough it had shot out across the kitchen. He had come in after his shower to find his flatmate wiping it from the window with some kitchen towel. That's where it had gone.

He went to the pub on his way to work. A sparkling water. A sparkling water with ice, and no, no lemon. The sharp temperature numbed his throat and with small sips he managed to get the liquid down in a little over ten minutes. Perhaps he should try a half pint? After all, he needed the calories, he had not eaten for a week.

The half-pint went a little too well and had led to a full pint of beer, and then a bottle of vodka, which he hid in his bag and gulped from every half-hour or so throughout his shift. Nothing happened, as usual. No one tried to break in. The rats and the rabbits did not succeed in escaping from their cages. A real, wild rat did not trigger a false alarm after chewing through some cable or other, which had happened once about three years ago.

At 2.50am Susan walked in. His heart skipped a beat. He swallowed, zipped up his rucksack and slid it beneath the desk. Then he scrabbled through his pockets for a chewing gum. He couldn't find one. He leant back on his chair as far as he could from Susan and put a hand over his mouth as he spoke.

'What are you doing here?' he said, as casually as he could.

'Monthly meeting,' Susan said. 'You remembered, right?'

Providing there had been no disturbances or threats they were all to abandon their posts for one hour before the end of the late night-shift and the beginning of the early night-shift, and the early night-shift were to arrive one hour early in order to attend the meeting. He had not remembered. Now he remembered. He wished he could find some gum.

'Oh yes,' he said, and said nothing further. He picked up his rucksack and walked off with Susan towards the lecture theatre.

They walked past the cages. Creatures shuffled in straw. Rabbits and rats sucked at the metal tubes of their small water bottles. On each bottle was a small, white label with a code printed on it. Some of the rabbits and rats were assigned to a control group and received nothing at all. Not even Drugged-Water. They were simply there to die of thirst. Luckier groups of control creatures had plain, filtered, sterile water at which to sip, and these rats and rabbits slept contentedly on the floors of their cages.

The huge warehouse clicked, shuffled, rattled and squeaked. Rats on the right, rabbits on the left. He and Susan walked towards the airlock at the far end of the warehouse.

Wine. Beers. Orange Juice. Sitting on a pop-up table covered with a black cloth by the entrance to the lecture theatre. Susan picked up a beer and held it by her thigh discreetly. He guessed there was an unwritten rule about drinking before your shift. He picked up an orange juice, drank a large gulp, and then excused himself. In the toilet he drank another gulp of orange juice and then topped the glass to the brim with vodka from his bag, then he returned to the lecture hall, picking up a beer on the way to kill the breath.

Luckily someone had sat next to Susan. He sat on an aisle seat towards the middle of the room alone and drank his vodka and orange quickly and then he began on the bottle of beer.

3am.

Rats. Rats.

The handling of rats protocols:

- 'If the rat has an ear on its back, handle the rat with gloves gently. Do not destroy the rat.'
- 'If the rat glows blue when passed over with a torch, do not approach the rat. If safe to do so; shoot the rat.'
- 'Do not shoot the rat in section 23b, 35c, 62n or 31n. Flammable material.'
- 'The glowing blue rats are the only rats unsafe to handle at present. All other rats should be able to be contained manually or with the Rat Box™.'
- 'Apart from the rats with ears and the glowing blue rats, no other information is required about the rats.'

He knew about the blue rats. The blue rats didn't escape. Didn't want to. The blue rats just slept.

The rabbits, however. The rabbits were complicated. He should have brought his notepad. He had left it in the desk drawer. He had been working on a picture.

- '…If the rabbit has one black ear and one white ear…'
- '…If the rabbit has a long tail like a cat's tail then…'
- '…DO NOT use Rat Box™ on rabbit variations 6 and 7…'
- '…Here is a picture of a rabbit with one black spot next to a rabbit with a tracking device, unhelpfully also coloured black and around the same size as the rabbits' black spot on those rabbits who have black spots…'

Rats.

Protesters.

Vegans. Tee-total. Shared accommodation. Rat-infested layabouts.

He felt a little wobbly. A little sick. Susan looked across at him and frowned.

At 3.50am he stood up and walked out. He walked back in through the airlock and through the shuffling, clicking cages. He took his notepad with the drawing he was working on it from the desk drawer. He placed it in his rucksack and zipped it up and slid it onto his back. He unhooked his flashlight and checked it once, twice.

'I'm going to have to report you,' Susan said.

He clicked his flashlight off. It didn't matter.

'You weren't going to drink this week, remember.'

He nodded gently.

He said goodbye to Susan and left her at the desk. He began to feel queasy. He walked along between the cages towards the airlock, shining his flashlight into the cages of rats. Red eyes reflected back at him. Some rats shot up to the bars and nibbled on them like they were trying to get his attention or signal to him in some way. Others squeaked. Others shot back into their straw. Those that were scared and did not have the comfort of straw bedding pressed themselves into the very back corners of their cages.

There was a glint of blue as he shone his flashlight across the water bottle on cage 378, and sure enough when he held the flashlight over the sleeping rat it glowed blue. It lay on its side, its claws curled up softly, breathing slowly and peacefully, squeaking gently. Never had he seen a more peaceful rat, a more sumptuous slumber. The blue rats slept through anything. They slept through needles, they slept through the screams of their neighbours, their brethren, they slept through fire alarms and news reports. They slept through vivisection. They dreamed of better things and they dreamed forever and ever.

He went home, drank the half of the blue-hued rat-bottle that remained, and he dreamed of the ocean on a warm day.

He was not going to drink this week. He was not going to drink ever again.

Breakdown
Anita Goveas

Mr Stephanu is out for his pre-bedtime walk, when he's pulled by Sugar the schnauzer out to the park to do her business then back to the cul-de-sac. Lindsay waits to pat the dog, leaning on her fence, singing Swing Low, Sweet Chariot to a bedraggled teddy and a ragdoll with no legs. They watch the woman in the road wobble on the yellow line, resplendent in her crimson sari and pink washing-up gloves, arms out-stretched, one bare foot slapped in front of the other. The hum of the traffic on the main road pulls at them all like hunger.

Mrs Parker always slows down near the cul-de-sac, on her way to get the newspaper every evening for her bed-bound mother-in-law, while her husband practices his ball-room dancing. Past the lanky man with the over-fancy pampered dog, past the latch-key kid and her destructive tendencies, vigilant against threats since her brush with a five-car pile-up six months ago. Dogs and children are unpredictable. But elderly women in pink washing-up gloves don't swagger in the road towards their potential destruction, it's a trick of the lowering sun, a ghost of her begrudging responsibilities. She stamps her foot down on the accelerator.

Mrs Chopra is invincible again, in her wedding sari and best jewellery, feet back on the earth in a way she's missed since Mumbai. Tell them to fuck off, she shouts to the pink-cheeked girl leaning on the fence, who has more imagination than all her own children put together. Go out on her own terms is all she wants, quick and simple. Until that whiskery dog runs off towards the sunset, she scoops him up before he hits the Nissan that's going too fast, his fur smells like grass and sunshine, and her tears don't bother him at all.

Up the Silver Cord
Rob True

Theron returned to his body to find his mouth trailing off a sentence that had not been spoken by himself. He only caught the last bit, something about chopping a donkey, climbing a hillside. But it had stopped, as he reappeared inside his head, faced with a few people looking blankly at him.

'It weren't me who said that,' he offered, by way of explanation of whatever strangeness had just spewed from his lips, as though something else talking through him was any less odd. The others looked embarrassed. He'd had this before, disappearing and then coming back to his body, with no idea where he'd been in-between. Just patterns for memory. That was the first time he'd been aware of his head saying something when he got back in.

Oh well.

He looked around, to make sure none of the vultures had taken anything, put another big stone on the pipe, lit it and licked it in one go. Holding the clouds down, he looked at shadow spiders crawling around him and then exhaled.

Later, the others had left, bar one. Little Dan soldiered on through the weird, wired atmosphere for the handouts. Theron stood at the window, checking for what? Police? Maybe. He sat down, stood again, looking out and there he was, a man staring straight up at him.

'Look at that geezer down there,' Theron said, eyes showing fear.

Little Dan peered out, but there was no one there. 'Where?'

'Look, down there. He's not even hiding!'

'There's nobody there mate,' little Dan said, a sly grin spreading.

Theron rubbed his face, unsure of everything. He sat down, took another lick on the pipe and inside his bone-box cinema, playing on a loop, Stan Laurel was saying 'We're not us. We're two other fellers.'

Back at the window, he watched, staring out. There was a long-limbed, naked, alien creature sitting on a deck chair, pretending to read a book, while spying on him. Theron stepped back from the glass in horror.

'Look down there. Tell me that monster ain't sitting there!'

Seeing little Dan's mouth and nose extending out, like a dog's snout, he punched him straight in the face.

'You're fuckin' one of 'em!'

Theron swayed slightly, gazing at his knuckles, wondering if the small man he'd just knocked down was real.

Little Dan got up, dazed and wiped the blood across his upper lip. Feeling the attack was worth what had been given to him all day and night, he thought better of complaining. He saw Theron setting up another bone on the glass.

'Why don't you stop doin' that and have something to calm down?'

Theron looked at him a moment, checking he wasn't a threat and reached for the spoon and syringe.

'Yeah, I know.'

He cooked a fix and shot himself up a smooth landing. Face slackened, losing the mad grimace, he slumped in his chair. Little Dan looked on, hopeful of another free ride from the schizo with all the tickets, patron saint of lost losers and lunatics.

Dryad
Rob True

The tension was killing us. She'd become distant. So far away. But she claimed it was me who'd been remote. Unreachable, she said. Like some invisible wall between us. Cooped up with her in that desolate flat. Together alone. So lonely. I was afraid that if I reached out and touched her, she'd vanish. It hadn't been right for some time. There was an atmosphere of doom around us. Or rather the atmosphere was around me and Sarah was losing her patience. Haunted by memories of us laughing that echoed through my mind. No laughter now.

We drove to a park on the edge of town. Green fields, deep woods. We'd gone for a walk to try and find some peace between us. She kept coming up with ideas like this walk in the hope of improving our situation. Long shot. I felt bleak and empty. No hope. I didn't love her. I don't think I ever had. I'd tried to convince myself I loved her because it was easier to take advantage of her that way. I was clinging on because I was afraid to be alone. Of everything falling apart around me, piece by piece. The bills, the cooking, the cleaning. Without her, I wouldn't be able to hold it together. She looked after me and that was enough. Or it had been. I'm not so sure what she got out of it, but there must have been something.

Sarah had made some sandwiches for a little picnic. We spread out a blanket and sat down at the edge of a field by the woods. Eating in silence, we looked at each other and smiled. It was a sad smile on Sarah's face. A mask that didn't fit. I looked away across the fields and, although the sun was shining, the whole scene looked miserable and forlorn. Melancholy clouds, threatening in an abysmal sky, tall grass, a broken-down fence. The saddest picture I'd ever seen. A shadow grew across the field, and the sky was green.

'Let's walk through the forest.'

Sarah nodded. We finished our sandwiches and strolled a little way into the woods.

I had led the way and when I turned back to say something to Sarah, she was gone. Tall trees and shadow. The sunlight reached the ground here and there through the canopies above. I heard her giggle and saw her run from a tree, and she disappeared behind another. I walked toward the tree grinning at our new game. When I got to it, she wasn't there. She giggled again, her laughter bouncing off the bark around me, and I turned to see her run from behind another tree.

She stopped behind a tall, terrible oak and disappeared again. Then I saw her run from a different tree. I was mesmerised. For some reason, I didn't even stop to wonder how she was doing it. I enjoyed the game. Chasing her from tree to tree. I remembered playing in the woods as a child. Hide and seek. I'd found a girl and there, behind a bush, for no apparent reason, she'd shown me what was in her knickers. It seemed to me; girls become strange entities in the forest. Sarah ran from behind a tree, giggling and vanished behind another.

After some time, the fun appeared to be finished. I couldn't see or hear her anywhere. I called her name, but no answer came. My voice sounded unfamiliar to me against the quiet of the rustling leaves. The trees all stood tall around me, looking down. Watching. Amused at my confusion. Taunting. A cold fear swept through my bones. The air grew thick, and the trees darkened. Branches reached toward me. It felt like something dreadful was about to happen. I walked back to the field.

There she was sitting on the picnic blanket looking a bit cross.

'What have you been doing all this time?'

'I was chasing you.'

'Eh? No, you weren't.'

'Yeah, I was. You was running and hiding behind the trees, and I was trying to catch you.'

'What are you talking about? I came back out here about half an hour ago when you marched off without me.'

'What?'

She looked me in the eye and pinned me down with an accusing stare.

'We came here to spend a bit of time together and you just want to go off by yourself. You didn't even notice I'd gone.'

I was baffled. It didn't make sense. I thought about the girl in the woods and tried to remember what she was wearing. If she looked like Sarah. I was sure it was her. I didn't know what to say. It was as though she was playing a trick on me. I thought it best not to say anything. A cold atmosphere crept back over us. It came between us and left us so far apart. We packed up and left without another word.

Not the Time
Izzy Arcoleo

And then it was winter. Cut glass quiet echoed, and she would've felt lonely except for the icicles that cracked between her fingers.

'Is anyone here?' she called out.

And the winter replied, 'Always.'

And she felt the love of the cold that wrapped everything up to rest and numbed the pain of dulling wounds, and cooled red scars until they faded to thin, white memory lines.

'It hurt,' she said. 'This year, I turned myself around until the ground beneath my feet was drilled away to dust. Nothing is the same as it was. I don't know any of the things I knew before.'

The winter nodded but was silent. The winter knew that it didn't matter if she knew nothing because this wasn't the time for knowing.

She looked down and saw the dust below her, glistening with frozen water, each particle shining and brittle and turning, quickly, into something new. She understood.

So she stepped out of the dust and into the snow. She sat, closed her eyes, and felt the world settle inside her; while the pores of the plants were closed and sleeping, she would rest too; and the searing hot spaces inside her began to temper, and close.

The world would change again, and she would be awake again. But now, no. This was not the time for knowing.

Only Up Here
Fernando Sdrigotti

Midday. I've been rolling around in bed since I quit last week. It happened out of nowhere: I pulled myself a double Jameson's during a busy shift and sat on the other side of the bar. What are you doing? I'm quitting. You can't quit. Yes I can: look. Go have a fag and come back behind the bar. I won't – it's too busy behind the bar. You've got to give me a week's notice. Silence. I finished my drink and walked out of the pub with the voice of the Cypriot telling me I was barred. I left with most of my money in my pocket; not that they would ever notice – they could never get the maths right. And then I felt like I owned the world, that I could go anywhere. London was finally smiling at me: no more bars, no more mopping the floor, collecting pints, long shifts serving wankers. The beginning of a new era; then it was the future already and the future of that future was full of promises. The high lasted for a couple of hours. Soon I realised I was unemployed. And I hit the bed. I must have been in bed for five days.

Not exactly five days in bed but five days of leaving it only to go for a piss, grab something to eat, smoke a cigarette, have a drink of water. And the same happened to Leo: he fell into introspection at about the same time – two days before me, actually. My moments of ecstasy and sadness were probably a copycat version of his, after he quit his job at the Bricklayer's Arms. He had come home hyperventilated, coked-up, speaking about his plans to go back to film school, how we should rent a car on Sunday and drive to Cambridge, Oxford, Kent, Cornwall, whatever, like Thelma and Louise. And then the bed. Just like I would some days later.

Midday all through this side of the studio flat and on Leo's side too. I'm head-to-the-pillow when the sun comes through the huge window. The smell of feet in the room, burnt cigarette butts, lack of personal and general hygiene, the mess all around us. We ran out of cunting cigarettes too, says Leo. Go get some, I says. Fuck off, he says, and didn't even raise his head from the pillow. Anyway, it's only a matter of holding on until tonight. Maybe I'll even fall asleep and wake up tomorrow.

By two p.m. I can't take it anymore and I leave the flat. It's stupidly sunny while I make my way to George's Kebab, just around the corner. I walk into his place with my stomach rumbling and don't even say hi until I've ordered my food: a large shish with humus and a can of ginger beer. Hello first, innit? Hello George! Sorry, I'm really hungry. No worries my friend we'll feed you. Nice to see you; where were you? he asks. I was away, at a training course to join the Royal Marines, I say. I thought you had to be British to join the army, he says. They've changed the rules now; they need people from other backgrounds. How did the training go? I passed it! Good on you, son. But I've changed my mind, I don't think the army is for me. Yes, don't join those cunts on anything. I won't! Large shish and humus and a can of ginger beer; there you go my friend, he says, and nods towards the back door.

Soon I'm sitting in the back room, watching my team 'back home' playing a shitty football game; the commentary is in Turkish – it's all very strange. Eleven thousand one hundred and forty-six kilometres away, I'm watching twenty two Argentine idiots chase a ball in real time. With three or four seconds delay, perhaps, but live. It's mind-boggling. From Buenos Aires and across the Atlantic, over the Ural mountains, BANG!, Istanbul, then picked up by a Soviet satellite who-knows-how-many kilometres above the atmosphere and BANG! (again) on the telly before me. I tell an old leather jacket-clad Turk about this uncanny situation. I think he doesn't understand me – he just smiles blankly and then goes back to his paper. I shut up and eat the kebab.

The other guy is here as well; the guy with the weird little eye, the second-in-command. He calls me 'my friend' too. He soon spots me and sits on the table with me. He asks where I have been I tell him I've been working overtime, managing the pub isn't an easy job, you see. Then I tell him they fired me. He seems confused, puzzled, or perhaps just drunk. He says something about these fucking English cunts. I tell him the owners of the place are Cypriots. He says they must be Greek Cypriots. I say I am pretty sure they're Turkish Cypriots. He doesn't reply and stops talking to me for a while. Then he says that there are cunts everywhere – he's absolutely right. He's drinking Raki and his eye, the funky one, gets smaller with every sip. By the end of the bottle he'll look like Thom Yorke. But before that happens my team scores a goal and I celebrate by closing my fist and saying yessssss. Little eye celebrates too – he hugs me and gets a bit overexcited and drops his glass on the floor. He curses in Turkish and leaves through the front door. The accident doesn't seem to bother the rest of the guys in the room – they're all busy looking at a laptop. Kebab people love gadgets – they are technological people. Little eye comes back and sweeps the floor with a broom. Stumbling and singing something in Turkish.

This incredible universe of brands, shelves, smells, little and medium-sized tins and cans, unpronounceable names and inedible processed meals.

The off-licence guy asks me where I've been. I tell him I was on a meditation retreat on the Isle of Man. I don't even know how

I come up with this. He doesn't say anything for a while. Then he asks me about my job, did I take a holiday? I say I've quit and he frowns. I pay for the beers, the Supermalt and the Jaffa cakes. Thanks. You're welcome. A frown, a clearly annoyed frown. He says that I have to work now that I'm young so that I can retire well when I'm older. I knew he would come up with some shit like that. I tell him that I've got a job interview in the City this week, for Royal Bank of Scotland, and that's why I quit my job at the bar and went on a meditation retreat. He says I should have quit only after nailing the job. I say I needed time to prepare for the job interview – god, I hate hard-working people. He asks me what sort of meditation I practice. I ask what does he mean with what kind. Vipassana, Zen, Mindfulness? he asks. It's all the same, I say. No, it isn't. He seems to know all about it. I say Singing Yoga Meditation. Singing Yoga Meditation? He seems confused. I tell him we do yoga, sing and then meditate. I don't think he buys it. It's a sort of New Age thing, very popular in Argentina and Liverpool Street. Never heard of it. It's a new thing. Then he asks me about 'my friend Leo' managing to sound the quotation marks, the homophobe. I tell him that he's still at the retreat, that he decided to stay a bit longer, he's getting good at the singing yoga but needs to improve on the meditative side of things. He quit his job too? Yes, he did. He has an interview at Warner Brothers the same day I have mine at Royal Bank of Scotland. You're doing fine, he says. It was about time, I say. He tells me to remind Leo that he owes him twenty pounds. I say I will. When's your interview, he asks. On Wednesday, I say. Good luck to you both. I thank him and walk out.

It's three p.m. and still very sunny. I cross the road and walk towards St. Leonard's churchyard. When I'm halfway there I feel I need to go for a piss. So I backtrack and head to the public toilets on the corner of Columbia and Hackney roads, some hundred metres up. There aren't many people around save for some hipsters carrying flowers and plants from the flower market. Perhaps I should go and buy a plant or just walk to the market, see people, maybe bump into someone I know, have a coffee, get some clean air.

A couple of minutes pass and the door remains locked. I look at a couple passing by, a girl and a guy; the girl with skinny legs, flat ass and huge tits, the guy very tall and pale, quite good looking, but he's wearing flip-flops and has huge bony feet. They stare at me when they pass – it must be my plastic bag. And they're gone. Some more people carrying plants, the phone booth; I start to get bored. I remember when I called Guido from this phone booth soon after I arrived. I called him crying, paying for the phone call with pound coins, saying that I was freaking out because I was feeling suicidal and was missing Buenos Aires. It was a very expensive phone call. Why do you say that? I don't really know; it's just this horrible idea I can't get out of my head: I think I'll kill myself. Have you been using drugs? No. Since when do you have this in your head? Since I arrived, I said, London is a shithole. I don't know why I called him, of all the people back home. I guess I needed to speak to someone and his was the only number I remembered at the time. Suddenly I ran out of coins and the call ended. It must have been a disturbing phone call, because he started emailing me like mad afterward, saying that I was very selfish calling him out of the blue like that, after we had agreed to let things cool down, that he had to ask around to find out if I was still alive, that I should have at least called him back to tell him I hadn't topped my head. I never replied to his emails but he kept sending them. I thought he would just let it go but he didn't give up. So I blocked him. He changed his email and I blocked him again and he changed the email address and so on: the whole process went on for a while. Until I tired and changed my email and gave it only to my mother and father. But he got hold of my phone number and started calling me until I changed my number too. I should have never called him that day: he's insane.

The door finally opens and one of the local crackheads leaves. He bows in a friendly way and I say hi. He's high as a kite and looks very happy. The door closes behind him and there's a sound of water; the word 'cleaning' starts flashing in red on the door and we both stare at it and it's fascinating. He gets bored and walks away. When he's walked some twenty metres he turns around and waves with a broad smile. I wave back at him, just about the same time the word 'cleaning' stops flashing. I put 20p in the slot and the door opens and I walk in. It looks pretty clean: no sign of drug paraphernalia, no weird smells, no small pieces of cotton. Perhaps he was really in need of a toilet.

I struggle for a bit first but then manage to piss with my plastic bag in one hand. A nice piss, longer than expected, but a bit dark, perhaps from having my kidneys crushed during my last few days in bed. It feels great to piss in a different toilet – I can see things are beginning to move. When I finish I leave without washing my hands because my dick must be cleaner than the faucet. The door opens and I leave. The door closes behind me and the flushing sound starts once more.

Sunny, so sunny. The traffic as a background mantra and traces of fumes in the air. I'm just sitting on a bench in the middle of the churchyard, checking out the tombstones in the distance and drinking my Supermalt. There are a couple of crackheads – others – loitering about. A guy, around thirty, and a girl, who could be anything from seventeen to forty-five. They've been around the yard, picking cigarette butts and putting them in their pockets and scavenging who knows what from the trash bins.

Now they're arguing by the church entrance. I can't hear what they say, but she shouts louder than him. She moves her hands like a Neapolitan, a lot of hands being thrown into the air in all directions – crack makes people very expressive. Or she must be communicating something very important, or maybe she just talks like that, like a Neapolitan; or maybe she is a Neapolitan. I've seen this couple before many times since I moved to Waterson Street. They hang around with the public toilet crackhead, mostly around the churchyard, although I've seen them walking up and down Old Street, frantically begging for money and tobacco from the wankers late on Fridays and Saturdays. Crackheads are always in fast forward, always in a rush to get somewhere. Many times I've thought I should stop one of them and ask them what's the rush. So far I've never done this and perhaps I'll never will: you don't want to stop people when they're on their way to score.

It's getting hot and humid now; it's getting dark: it'll rain. I light up one of my counterfeit Polish Marlboro. Smoking feels funny: smoke gets denser and the cigarettes smokier. The fag doesn't taste right, and it smells weird, and I can't tell whether it's the humidity or the taste of Eastern Europe.

Back in the off-licence I buy a new lighter, a can of tuna, mozzarella, baked beans and crisps. I ask the guy to swap my cans for cold ones. He agrees but gives me an evil eye and checks the cans haven't been opened. I know he thinks I'm a lazy fuck and that he doesn't trust me; I don't trust him either. He's always checking the CCTV screen when I walk to the back of the shop and I'm always checking the expiry date on the products. He tells me once more to remind Leo about his twenty pounds. I say I will, and think to myself that he's bound to live out his days behind the counter of his tiny shop, until he gets his throat cut from ear to ear by one of the churchyard bums. But I don't tell him that.

Things are better next door. No need for CCTV when you have a large kebab knife behind the counter. I buy three more packs from little eye. *Palenie Zabija. Palenia Zabija* I say, *chcesz papierosa*. Eight pounds my friend, he says. Three for eight pounds. Even if they taste like shit: long live the EU, long live Poland and continental cancer.

Soon I get home. I open the door. Leo is still tucked under the sheets. He looks at me when I enter the flat. Morning, I say, I got us food. Morning, he says. It's four thirty. He doesn't reply and I'm starting to get tired of his self-pity. I'll cook some food, I say. More silence.

I walk towards the kitchen area and open a drawer and get the tin opener. I open the can of tuna and empty it into a medium-sized bowl. I open the baked beans and mix the beans with the tuna. I put the mix in the microwave oven, set it for three minutes. While the tuna and the beans are turning I put the beers in the fridge. Then I get the mozzarella out of the pack and lay it on a plate. I watch the bowl turn in the oven and soon the thing beeps a couple of times. I cut the mozzarella in two and then open the oven and get the bowl out and empty some of the tuna and beans from the bowl into the plate; then I put one of the halves of mozzarella in the bowl. There you go, you need to eat something, I say, holding a plate to Leo's face. I'm not hungry, he says. Eat anyway; I've got cigarettes, a lot of them; but no ciggies until you've eaten. Which ones? George's or the cabbies'? George's. Lights or reds? Lights. I like reds, he says. I don't, I say. I leave the plate next to Leo's bed and go to my side of the room. I'm hungry and I eat fast. Before I finish my plate I see Leo grabbing his. He starts eating, slowly.

It'll rain, I say. Yes, he answers. It's very muggy out there. Yes, it feels muggy in here too. I got us some beers; I thought we could go to the roof, drink beer, smoke, listen to music. It'll rain, he says. We can hide under the water tank. I'm not sure I want to go all the way up, he says, sorry. No worries, I say, I'll go by myself.

I finish eating from my bowl and leave it by the side of the bed. I move my clothes around until I find my small CD player. I press play to see if the batteries are still good – it would seem so, at least the CD seems to be moving: THESUNDAYSTHESUNDAYS THESUNDAYS. The letters become one large white lump and I press stop. I can feel Leo staring at me but I don't look back. I get my cigarettes and keys, grab the beers from the fridge and leave. I'll be on the roof, I say before I close the door.

The parking lot and the flats all around. Three blocks in a square of which the fourth side leads to an alley, some more workshops, or the end of the world for all I know. And here four floors of huge windows, reconverted workshops, tall ceilings and cold lofty spaces – places never meant to be lived in. There are traces of fabrics scattered in the lot and some weird cylindrical props. A huge cardboard palm tree lays next the overfilled garbage skip. A flash flares in one of the few flats with curtains. Someone shouting in Italian below me. A girl laughs somewhere. And five cool-looking people are barbecuing something on the roof to my right. People are going about their lives in their flats and the sky is bright yellow. I haven't opened a can yet, I haven't lit up yet, I haven't even pressed play. I'm just sitting here, under the water tank, looking.

Thunder, finally, and Leo's hand resting on my shoulder. He sits by my side, wrapped inside one of his sheets – a stinking greasy-haired Jesus Christ. I pass him the Polish Marlboros and he lights up. I'm glad you came, I say. It's breezy up here, he says.

Beers are opened – no need for a toast. We drink in silence and smoke. We both look at the sky. It can't be long before the clouds fall down like sacks of potatoes. But the barbecue people on the other roof don't seem to care. Perhaps they haven't even realised or perhaps they've reached an ideal state of unawareness of the things around them. Shit, he says, it will rain like in the Bible. Yes, I say. I've left the windows open, he says. Don't worry Leo, we're only up here. He nods and I press play. We stay there under the water tank, listening to The Sundays.

And then it starts raining.

Everything is What It Is
Fernando Sdrigotti

To Mark Fisher

That's a bateaux mouche, it's packed full of tourists, some of them wave in our direction, people always wave from boats, god knows why. And a horn, like a foghorn yet different, perhaps doing what all horns do but in French. And Île de la Cité, Square du Vert Galant, the Seine. And this urge to scream something, anything, not even words, perhaps just howl, puncture my lungs howling, shatter every glass around me, the lenses of all these needlessly big cameras, the windows of the Louvre. I know it's rather pointless but the urge exists and I need to acknowledge it. Acknowledge the urge; it is what it is, this urge, it can't be escaped, nothing can. Everything is what it is. And the sun is sinking west, that's what it is too.

And lovelocks everywhere – gold and silver, and even red, green, and blue sparks. Lovelocks in the Pont des Arts as there were lovelocks just a while ago when we walked past the Pont Neuf, as there are lovelocks anywhere where anyone with an inclination for clingy declarations of love had the brilliant idea of leaving a memento of their fear of dying alone. You can buy them off Amazon now; they can be personalised with the names of the involved parties; that's what it is too, no point in fighting it. But that's not here, it is what it is somewhere else – I'm drifting. Here is the bridge, the river, the lovelocks and the tourists. And the year abroad students. And the Americans – almost everyone is an American or could be one. And many of them are drinking their tepid wine. Young and carefree and drinking their tepid wine, just like every Sunday in this same spot. Carefree, beautiful people, not very bright, doing stereotypically Parisian stuff: tourists.

I'm drifting; I'm judging – breathe.

Then breathe again. Etc. Etc. Etc. Repetition. There's a rhythm; you need to connect with this rhythm, or so it goes, find something that brings you back to the present, take things in, kill the mental feedback, the brass orchestra, the trombone solo out of key, the noise. So I take it all in, keep taking it all in, trying not to shut the trombone player down with a mental sawed-off shotgun but hoping it'll go away, which is already a way of failing, because that's not what it is. But I still make a case of taking it all in, trying to do it non-judgmentally, like the guy said – if I fail at least there's that, the trying. He said I should be in the present, shouldn't judge the present, and shouldn't judge my thoughts, or try to shut them down, just let them be. He said many things, this guy who was peddling some life advice that sounded right to me yesterday. Advice which came across as something sensible: be where you are, don't punish yourself, this is the only life you've got, do things, your breathing is like a bell – I don't know exactly what this means, but it was a nice image, the bell. And it helped. It was bad before yesterday and it worked when I went to the talk, after Chris insisted I go, 'because it can change your life around, mindfulness,' and it was even in English, organised by some British *expat* NGO that cares about the mental health of monolinguals. And it was free – there wasn't a lot against it. And like I said, it did work, at least for a couple of hours; I found some form of peace, I think. He seemed like a decent guy, even if most of what he said was bordering the obvious. But sometimes you need to hear or read the obvious. Grab a book by Mark Hiller or Peter Coutinho and surrender to the commonplace, sink into the banality of the obvious, drown in it. The cliché preached as the ultimate truth – sometimes that's what you need and that's what it is too, when what you need is that. Sometimes what you need are basic ideas delivered in short sentences or even via lists or bullet points, repeated to you as if you were an idiot.

TO BE HAPPY:

* Don't overthink
* Don't overthink
* Don't overthink
* Don't overthink
* Don't overthink
* Don't overthink
* Don't overthink
* Don't overthink
* Don't overthink
* Don't overthink

But this is NOT what it is right now and I'm drifting once again and I can tell I'm full of spite and that's a recipe for disaster. Maybe you have to call the cynicism off. For even just an hour of this guy delivering his commonplaces to an audience of desperate idiots yesterday was better than nothing, better than the angst of the previous weeks, the tuba and the trombone and the fucking English, French, Dutch, whatever horns, playing at the same time, not hitting a single note, reminding me over and over again that nothing makes any sense, for the sole reason that nothing has a sense, that's how things are. Once you realise that things have no sense there's no going back. Once you see things for what they are you are fucked. And I guess I hate him, now – this meditation guy – because he made things making sense sound so easy, so effortless, he made it sound like there was an alternative to the despair that comes with feeling alive, and things even worked for a couple of hours and then everything stopped working and I can't make then work again and I feel miserable again. So I will have to come back to one of his talks, take some more pointers, more mental notes towards a voluntary lobotomy, even if that's already a form of not being really there; not the lobotomy, I mean all that thinking I will end up doing, the battle between the side that thinks and the one that wants to stop thinking, and I will try and fail again for the sole reason that nothing ever came easily to me, because (like I sort of said already) I figured out long ago what things are like, which is not what it is, apparently, if I'm getting this mindfulness stuff right. But maybe that's what it's all about, to cling to whatever works, while it does, however sad and pathetic this is. Make sense of things whichever way you can, while you can, and stop thinking so much ahead or into the past or thinking that things have to be so complicated and perhaps think when you have to think and stop thinking when you have to stop, and maybe just think about the now, this precise moment right here, the bell, because it's my impression it's impossible to stop thinking completely, there'll always be thoughts, and there'll always be me reminding myself about myself, that I'm a grain of sand in the middle of the desert and that nothing has any meaning, if I could be dead the next second, no one knows – how can things make any sense like that? And maybe then and there it was a matter of paying attention and actually using my brain, and maybe the 'don't overthink' thing – and other versions of it – need to be taken metaphorically. Perhaps it means you don't have to think about how things really are but think about what it is, at that moment, that precise moment and nothing else. Perhaps it's about doing what you have to do and not doing what you don't have to do. Maybe that's also what it is. Or maybe it's the opposite; I don't know; I'm confused now, but I swear I keep trying to make it work. I want to make it work and I want things to make sense – there's that, which could be actually counterproductive. But maybe I'm just damaged, like a broken machine, and I just wish I could give up and start thinking in lists and short sentences or at least not to find them stultifying. Maybe I should buy a self-help book; maybe there's a self-help book to teach you to take self-help seriously.

But here: here once more – here is what it is. This place, the Pont des Arts – that's what it is. And we're also drinking our tepid wine. I have a drink and tell myself that the wine is tepid, which sort of ruins the wine for me, but it still brings me back to something, at least to the fact that the wine is tepid, and it is tepid now. We've been drinking since lunchtime and we're drunk. Not off the trolley drunk but drunk nevertheless. Chris is merry – he's said several times that he's merry, for the girls he started chatting up (in English) to hear. And I pretend to be merry – I even smile. But I'm here in the present and here and in the present what it is – once more, against my attempt not to think about it – is feeling that nothing – absolutely nothing at all – makes any sense: life is a joke, a perverse joke, you get the drill. The feeling is like a stain of grease on everything, and I can't make that go away even if I'm so much in the present that I could die. Now this is I, feeling like nothing has the smallest point, nothing makes sense, in the Pont des Arts, on a warm Sunday, wanting to die or to stop thinking, while the wine is tepid and the sun is singing its swan song, and my thoughts are getting corny, and I'm not only leaving the now but I'm searching for those picturesque images like everyone else over here, because that's what people do in Paris, right? But maybe this is also mindfulness: this awareness that nothing makes any sense, that I can't stop thinking about that even if I think about the present, and that my mental images aren't necessarily that bright, that I'm as guilty of cliches as your random cretin carrying a DSLR, taking pictures he'll never see again and that will be lost in the Cloud when he dies some years down the line. Maybe that's what it is? Still, if it's not mindfulness at least is another place from where to start, from where to unpack who I am and what this is all about, although I'll end up hitting an existential wall, which apparently isn't what it is, for some reason I still don't get. Perhaps; I don't know. In any case it's clear I'm rather selfish to be licking my wounds like this, when other people have to deal with more serious shit, like a terminal disease, unemployment, the death of a partner, war, bunions, bad breath, piles, a tiny cock, what have you, on top of things not having any sense. But, hey, I need to avoid letting it become guilt. Nothing good can come out of guilt: guilt is selfish – someone said that, the guy might have said it. Or maybe Chris did. Or maybe Mark Hiller or Peter Coutinho tweeted about it, because there's no way I'd come up with that on my own, even if a child could, and yes it was Mark Hiller who wrote it in his latest book.

DON'T FEEL GUILTY:
* Guilt is selfish
* Guilt is selfish
* Guilt is selfish
* Guilt is selfish
* Guilt is selfish
* Guilt is selfish
* Guilt is selfish
* Guilt is selfish
* Guilt is selfish
* Guilt is selfish

So I tell myself that what it is right now is that I'm living in Paris, that I have no right to wallow in self-pity with this loops about nothing having any sense. And I have no right to feel guilty about clocking that things make no sense. Basically there's no need to lick my imaginary wounds, because everything there is to everything is this moment, this now – don't beat myself up but don't pat myself on the back either, that's what I should be aiming for. And everything is a possibility now: all the roads are open, I'm only 41, and I still have a lot to live and some things to give and perhaps things will make sense a couple of days, weeks, months, years, or perhaps just seconds from now, or I might get used to the lack of sense, and that's the beauty of life, or at least just its point, this constant surprise, yes, perhaps that's its point. And I even have a relatively good job: I make good money, I'm my own boss, I work the hours I want, I live wherever I want, and I will very likely work until the day I drop dead because I won't have a pension or a house of my own or nothing like that, but at least the work is rather stable and I'll never starve, that's quite certain, even if the rest of the world is falling to pieces around me, everything is going to the dogs, everyone is working 120 hours shifts and expecting everyone else to do so, and robots will sooner than later conquer us, take our jobs, fuck us in the arse and drink our spleen in their robot cocktails. But things are still going well for me and I should be thankful – and this is another reason for stopping being such a wuss, and here's the guilt once more, fucking god, here's the guilt and as I tell this to myself I also tell myself that I'm not only feeling guilty but overthinking and remember what Mark Hiller says about overthinking, I'm overthinking and not being here and now, and I tell myself that I don't always have to buy or even engage with my thoughts – and yes, the guy in the course said that as well, although Mark Hiller or Peter Coutinho could have said it too, they might as well be the same guy, I have a sip from my wine.

'He's not depressed, no, he's really into meditation,' I overhear Chris say to one of the girls, both who speak English with an accent I can't quite place. I also forgot their names, as much as I had forgotten about them while trying to be here and let things be what they are, only to be trapped by my thoughts, always my thoughts. I only know that they are very young (twenty or twenty-one the most, perhaps less) and quite pretty and that makes me feel worse. I feel like one of those old creeps who go to nightclubs until they are sixty-something, leaving a stream of piss wherever they walk, trying to turn back time by fucking the young, with a limp dick. 'How cool!' says the one with the ponytail and I smile at her and she smiles back at me and her smile is painful to watch, so much youth, so much untainted beauty, her smile is so open – it's terrifying.

But I'm not that much into meditation – I'm actually depressed and if I'm not depressed – because the word has lost its value these days where we wear our plights like a badge of honour – at least I'm quite lost and can't figure out how to go on, what for, how not to jump under a bus, from a building or into the river with stones in my pockets, take an OD of Paracetamol, what to go on for, if nothing makes any sense? Although I'm trying for things to make sense and that's why I went to that mindfulness thing, after finally listening to Chris, who may be a functioning alcoholic but still gets some things. A couple of months ago, when everything seemed to me just like a bad dream that would vanish in the morning, he started to tease me with this kind of stuff, 'stuff that can help you grow as a human being,' he said, 'you need to stop thinking so much about yourself and try to see the bigger picture'. So, in order for me to get the Bigger Picture, he would drop passing references to this or that, things that sounded like nothing at all to me but that suggested other realities, possibilities, ways out. I never got my head around this kind of mystical stuff but Chris made it sound promising, like there was something out there that wasn't just this, but that was fine anyway, which was another form of things being what they are but that it didn't entail things not making sense. The Bigger Picture was perhaps something that gelled everything together, something that made all our problems rather ridiculous, an order, a logic, something mightier and more important than our ephemeral and short human lives. And then we watched two documentaries with English subtitles that he downloaded from a torrents website. The first one a film about some guy called Gourdief, where everyone was dressed with very furry clothes, and it was snowing all the time, and there was a lot of esoteric chit chat that I could barely follow. And then one about how every religion is actually a variation of the same pagan rites. In this one a Buddhist monk talks about being in the present which is sort of coheres with what the guy said in the talk yesterday, but then a lot of things happened – there was a lot of information, the film seemed to be about everything, and this confused me quite a bit, because from being in the present we ended up in 9/11 and how everything was a big coverup, that it wasn't really Bin Laden who did it but the Bush administration and I think probably Israel too, which seemed disconnected from the rest of the documentary, although it might be my bad, because all things are connected, aren't they, at least to people for whom things make sense, and antisemites. And then, finally, out of nowhere, Chris introduced the seed of this idea that I should try mindfulness and that perhaps then things would make sense. 'You should try mindfulness; things will make sense like that, perhaps,' he said. And I just replied 'OK' because it felt right at that moment and I didn't have any other words to say. And I was left there, in what felt like the beginning of a journey of some kind, even if the journey went nowhere. And if it went somewhere I can't tell. Until yesterday. Or so I thought until everything stopped working once more, just a couple of hours ago, when I saw things for what they are once again, which somehow isn't what it is but something else.

'I don't care if your boyfriend dumped you. Look at him,' says Chris, pointing at me. 'You wouldn't know the shit he's been through. Did he deserve everything that came his way? Probably, because he's not very clever. And to be fair: he's his own worst enemy, quite selfish, and maybe he has to go through this, grow out of this – maybe that's his cross to bear – maybe he himself is his own cross to bear. But he also chooses to be well: he chooses to be well, believe me, even if it sounds contradictory. He chooses to regain control over his life, he's trying to be better, he's into this meditation thing, in some kind of spiritual journey now. So, yes, I don't care if your boyfriend dumped you. You should learn from him,' he says, squeezing my left shoulder: 'you have to work with what you've got. Does he have much to work with? No. Very little. But he's working. And that's something. We all have to work with what we've got. We come with a toolbox, get it? You can't go buying tools all the time, can you? You'll go bankrupt or run out of space for the tools. So work-with-what-you've-got!' I can tell Chris is very drunk now. But the girls are staring at me and I feel like I need to say something.

So I say 'yes: pain is unavoidable; suffering is a choice,' quoting something either Mark Hiller or Peter Coutinho tweeted. And the girls stare at me in silence; and he stares at me too, Chris. I can't tell whether he realises that I don't really believe what I'm saying because right now I don't even know what the point of anything is, even with all this mindfulness I have been doing since yesterday. But hey, pain is unavoidable, suffering is optional, I think; pain is unavoidable, suffering is optional; pain is unavoidable, suffering is optional; and although I'm thinking and getting involved with these thoughts, at least this makes sense. It makes sense that suffering is optional, that this need to scream into the river, to howl, to destroy my throat in the process will go away and that if things don't get better now they will get better later. I just need to really want it. That's all I really need. I just need to want this to end. It's always about wanting. There's nothing but wanting to it. It's all in my hands. It always is.

THE EVENING SHIFT
Holly Watson

Good evening Madam, it's Holly calling from Stay Bright Windows, if you could replace all the windows and doors in your home with none of the extra cost involved how many would you do 4, 5, 6 or more? Sorry madam, I'll take your number off our system now... alright calm down... I'm just trying to get a bit of cash before Uni so I *can* get a proper job... Yeah well I'm sure the police and Ann Robinson have got better things to do than deal with some doyle who doesn't need her windows replacing.

Good evening Sir, it's Holly calling from Stay Bright Windows if you could... erm, jeans and a hoodie... I'd rather eat dog shit you dirty prick...

Good evening Sir, it's Holly calling from Stay Bright... Oh I'd love to fuck off, I was thinking St Lucia maybe.

Good evening Madam... Mum it's me just go along with it for a bit my supervisors watching... How many windows was that madam? ... Right he's gone, fuck me there's some arse holes out there tonight...what's happening on Neighbours?... Oh yeah, sorry I forgot we watched it a lunchtime. I'll be back about nine if I haven't topped myself... I'm joking... I know it's not funny. Shit he's coming back, save me the chicken and mushroom one... Fantastic Madam one of my colleagues will be round to talk you through the glazing options next week.

Good evening Sir, it's Holly calling from Stay Bright… Jeans and a hoodie… sorry you want me to shove it up your? Oh god, you've already done it, well make sure you use plenty of Sudocrem after.

Good evening Madam, it's Holly calling from Stay Shite windows if you could replace all the windows in your home…

Good evening Sir, it's Holly calling from Stay Bright Windows… Jeans and a hoodie.

I Get Weird Dreams
Ben Stone

If I see a rerun of Buck Rogers in the 21st Century, I'm sure to be in it. I'll be admiring my slightly effeminate boots as they foley the white corridors when suddenly it's like, Holy shit, these are the corridors in Buck Rogers! Shooting down the tubes going Woohoo! into space just before the bad dudes attack, I realise I must have been watching Buck again and what kind of pizza do I want? Whatever's in the show – the launch bay, his cool if kind of thinly-drawn high-gloss white pad and control room where pizza can be radioed for – I get to live it. It's pretty cool.

For this reason I don't watch horror. One time I accidentally watched 28 Something Later after I ingested whatever it was I found down the sides of the couch and unable to even look away it was awful. Sure, there was light relief how you could run down helpless civilians and just go nuts, but then there's also being chased by the infected proper house to house while they do flying headbutts in through the walls and windows. Even it wasn't in the movie, you ever seen a dude eat his way through a door? Nightmares within nightmares is wooden door eating, let me tell you. Also getting trapped in a basement and weathering the endless torrent of peeps hell bent on getting in takes its toll. When the flashlight you find yourself holding reveals all those hands clawing at the grille are only down to bloody knuckles, knuckles alright, you know you're in for a long night. Blood spurting everywhere as another finger drops onto the pile before you, you switch to breathing through your nose so none lands in your mouth. Even nose-breathing gets old fast, infected blood in your mouth would be worse. Maybe really so. And that sound they make like unhappy babies on bad acid just going on and on for hours, please. Sure, you survive, but my advice is maybe you should watch something else next time.

Like porn for example. Needless to say, with my condition, I watch a lot. A lot of porn is fun, sure, but even fun gets boring after a while. I know you won't believe it since they're called stars for a reason, but even porn is passé on repeat. Maybe a bit of dialogue wouldn't hurt. Maybe a little 'Look, there's a giant reptilian thingo destroying the city (cut to giant reptilian thingo destroying the city), so let's get our clothes off since we're going to die anyway and you don't mind if my buddy Mr. Ed here joins in, right?' But no. No, that would be a cliché. My extended advice is when fun gets boring, take a break from the pounding of indents on the sofa and find the kitchen. Make a sandwich and watch yourself eating it in the TV's hall of mirrors all around them. A favourite is this one where there's an infinity pool they're doing it next to in the Hollywood hills. After commentating for a while like 'Donald Bumsfelt at sixty-eight strokes a minute has really hit his rhythm, folks.' And, 'Is that smoke coming from Gina's mineshaft or lens-flare I ask you, dear viewer?' Do some underwater laps like the original Aqua guy who comes on after Buck.

Better than porn IMHO are music vids. In those dreams, everyone's not only beautiful but cool in unspeakable ways. I think it's the young directors. Their hipster beards and label-less clothes explain who is cool but why is not. Stripped back and slowed down, there's comfort in the untold coolness of barely existing. Find yourself wandering a nightclub where models standing on tables are shaking and you know you've made it. You got there in a stretch with a Patrick Bateman grinning for some reason that's not about money. And before you groan if only life was like this, realise a third of it is.

Another dream was like the robot formerly known as Voltron. Related was this musical montage like South Park after sniffing cat-pee. I don't know which from what here, but any mission in geometric space where lilac mountains are bridging digital black sky and life is sweet. Give me comforting lichen green plains and circuit board cities and piles of fingers are so passé. With cat-pee in the mix, Seventies' sexploitation via a special forces dominatrix in a cutaway black catsuit is inevitable. South Park's cool because people really are two-dimensional.

Dreams are weird but also fun is basically what I'm saying, but they also make you think. They make you think that if the world out there is really in your head, then where are you really? Are you out there in what you're seeing because you recognise it in your head? Because without the models of the stuff out there, what would it really look like I'd like to know? A table and chair in a room next to a window looking out onto a shitty little treeless yard is suddenly Lavender Mist? Is it a model of a model or are your eyes really open?

To answer these questions, the court sent me to this dude who hooked me up to wires inside a big doughnut machine. Later on the screen of my mind, I could kind of see me moving around the models and interacting with them but splotchy red blobs aren't shaking booties in nightclubs. It's back to weird rather than fun as far as red splotches are concerned. Models of models in the soap next were these women maneuvering against each other to marry this dude kind of like a human puppy every female has an overriding instinct to squeeze, but as squirming splotches of variable redness, were a total come down.

Even you can do what you want in dreams, to be is something that can get away from you. A Tarantino joint where you're a Nazi or plantation cracker and that could well be the end. What I mean is you think you know you but you don't. Not really. The Nazi committing crimes against decent peeps is you your mum held in her arms? That's you she kissed on the cheek and smoothed hair from your eyes and now you're Tarantino-ing? Believe me on this one: you go cracker and you won't see you going 'til you're gone.

Pretty much, dreams are a test is what I think the message is. The court's judgement of what I finger-quote 'allegedly' did to that American Werewolf in London extra isn't something I vouch for. His fingers they pumped out of my stomach was his word against my lawyer's, but also the elephant in the room. Disgruntled models of models in TV's halls of mirrors aren't supposed to sue you either, but that's just how weird things can get. Sure, the aforementioned werewolf incident wasn't pretty, but those photos the prosecutor kept handing around simply begged the question, what's actually real anymore?

Everything? Nothing? Something sensorial in between?

Never turn your back on a dream is also important, especially when that dream is within reach of a brick they can bring down on your finger-focused head. Never say the dream is over is worth a go, while give my regards to Brooklyn dreams goes without saying. The dreamer has left the building reveals the predicament people with my condition are in, and even though dreams can't buy you love, in the heartbreaking Hunger Games of Syria news, love only buys you nightmares anyway. Dream on, I think we can say, is self-evident rather than choice, while running down the dream is easier said than done.

Axel Rebuilds the Empire
Ben Stone

1. Axel

There's a knock, and the woman whose office it is, says, 'Come in.'

On her tablet's screen, I zoom the door handle, chrome, turning on hot-pink laminate, and a smallish man appears silhouetted from outside. This is Axel R, an elderly gangster, whom inferenced, gets canned applause.

'Close the door please.'

Axel does so and looks around the long room. He eyes the young woman, a doctor plus, who's my, well, behind her huge natural grain desk. Extending almost as far as the first window of the granny-flat office, he takes a step and sees through its Venetians the main house up the gently sloping yard. If there's actually an audience canning whatever, I add him up, that's where they'd be.

'Have a seat.' The woman in her lab coat doesn't look up from her notes. We watch her close the file, note the time on a slip on the front, then open another. 'Can I help you?'

'Axel R?' he says like she should know.

Bri flicks at our tablet for the name. 'And R is for?'

'Rated?'

'I see.' Which she kind of does even though she's still writing.

2. Bri

A minute's silence as the woman behind her desk closes the last file and takes a look at Axel. This is Bri M, my boss according to implied subject-positions, and she also gets canned applause (though Axel's pretty certain it isn't as enthusiastic as his).

Nearly triple her age, Bri's inferencing is kind of other person's creepy grandpa, kind of vampire thing with that expensive dark suit. We watch him go to sit on the quite average office chair facing our huge desk, but then he sees the old if comfy sofa-chair nearly under the window where, he assumes, his audience must be.

We watch him get comfortable in the big, soft cushions. More or less facing the door, the hot-pink laminate and angular handle, chrome, makes him uncomfortable. Modern, too much so, it's not hard to interference, and he turns right so that's he's facing her, Bri, tucked away behind our massive desk.

'Do you have time?'

Performative slouching, we analyse him, performatively bored. 'You didn't make an appointment with my bot, Kay?'

'No.'

Sitting back behind the big desk, I see Bri feeling her hands on the fabric of her executive chair. 'Not really.'

'Then we won't be long.'

Bri realises he knows her and she kind of knows of him. Everyone in this part of town does, der, but while he remains on that side of the desk, she's thinking she can handle it.

'I provide two services,' Bri says, 'that can, if required, be applied in concert.'

'How unusual.'

'On the one hand,' she lifts a brown hand, 'I'm a defence lawyer and attorney, while on the other,' holding it up, 'I'm a registered psychiatrist specialising in psychedelic therapy.'

'All by twenty six,' Axel creases up.

'Okay,' Bri says clasping hands on her huge desk. 'That's not weird you know my age.'

'Your parents must be so proud.'

The legal psychiartrist watches him. Clearly, mention of her parents at her age and still pretty much living in this office and two bedder granny flat out the back of the family's big old gothic house with me is not okay. 'I got lucky.'

'I wasn't as lucky to begin with.'

'I see.'

'I suppose you know the rat story?'

Bri keeps her pokerface going. 'Everyone's got a rat story.'

'So you know me then.'

'That depends. Who do you think you are?'

Axel shrugs. 'Undisputed ruler of the extending burb and targeted satellites, if they know what's good for them.'

'Oh,' she says. 'That Axel.'

'Yes.'

'Okay.'

'But you knew that.'

'Perhaps.'

'Great nephew of Pete The Elite?'

'I know my history.'

'Yeah.' Axel's happy to have her think. 'I get mentions on The Tate Show and War Room all the time.'

'Is that a fact?'

'You'd better ask somebody,' Axel confirms.

'What would they say?'

'Specifically?'

'Sure.'

'They talk about how he's back.'

'Meaning you.'

'Yes.'

'You personally or?'

'Not retaking as much as refilling a power void.'

'There's a void?'

'That's funny.' He doesn't laugh. 'Logically speaking, if it's not owned and controlled, it's not worth anything.'

Bri says, 'That's one way of looking at it, I suppose.'

The legal psychiatrist hasn't looked away from him or even moved, but Axel hears a drawer behind the desk edging opening. Axel watches her empty eyes behind those large glasses as she fumbles for something.

'They also say how no one thought he could.'

'Which is you in third person.'

'They say how peeps said those days were over.'

'But they're not.'

'Because then they took a house.'

'They did?'

'Then another, and now here he is with me, being you, the office of Bri M, legal psychiatrist.'

'It is a thing,' she assures him. 'I have the papers.'

'The NAD.' Axel watching for reaction sees Bri put something in her mouth. 'What was that?'

'Neighbour's adult daughter?'

'You put something in your mouth.'

Bri settles in her doctor's chair. 'I also have conditions, Mr. R.'

They watch each other.

'Axel.'

'Okay.'

'Any good?'

Bri thinks about that. 'Relative to?'

'Interesting.' Axel's piqued. 'Try me.'

Bri awkwardly dry swallows the pill. Axel R, she thinks, the mafia godfather of this side of town, is sitting in her office and he wants to try something that she can provide. She has things to provide, lots of them as it happens, some tucked away in the vast desk's drawers, as we've seen, but moreover, one of the new molecular printers we've been getting funky with, tweaking parameters and compounding all kinds of agonists and whatnot.

'What are your symptoms?'

'Well, you know.'

'Probably.'

'Total control is not an easy thing.'

'I can imagine.'

'There's always resistance.'

'Foucault.'

'Discourse control to enforce.'

'Althusser's interpellation.'

Axel nods at the door he's more or less facing. 'Take that door.'

'Okay.'

'Hot-pink laminate with a modernist handle, chrome, ironically postmodern in its *I'll never turn on you, Axey –*'

'Axey?'

'So I'm forever.'

'That's what it's telling you?'

'That door,' he insists, 'is an 80s rerun in the flesh.'

Looking at it, Bri's hand goes to her mouth. 'I think I see it.'

'You did it again.'

'*Top Gun* and *American Psycho?*' Bri distracts him with. 'The book, not necessarily the film.'

'The Coreys,' Axel remembers.

'Who would've been more or less your age?'

Axel is clearly an elderly man but stiffens at the implication. Eyes still on the shiny pink door with its chrome handle, he asks, 'Who is we?'

Bri doesn't remember mentioning her *we*. 'Me and my assistant?'

Looking left, Axel sees a smaller desk in the far corner by the other window. 'Andre.'

'Right again.' Doc Bri opens another drawer. 'Not creepy at all.'

'I'll tell you something you don't know yet.'

Bri doesn't even try and hide another hand going to her mouth and licks a finger pad. 'About my door?'

'Then you can then relativise my symptoms.'

Bri does the calculations. Legally what she can write versus plausible symptoms and deniability if push comes to shove. 'Good enough. Shoot.'

Axel looks back front at that stunning pink door. 'That handle, chrome, postmodernist ironically modern.'

'Yep, yeah,' she moves him along.

'It used to tell me it was forever.'

Bri looks at it then back at him. 'The 80s were?'

'That handle.' Axel focuses it as Bri toggles compound parameters on the tablet connected to a dock holding a narrow black rectangular block. 'Horizontal chrome, like a chrome horizon that won't turn on me who isn't just anyone?'

Doctor Bri tweaking hard, 'No-one is just anyone.'

'The greatest tragedy of the century?'

Bri notes that down on her pad. 'And what do you think that means?'

'It means enough to start my tab running.'

I can tell, Bri is starting to feel the effects of the pharma she's being doing sneakies with. Why does she do this? She wonders as her head momentarily rollercoasters and I parse her data. In a running notation, I note that agonist-wise, that one's anti-depressive where everything is more or less funny in it's own way.

Great for reframing PTSD root experiences and you, I note on the table, will just have to serious it out, doll, for a few minutes until it transitions into clear-headed positivity with a half-life of five minutes.

'Perhaps to you,' Bri says and slides the undocked black object like a weekly pill strip across the vast plane, 'some of these will seem outrageous, like that door.'

'Yes.'

'They will seem to you to affect your thinking.'

Axel leans over the sofa chair arm and takes the rectangular strip at full stretch. 'Okay.'

'But remember that they are nothing that is not you.'

Flinching at her suspect Yoda revelation, one of the little lids hinges open and Axel sees an almost luminous purple circle the size of a finger pad inside.

'What is it?'

'Molecular print. Molp. Half-life usually five minutes with clear dissolution.'

'We're moving in this direction of course.'

Counsellor Bri says, 'The royal we as in generalised third person?'

Axel sticks his right pinky in. 'As in me.'

Almost instantly, Axel's mind is a golden fountain erupting from the centre of his head and covering the room, including her, with golden flow. 'Holy shit!'

'Am I right?' Bri squirms behind her huge desk.

Axel looks back at door.

'As I can see on my scans,' Bri's looking at her tablet, 'blob, blob, blob, this particular door with that particular handle, chrome, is triggering circuits in your brain, blob, blob, blob, associated with the 80s and almost, according to Kay here, Greek tragedy?'

'The biggest,' Axel's reliving its all-encompassing hot pinkness. 'And there was even an actual door that you knew then.'

'It's actually that door.'

'Okay.' Bri tries to give it a chance. 'Like specifically?'

'Did you put that door there?'

Bri does her best to keep her face behind her big nerdy glasses professionally vacant. 'I grant you I did not.'

'Well then.'

The legal shrink nods he's got her and leans out over the desk for the boxstrip.

3. Laplov

The 1980s handle, chrome, turns and Axel inferences canned cheers for a man in a grey business suit who enters and closes the pink door behind him. This is Laplov.

'Did you hear that?'

Bri redocking the boxstrip, tells him, 'Excuse me? I'm in session?'

'It's quite warm out there.' When he gets no reply, Laplov looks at the young woman behind the huge desk and then looks at his boss. Clearly, Axel is philo-pastry'd, he's realising, like really pickswillzed on something, and she, the NAD, Bri, my boss, looks busily suspicious about it.

'When Laplov walked in,' Axel tells Bri, 'there was distinct canned audience appreciation ala 1980s sitcoms.'

'You work for Axel,' Bri adds it up. 'Not in the slightest even creepier.'

'We don't hear it boss.' Laplov has his phone out and doomscrolls messages.

Axel tries to smile but it's a grimace on his pink face.

'So, the ol'sitcom canned laughter, eh?' Bri tweaks parameters that I slightly less tweak back. 'I may have something for that.'

Off-chops on the tail of whatever she's given him, there's that disembodied off-stage laughter again and he creases up embarrassed. 'Well, if you say so.'

'Boss,' Laplov steps in. 'I've looked at the numbers and inside,' meaning the main house. 'It's not good.'

'What's good but?' he says.

'It's not.'

But Axel's doesn't want to hear it. 'Take that song contest star there.'

4. Marissa

Laplov and Bri turn to the framed poster right of the door.

'Marissa?' his No. 2 notes.

'Good or not good?'

Laplov, 'Well, you know.'

'Mouth open, eyes squinting ready to sing the stadium's brains out?'

'Well.'

'Marissa's O.P.' the doctor says.

'I had a share in her.'

The legal doctor hesitates. 'As in?'

'A large one,' Laplov confirms.

Oh jeeze, Bri realises as Axel creases up. Toggling the full spectrum scanner on the tablet, I transcribe the blobs for her, such as: …yuk yuk yuk, gets bit crazy with the boys, yuk yuk yuk… and in another part of the model, there's the phenomenological subjectivity that is 'Axel', re-consuming her eyes slit and mouth open really feeling it.

'Do they?' Axel wonders. 'Like really?'

More, is what Bri knows from our work with trauma victims of men like this. Even the agnostic professional in her sucking for air, Bri fingerprints the little open box with a luminescent pale blue circle and gasps, 'Do you think they do?'

The buzz is intense, like a stadium-banger climax ballooning in her legal medical mind.

'Like how a dog on a leash still feels something?'

'Oh wow.' Bri can barely take it. Really feeling that patriarchal leash a moment, the truncated agency, the vulnerability to an owner's whims and wants, the compound mercifully wanes as quickly as it came.

Axel says, 'That's just how the world is.'

'Yep.' Laplov doomscrolls. 'But boss, the house –'

'She knows it too,' he ignores him. 'Look at her.'

Instead, correlating concerning blobs I'm parsing on the tablet, Bri says, 'It's men like you, you're saying?'

'We exist.'

'We do,' Laplov confirms.

'Affecting things.'

Clearly, I inference, the primacy of his feelings is a metaphor for power.

Bri sighs and looks at him. 'It's a lonely way to see the world, Axel.'

Axel wants to laugh and indicates Bri to his red righthand. 'You see this?'

But Laplov's seen better and shrugs.

Relieved at least that Marissa, wherever she is now, has escaped these old vampires, Bri plugs the boxstrip back into its dock and starts prescribing. 'Ever feel I'm so ronery?' she references Team America' North Korean dictator. 'The pointy end of the pyramid type thing?'

Laplov stiffens but Axel's flexing a suited arm.

'Look at you,' he baked-as dotes on steroidal biceps. The last of the purple dot bouncing around his cognitive walls, Axel's toned if age-flabbed muscles are still powerful, he's sure.

'Impressive.'

'She's taking the piss.' Laplov glares at the legal psychiatrist.

There's canned oohs and Axel looks around. 'Right there. Did you hear it?'

'As in an audience?' Bri's watching his blobs.

'That's right.' Axel looks for it. Once more, he settles on the window behind. With its horizontal slit blinds through which they glimpse the main house, he sees a few of whom he expects are his guys milling around on the back lawn.

'I may have something for that.' Bri works the tablet with my help and the molp printer starts microwhirring.

'Great power,' Axel says of his biceps as his man and Bri watch. 'As strong and hard as a man half his age.'

'Oh yeah?' the legal doc's not sure about third person here. 'Try this.'

'A third even after I finish with him,' Axel creases up.

Reaching over, he takes the fingerprint strip. He looks into the open one and sees a little pollen-yellow circle pulsing inside.

'Boss, is that really a good –?'

But Axel's already put his pinky onto the pollen ring.

Almost instantly, that look of horror on the patient-client's face is he's interoceptively having a moment. Ignoring Laplov's elevating disapproval, we watch Axel's blobbed subjectivity on the tablet shrinking down and down the fractal that goes down forever. As he's doing that, conversely the room, world, everything that's not him, Axel, expands at a proportional rate. 'The half-life of this one,' the doctor reminds them, 'is about three minutes.'

Laplov pales. 'Boss?'

Monstered, like totally Dortmunted, Axel gasps, 'This is how the fucking opposite of power feels!'

'Interesting,' Bri jots notes on her pad and takes the fingerprint strip back. She docks it and with me, Kay, balancing compounds, matchmakes the next course.

'Terrible!' Axel cringes into the sofa chair. 'Just awful!'

'Boss!' Laplov's concerned.

Interoceptively this tiny bug waiting to be squashed in the old crusty cushions under the window, Axel's so depressed by his own nothingness he can barely stand it. 'I'm so small!'

'Yep,' Doc Bri tells him. 'Ontology come ego death.'

Laplov gives her his most reptilian stare.

'Suspension?' Bri shrinks as much as she can down behind her vast desk (where she can also open drawers more easily).

'You better know what you're doing,' Laplov warns.

Awkwardly, the legal doctor leans over the desk pushing a shiny yellow clipboard with consent form across its acres. With Axel radiating sheer terror, she telescopes a stainless steel pointer and awkwardly pushes it the rest of the way to him.

'I'm nothing!' he cries. 'Nothing!'

'It'll swing back,' Bri assures them both. 'Any moment now.' To Laplov, 'Interoceptively, "you" get to "feel" – see how I'm using those words – both sides of the self relative to world. You want to try some?'

Laplov, phone in hand and hands on hips, just looks at her with his dead eyes behind feelingless glasses. That look, I transcribe for Bri on her tablet, is: do you have any idea how many people just like you we've buried?

'But, oh wow.' Axel starts the return journey. He's emotionally expanded back to himself but then he just keeps going. 'Amazing!' he says, getting bigger and bigger.

'See?' Bri tells Axel's stooge.

Axel flourishes his signature and shoos Laplov away. 'I'm inescapable!'

'That's what I'm talking about,' Bri encourages them with her results.

'I am your fucking space and time!' Axel says as he expands and expands like an interoceptive balloon. 'A singularity gripping all in orbit even!'

Doctor Bri, 'I know, right?'

'The Nothingness on *The Neverending Story (1991)*, advancing mercilessly into more and more houses!'

'Okay,' Bri equivocates. Hands creeping back to her desk drawers, 'That's different, but I get where you're coming from.'

Fluffed-up, Axel looks again at that satellite posing as sunrise in her framed poster right of the door. 'That song contest winner.'

'Marissa,' Bri notes.

'Screaming at a photoshopped stadium on top of the world –'

'Uh huh,' doctor Bri notes in her pad. Laplov watching her, she says, 'All confidential.'

'She's not the real story at all!'

Bri writing and writing, asks, 'And how is that?'

'Oh no no, mon cheri,' Axel mansplains. 'Because you see that curtain behind her?'

Bri, the young woman whose poster it is, intuits, 'The one where behind it a man is making her great again?'

Axel's nodding. 'He's deploying her!' he mansplains harder. 'And she –'

'Marissa.'

'Whatever you think she's feeling –'

'Which is a lot.'

'She's just a shiny lure attracting more prey.'

Adjusting the next compound on the tablet, Bri says, 'Well, that's one way of looking at a relationship.'

'A human funnel!'

'Boss.' Laplov tries to get Axel's attention.

'Channeling money to the man!'

'What are we doing here?'

There's canned laughter again that Axel hears and he turns sharply to the window. Through the Venitions, across the lawn like backgrounding it, there's the big old gothic house that after today will be his.

'And yet such eyes,' Axel says.

'Yeah,' Laprov remembers.

'She's beautiful,' Bri offers.

'But it's not her moment,' Axel turns back to them. 'It's the man's in the shadows.'

'Oh please,' I, Kay, Bri's AI, womansplains Axel on our tablet.

'And worse.'

(narrow-eyed schadenfreude emoji)

'Awe.' Bri likes it.

'He's already found someone better.'

Bri looks up at her patient. 'The guy behind the curtain has?'

'A bigger funnel like.'

Bri uses her telescoped metal pointer to push the fingerprint strip back across the vast wood. 'It's just business, you're saying?'

'More beautiful, more talented, more her who then disappears.'

'Brutal,' Bri ventures.

The two men share a glance and the legal doctor silently freaks out how right she is.

5. Borg's man

Laplov flick-scrolling his phone resigns himself that Axel has that look again. Clammy sweat beading on temples, paranoia bubbling out of control just behind whatever it is this latest quack is giving him, hearing the canned laughter again, it worries the Number 2.

But what can you do when, despite what just happened, Axel's looking in the open fingerprint box again?

'Blue?

'Royal blue,' Bri sells it.

Axel puts a pinky onto the little coloured ring. 'And Borg's man?'

Laplov says, 'We've got him at the hotel.'

'And?'

Looking down his glasses as he taps away on his phone, 'Doesn't know apparently.'

Axel rolls his eyes as Bri takes the boxstrip back and redocks it. The rebound expansiveness where he felt like the god he kind of is long gone, Axel asks his legal psychiatrist, 'Is royal blue supposed to feel like something?'

'What is feeling anyway, right?'

'You see this?' Axel flatters her to Laplov.

'Meh.'

Bri tells Axel, 'Now, think of your family.'

Axel just stares at her, and then it hits him. Actual love. For his adult daughter not too much older than the legal doctor here. Less so for his wife, Trina, sure, but as a human being, human to human, Axel's feeling her bigly. There's even some for good ol'Lappy watching him with concern.

'And how's Marissa now?' Doc Bri prompts.

Laplov doomscrolling sighs they're back to Marissa.

Axel to his stooge, 'Whatever happened to that poor thing anyway?'

'A sweet girl,' Laplov sidesteps.

Axel has the sensation of at least pretending to feel bad about what happened.

'And how about now?' Bri prods.

'Oh wow, 'Axel confesses to the doctor. 'Really Mount Panoramaed here.' He shifts in the spacious sofa chair and says, 'Thriller times K2 and we're just getting started.'

'Interesting.' Doc Bri sneaks another tablet.

The old croney doubletakes. 'She just put something in her mouth.'

'She does that,' Axel tells him.

'And this "Borg's man" guy?' counsellor Bri gets them back to.

'That's right,' Axel tells her. Off chops, there's no way he can't say, 'He has a family too, of course.'

'But Drasko did the numbers again,' Laplov heads off the touchy-feelyness. 'The shipment's short.'

Bri and I watch Axel side to side his pencil brows. So they have his man, I inference his blobular thinking on the tablet, and though this Borg guy should pay, it's his proxy instead doing the screaming.

'I see,' Bri adds up.

But that's not all, I tabulate, because on royal blue, hurting Borg's man because of Borg, or even because of a clerical error, he's hurting the man's family, which right now hurts him, Axel R, in this weird and unfamiliar way. Not really knowing what to do with it, he squirms in the sofa chair unable to get comfortable.

'Boss?' Laplov looks up from his phone.

And then the feelings dissolve and Axel's back to feeling nothing like he normally does.

'I think that's progress, right?' the doctor asks.

'Like Marissa,' Axel sniffs as normally as he can, 'Borg's man thinks he's feeling something of his own.'

Laplov chuckles. 'Little toes being cut off, for starters.'

'Ha. Yeah,' Axel creases up.

'In the Chair,' Laplov explains, 'watching himself gag-howling on loop, snip snip, for,' he checks his watch, 'sixteen hours now.'

Oh boy, Bri's writing on her pad. She looks at Axel, 'And is that really productive?'

'Which room?' Axel looks like he might drop in.

'One-Two-Four.'

Totally Swiss-cheesed coming down the overlapping short half-lives of whatever she's given him, Axel crinkles up at the thought. 'All work and no play makes yada yada.'

'Ha,' Laplov realises. 'So true boss.'

'But what about that feeling?' Bri wants to know. 'How we're all connected?'

'So monked,' Axel admits. 'So totally Gina-fatsuited.'

Bri sighs. 'Not a total loss then?'

'Not yet.'

'Anyway,' Laplov moves things along, 'the papers are on their way, boss.'

'Good. Because you see that 80s rerun right there?'

Laplov looks around at the hot-pink door.

'That's our *Red Dawn*, (1984).'

Laplov hesitates. 'But it's pink, boss.'

'Whatever.'

The old croney extends his distaste around the rest of the room. 'But this place? Seriously, boss? It's more trouble than it's worth.'

But baselining after the weird experience of so-called 'feelings', Axel's less interested in his minion's opinion than what the next little coloured circle may be. He doesn't have to wait long to find out, because Bri toggling and sliding parameters on her tablet, I finish and print it.

6. The Rothko

This one is flightgear orange and hits him instantly.

'Yeah?' Bri watches her patient's face go through the motions. 'Am I wrong?'

For Axel, his subjective point of view – his SPOV, as doctor Bri who's watching him with Laplov, has come to think of it – has detached from everything. Dissociated, Axel realises may be the right term. In fact, from this elevated, outside realm he now inhabits, the world, including these two human insects and even himself to some degree somewhere down there, it's just happening and cannot be stopped.

'Anything else?'

'The Rothko.'

Avoiding eye contact with the gangsters, the doctor clarifies, 'The royal we again?'

'Last week.'

'Boss,' Laplov sighs and doomscrolls messages.

'For it's own safety, he told the Midchis.'

'Yep.' His number two doesn't want to talk about it.

Axel and the legal doctor watch each other.

'So, what?' he wants to know. 'This one is tell everything like it is?'

'Pretty much,' Bri tells him as straight as she can.

'Huh.' Axel's impressed. Torture is never going away, he's not worried about that, but absolutely knowing even after you've been over and over the subject is, well, satisfying.

'And the painting?' Bri reminds him.

'The Midchis,' Axel recalls, 'were huddled together on their sofa. The look on their faces was, well –'

'Yep,' Laplov grins.

'As men, my men,' Axel creases up, 'unhooked the big painting from their wall.'

Bri finally on the verge of freaking out squirms behind her massive desk. 'And you felt?'

'They took its sides.'

'I'm seeing it.'

'Frameless as painted with endearing bleeds.'

'Very arty.'

'Revealing strapped machine pistols, knifes and ties, blinds and gags.'

Bri somehow swallows another pill as she writes in her pad, 'Gags.'

'And then they're holding it against those pitiful sobs like, here boss, it's yours now.'

'A picture,' Laplov explains like he's selling insurance, 'soaks up a thousand screams.'

Bri really struggling beneath professional detachment watches Axel nod because it's true.

'Like Dorian Gray's portrait,' Laplov paints a picture for the Doc, 'blue chip art unsoaks years of blood from hands good.'

'An interesting way of phrasing it.' Then under her breath looking down at the desk, 'Did you get that?'

Another female voice, mine, answers, 'Of course.'

Laplov, 'Who is that?'

'AI,' Bri tells the men watching her. 'It's being quiet again, so.'

When they keep watching her and she knows that they must be noticing because her hands are creeping into her main drawer, the legal shrink adds, 'To organise the information for therapeutic outcomes? And it's confidential and encrypted?' When they're still watching her, 'It will defend itself if any unauthorised access is attempted.'

Axel studies buffed and manicured fingernails. 'No browny red crumbles these days.'

'Ha.' Laplov feels nostalgiac and scrolls.

'Now I check my Swiss movemented bling on smooth pink.'

'Yep.' Laplov can't argue with that one either. 'Anything else boss?'

'Don't look at my dick.'

Laplov clears his throat and shoots cuffs. 'Not me boss.'

'Also, there's a Maleovich next door to the Midchis I'm hearing?'

'You got it boss.'

Axel waves him off. Laplov turns chrome as he exits, cuing canned applause.

'There it is again.'

'Yep.' Doc Bri notes my scan annotations on our tablet screen. 'We've got blobbage.'

The bright outside engulfing Laplov, doctor Bri sees glints of gun barrels and shadows milling nervously.

7. Pete the E

Legal doctor Bri M docked the fingerprint boxstrip is tweaking another compound with her AI, Kay, me, as Axel settles in to watch the 80s rerun.

'That door, if I'm feeling it correctly.'

'Feeling is interoceptive, so.'

'You keep saying that.'

'There was a particular day,' Bri doesn't look up, 'you were watching the door, that one or one similar, and the handle.'

'Chrome.'

'Turned.'

He was in his young daughter's room watching her sleep when Axel got the news.

'My great uncle,' he says, 'Pete the E, master of all as far as the eye could see, was dead.'

Bri knows the story.

'His sprawling empire,' he says distantly, 'on fire. The age the Corey's were, I was a year on average older, I'd just started cutting my teeth on the population when, poof.'

'When you say, "cutting your teeth".'

'Decades,' Axel says of the door. 'Centuries even, collapsed overnight.'

'It's happens to the best of them,' Bri tries to console him with. When that's the wrong thing, she tries for, 'It's the general pattern?'

'Yeah, well,' Axel chuckles to himself. 'Everything is not actually built equally, so.'

Bri is back and forthing with me in disagreement to a compound parameter and is in the end agnostic. 'Iterations of patterns, and agree to disagree?'

'It should never have happened.'

'Naturally speaking, periodic extinction reshuffles the deck.'

Axel stiffens. 'Infighting, insolvencies and then the power vacuum, it was everyone for themselves.'

'People were relatively free, you're saying.'

'Chaos,' the aging godfather recalls bitterly. 'Too young to resist the tide, no amount of blood spilling could stop ol'Pete being swept into history. Bitter years of wilderness followed.'

Bri's hand on autopilot sneaks another pill. 'I bet they did.'

'The humiliation of irrelevance.'

'Uh huh.' The legal doc's quietly freaking out with the gravity of it.

'The patronising "concern" of exonerated enemies downtown.'

Bri tweaking parameters makes herself breathe. 'That must be exhausting.'

Staring at that beautiful awful hot-pink door, its handle, chrome, he says, 'A dark time.'

And yet so liberating for most, Doctor Bri's mind reels.

Undocking the boxstrip and tapping her tablet, a lid servos open. Axel leaning over the massive expanse of wood takes it and sees a luminescent pink finger-pad circle pulsing inside.

'The I-told-you-so sniggers behind helping hands,' he says, 'as my great family was reduced to petty crime preying on the new "public".'

Doc Bri musters all her professionalism not to melt into a puddle on the floor. The fact is, she hasn't forgotten, associated thugs killed her Grandma J.

'But slowly, patiently,' Axel says, 'I learned to reframe this new idea of freedom.'

Ripe for the picking, Bri reads my inference of his FS blobs, was firstly the idea.

'Freedom equals chaos.'

He decided what was worth what, I reconstruct it, and restructured the gang accordingly. He found out about the node, which is that blob, blob, blobbing, and they dug through the floor of a house they took and metered it. Then they took another. He waited for the tide to turn as it must, and now, my dear, I explain to Bri, he's here.

8. Randy

Canned applause as the pink door opens and a wiry Asian man in a high-street business suit enters. This is Randy, the United Front boss of locally owned businesses and a proxy for Fang's sprawling East Side Emporium, and Axel rolls his eyes.

Fronting them, Randy looks counsellor-shrink Doc Bri up and down behind her massive desk and stiffens. 'When you said you'd be here, Axel, I didn't know that.'

Bri glances between the two old men. Baked-as on her own tweaks and barely believing where this new client is taking her freak-out wise, she tries for, 'Um, we're in session?'

The business slash party man stares at Bri until she's back to tweaking compounds.

'This place, Axel?' Randy parrots Laplov but doesn't look around. 'Really?'

I add that to the increasingly ominous context but Bri's already there.

'We've added it up and don't think it's a sound move.'

Axel, Bri sees in the blob, blob, blobs of my inferenced scan, does this big eye roll performance. 'This is not just another house, Randy,' the godfather schools him. He creases up his gangster smile and says, 'Annexations are the returning of property to the rightful owner.'

Your move, Randy, Bri chews on her pen.

Blob, blob, blob, I translate, he's alarmed why this Bri person, you hon, is getting this precious time with you, Axel, when, blobular inference extrapolated, you must know as much a we do that she did several units of a George Saunders' Studies of Russian Lit. Twice Removed course (GSSRLTR), while completing her accelerated law and psychiatry grad school and placement, making her, which is you babes, suspect?

'Nevertheless,' Randy actually says, 'reconsideration is advisable.'

Dissociation receding as quickly as it came and leaves Axel flat. 'Duly noted. Now if there's nothing else?'

'But more importantly, Axel,' Randy is ready with, 'if we could discuss the partnership –'

'You see this?' Axel indicates to Bri. 'All day every day.'

'The shackles of great power,' she spells out on her pad.

'You know that song, Randy? Axel studies his bloodless manicure. "Bitch Don't Kill My Vibe?"'

The sheer crudity of it throws the rep. Of course he knows: it's Kendrick Lamar. But should he know it in *this* context? Soft little hands clasped behind his back, Randy's suddenly interested in looking about the room.

To the right of the disturbingly pink door with its angular, kind of space age chrome handle, Randy recognises the song contest poster of Marissa.

'His boss, Fang,' Axel tells his new legal doc, 'had a stake in her too.'

Randy makes sure the doctor slash GS Russian Lit. Twice Removed unit completer doesn't see him remember those white letters above her light-lined dresser.

Blob blob blob, all you need is love, I reveal on our tablet.

'The partnership, being unlimited,' he emphasises, 'cannot wait, I'm afraid.'

Axel rolls his eyes like is this guy still here? 'Laplov has the details.'

'We've talked to Laplov,' Randy says of himself. 'But it's we who need to talk.'

Axel looking dead-eyed at him like that, Randy finally gets he's on drugs. Who isn't today? is different in his case, and worse, he's making moves on this nobody doctor slash lawyer as much as her family's house that has unwisely let the wolf in.

Seeing him see her see this, Bri fingerprints.

'Let me have that lime one again.' Axel pushes the boxstrip back.

'It does have a difficult start. Do you consent?'

Axel chuckles. 'Did I the first time?'

'The first time,' Bri says, 'you couldn't have because you had no context.'

Beyond seized Rothkos, I show Bri how his unmistakable blob, blob, blobbing is a man who's tortured and crushed last breaths from more people than he bothers remembering. So there's that, in other words.

Regardless, Bri activates the splice-lime circle box and its lid microservos open.

'Axel,' Randy lubes up the older man before he can get his pinky in there, 'I've been asked to talk about the gas side of the partnership.'

But too late, because Axel's suddenly sitting on a foggy hillside as it reverbs cool intrigue about him. 'Cool,' he says.

'But Axel –'

Swatting playfully at impossible softness, he says to Bri, 'See what I put up with?'

Bri's tweaking parameters and doesn't look up. 'The give and take of business?'

'In their case,' Axel indicates the hovering businessman, 'it's mostly take.'

There's multi-modal oohs as effectively Axel scores a little slap on Randy's red face.

'And there's the audience.' Axel rolls his eyes.

'Canned oohs?' Bri's looking at her tablet.

'You heard it too?' Axel's almost afraid to hope.

'There's are some blobs that definitely look sussy,' she admits.

Huh, Axel thinks with his luscious fog. He looks at Randy like, *See?*

But what he doesn't see is what I'm showing Bri, and that's that those contextual 'oohs' were actually because Randy's eyes are now black and white spirals turning down into singularities as he does much feared Discourse Control.

'It gets you thinking.' Randy's eyes spiral.

'It gets me thinking,' Axel says.

'Who owes what when in a nutshell.'

'Nutshell,' Axel confirms.

'And that's our point, Axel. We believe.'

But Axel's an old pro from the East Side days and sidesteps out of Randy's grasp.

'Impressive,' Bri notes.

'Not only to avoid bloodbaths,' Axel says.

A bead of sweat on Randy's forehead as he finds himself repeating, 'Bloodbaths?'

'Wow.' Bri looks up from parametering another compound print (with my guidance).

'The bread and butter of how great power works,' Axel tells them.

Randy in turn breaks free. 'What was in that?' he asks of the boxstrip Axel pushes back across the vast desk.

'Hillside fog,' Axel says.

'Good name.' Doctor Bri redocks it.

Randy in his expensive and slightly shiny dark grey suit isn't sure.

'Take the Slatts.'

'The what?'

'The Slatts.'

Randy looks at Bri who doesn't look up from my tablet.

'The who owes what in a nutshell?'

Randy stiffens having his lines fed back against him.

'Even they lost their home six months ago to my expansion along Figgaro?'

'Okay.' The rep gets it.

'And they in their Slattness have the gall to ignore invites to my party last weekend?'

Randy was there of course. A lot of people. Barely knowing the Slatts from a hole in the ground, he can't remember if he saw them or not.

'Your wife Trina's party,' he goes for.

'I was there,' Axel tells him.

'Yes.'

'So effectively, it was mine.'

'Okay.'

'I didn't actually ask them myself, but you get where I'm going with this.'

'Yes.'

'Because if I did ask them directly.'

'Yes.'

'And they still didn't come.'

'I see.'

'I'm taking on a cost.'

'Yes.'

'Because their risk, if I asked, well –'

'Yes.'

'How big do you want your risk?'

'We don't.'

'When I've got the bomb and you don't?'

'We do.'

'Scale-wise,' Axel tells the doc as he takes the updated boxstrip, 'everything else is downstream. What's this purple one?'

'An iteration on Close-Up 27.'

As Axel puts his pinky into the open fingerprint box, Randy calculates.

Even I probably shouldn't, but since Bri hasn't stopped me, Randy's blob blob blobbing, I tell her, reads like the Slatts feigned they didn't know it wasn't Axel's party but that's not going to save them now.

The party, Axel's wife Trina's officially, happened soon after next door's annexation. With its jackpot subnode Axel's people found underneath, he literally had power over several more streets and celebration was called for. Walls were hastily punched out and the whole thing soullessly redecorated ala Melania-coin chic. In fact, some of that noise Bri had been hearing was the fence between it and the last place being knocked down. His palace sprawling as fast as his people could slap it up, Axel's world was now literally just over the mock-orange Randy could see through her Venetian blinds.

Officially a who's who, Randy wore black-tie and had drinks with various important people from the city. Including, of course, re-mayoral hopeful, Dunalt, on the cola, if I'm inferencing the data correctly, and his would-be mayoral entourage of clown-car actual drunks. Hedgehog, for instance. Though people like the Slatts were not important enough to be missed, blob, blob, blob, Randy gets that neither can they be allowed to claim plausible deniability because what's a court without the subjugated?

'Next time then.' Randy cuts his losses.

Axel and Bri look at him.

'What?'

'The price of the gas we are getting for our special relationship?'

Axel bristles. 'You see this?'

'I'm not sure,' Bri hedges.

'If Fang wants to talk about the price of gas, Randy, he can send his fat arse to me instead of some pissant like you. Yes?'

Randy reddens imperceptibly. 'Very well Axel.'

'Don't let the hot-pink 80s whack your arse on the way out.'

Canned laughter as a chastened Randy the UF guy glides on out of there.

9. Dunalt

Watching the door again, Axel says, 'These people!'

Cue 80s rerun canned laughter and Bri says, 'There's that blobbing again. What's his story anyway?'

Neneh Cherry, Buffalo Stance, 1988, Axel nods. 'I give and I give.'

'My advice is you need to find some me time.'

But the handle, chrome, turns once more, and canned applause draws in a big lumbering unit from the light. He winks at the window where he's pretty sure his adoring audience must be and grins bigly. This is Dunalt.

'You know how long I had to wait out there?'

Axel is less happy to see him than even Randy. 'What the fuck are you doing here?'

'Hey there,' Dunalt tells Bri's breast area. 'You know, that's a nice labcoat, sweetie.'

'We're actually in session,' Bri tells the big blonde.

'Course you are, darlin,' Dunalt grins full-press. Edging closer, 'You know what? Jeff. The Big J. He woulda loved ya.'

'Dunalt,' Axel snipes. 'Stop fucking talking to my legal doctor.'

'The first two,' Bri chews her pen thoughtfully, 'you weren't swearing.'

'Legal?' Dunalt's interested. Then saliciously, 'Boy, could I use one-a-her about now.'

Encouraged by Bri freezing-up, Dunalt shuffles another step and says, 'You ever worked a campaign, darlin?'

'What do you fucking want?' Axel's had enough. Dunalt, he well knows, will grab a private part, sometimes even a young male's, who knows? within seconds should everyone accidently turn their backs at the same time. Trina, his own adult daughter, lock up your women, Axel has it, because the blonde unit's a PP hound and about as smart after the fact.

Canned laughter as Dunalt, his little hands up, retreats. 'Well, as you know,' he tells the godfather, 'I'm running for re-election.'

Axel rolls his eyes. 'How quaint.'

Hostility, my doc Bri notes.

'Yeah.' Dunalt, shameless, grins.

As (de-facto incumbent) mayor of West Side going for the CDB's seat of power (not actually again because he doesn't count the last time), Axel's now bumping up against this guy who seems to have no idea of what he could actually do to him.

'You know how hard it is to steal elections these days?'

Axel exhales bored with it. 'Just say it's rigged again, already.'

'Yeah.' Dunalt does this little performance of *if only*. 'But then you got the me-di-a.'

'Fuck the media. What about Mudorc?'

'You got Mud-orc.' Dunalt spells it out for his loving audience. 'You got all these dummies who believe anything, like really, anything.'

Axel knows them well. 'And?

'Well…'

Bri in clinician mode watches the two men watch each other.

'What Dunalt? Make it quick man.'

Instead, Bri sees Dunalt look longingly at what Axel has. If not longingly, then covetingly, specifically me, his maybe doctor-lawyer, Bri gets.

'But if we cut some kind of deal, Axey, well then…'

Axey hits the little ice-blue circle again and feels his head corkscrew. He gives a satisfied gasp of, 'Just wow,' then says, 'So vastly soft!'

'Vastly,' doc Bri is noting it down, 'soft.'

'So ethereally hillside fog but clear,' Axel confirms.

'Like skin?' doc Bri wants to know.

'Impossibly close yet far, far away.'

'Star Wars,' Dunalt says.

With a half-life of only a minute, Dunalt's actual 80s vibe kills it and Axel passes the boxstrip back to Doc Bri.

'You should try my prints,' Dunalt tells Axel. 'PP.'

But Axel's annoyed the big unit's still here. 'You pay the cops and own the courts. What's the problem?'

Dunalt shrugs. 'No offence, Axe, but,' looking around, 'it's not exactly Central.'

'And your point is?'

But Dunalt's back to coveting Dr. Bri to care what he means. 'No more e-lections,' he monotones. 'Just like you.'

Bri sees Axel bristle. Then calmly, 'I have elections.'

'Election elections I mean.'

Axel doesn't give a shit either way, we both note, but wants this Dunalt guy to crawl more naked into his pocket before he kicks him out.

'Trina's party.'

'I was there.' Dunalt doesn't even try to deny it.

'Even Trina's party,' Axel draws him in, 'it was a good party.'

'It was a good party,' the blonde fondly remembers. 'A party party.' His people making sure no one saw when they found out, Dunalt got taken care of.

'A different kind of party now I'm a respectable businessman.' He holds up bloodless hands.

Bri watches as Dunalt, clearly a psychopath, subsumes further into envy. 'Yeah,' he says. 'That Rothko,' and nods sadly. 'Nice touch guy.'

'For great power, comes great opportunities.'

Dunalt is salivating. 'That's what I like about you, Little A.'

'Axel,' Axel says, making himself even more at home on his legal doctor's sofa chair.

I show Bri his blobs on our full spectrum scan. Transcribing as much for the record, Axel thinks even Dunalt's got people, he doesn't have GRUSUM. Second to none social media disease, blob, blob, blob, surveillance, troll farmers and producers of wrongest stuff you can think of, they do what his ship of fools couldn't even dream of before breakfast. Further blobs could be, I stretch I admit, that Axel knowing people knows Dunalt's a psycho, confirming our mutal observations, but the slow-zombie type and in his advancing years, more controllable.

'I'll get back to you.'

'Awe, come on, Axe-man,' Dunalt man whines. 'It'll be yuge!'

'Meh.'

'The biggest thing in history.'

Axel bristles. Blob, blob on Bri's tablet, he's like what does this dumb blonde combover know about history?

'No one's ever seen anything like it.'

'I said I'll think about it,' Axel says.

'I can't do it without you, ace,' Dunalt resorts to slippery crawling. 'Your good ol'boys. You know what I mean.'

'That's the 80s.' Axel indicates the hotpink door.

Dunalt faces it. 'You know I was kind of in *American Psycho*?'

'That's so cool,' Bri makes the mistake of saying.

Winking at her, which means a follow up, Dunalt turns with blobbage of canned clapping, and briefly doing a little jig for the window audience, turns the handle, chrome, and exits into blazing afternoon glinting steel.

10. Mudorc

Canned stuff just keeps coming as Axel rolls his eyes for the hundredth time that session. Like he has to have the fittest eye muscles and brows in the nation. Because as soon as Dunalt's out of there, the pink door with it's groovy angular handle is opening again so a wiry old man in an expensive suit and peabody glasses can push through the crowd and slam it shut.

This is Mudorc, the really old media barron, and he gets canned applause blobs.

'Now listen, Axel.' He turns from the door. 'We may have a problem.'

Axel says, 'You have a problem. I have this. The mauve one?'

'Yeah it's an ego lateral agonist?'

'Meaning?'

'Another kind of detachment due to isometric acuteness to environment.'

'So, indifference?'

'Great.' Mudorc puts his hands on hips. 'Look, Axel.' He gets serious. 'There's no way to do it.'

Axel puts his pinky onto the little luminescent mauve circle and instantly feels like he's looking at Mudorc from a distance. He hears himself say, 'There's always a way to do it.'

The media baron glances wearily at Dr. Bri.

'We're actually in session?' she notes for the record.

'At the party,' Axel tells counsellor Bri, 'Dunalt, the big doofus, went and hurt a wealthy patron's seventeen year old daughter. Seventeen. A sexual encounter, according to a private medical report,' (at this point, Bri sees on my screen blob, blob, blob, get him out of here! Activate damage-control!) 'that no one knew was happening until it was too late. Worse,' Axel continues, 'it'd turned bad just as his own people found him. He'd broken both her arms.'

He lets that sink in.

Axel says, 'Not one but two. Which Mudorc here just can't believe.'

'At your party.' Mudorc lays some pipe.

'My wife's party.'

'Your wife's party,' Mudorc grants. 'And on the edge of it getting out?'

'Don't let it out.'

Mudorc's like it's not that simple. 'I just won't endorse him.'

'You have to.'

'How don't let it out?'

Blob, blob, blob, Axel it appears is not enjoying being talked to like this in front of a young female employee (ha you!) and hence that kind of creasing up.

'Well,' Axel does Axel, 'if you have to ask somebody.'

And we watch them creepily chuckle at nothing in particular.

Mudorc reads the room despite himself. Have you had people killed? is how Axel's looking at him. Indirectly, sure, but knowingly?

'It's whatever the blackbox says it is,' Axel tells Bri and taps his temple.

'Decentred subjectivity,' doctor Bri notes.

Axel stoned so far into himself nevertheless indicates her to the yet older man. 'You see this?'

'It's whatever I say too,' Mudorc says, 'but when it's out.'

Axel even more off his chops than before, if, he realises, that's even possible, waves off the media man. 'You feature Trina in flattering and distinctly bloodless clickbait on your society pages.'

'We do.' Mudorc, phone out, doomscrolls. Straightening and looking around the humble office, he notices the song contest poster, Marissa, next to the door.

Blob, blob, blob, I had a stake in her too, I, Kay, transcribe for Bri.

'The media mogul is something of a great power himself, you know?'

'I see,' says the legal doctor, Bri, from behind her big glasses.

'Well,' Mudorc performs, trying not to gloat. 'We do our bit.'

'If, you know, being a parasite on society's arse can be considered great.'

The wiley media man steadies on his insectoid legs. 'If you weren't so far up Dunalt's useful idiocy, Axel.'

'Ha! Because he is too,' he tells Bri.

Clearly nearing the edge of not freaking out, doc Bri says, 'Go on.'

'So far,' Axels tells his doctor, 'neither of us have actually poked out his mouth by accident.'

'Ha.' Mudorc also thinks it's funny. 'Nor each other's, for that.'

'If I'm sticking out of you, my friend, trust me,' Axel jokes, 'you will know it.'

Bri observes, 'So the relationship works until it doesn't.'

'No honour among thieves.'

'None.'

'But I would be lying,' Axel admits, 'if I said I didn't covet the business model.'

'Ha,' Mudorc says again but stops himself admitting it.

Regardless, Bri's nodding as she sees their two way blob, blob, blobbing as he thinks it anyway. While I've got her attention, I relate them to Dunalt's covetness score I logged and then them together on the spectrum, all the while simultaneously doing just as interesting pharmaceutical compounding with her.

'Yes, well, my dear,' Mudorc says, 'that's why the world has me already.'

'Power in his case is its simplicity,' Axels mansplains to Bri.

'They willingly come to you.'

'Yes.'

'He provides sport for the masses,' Axel says.

'Yes.' Mudorc is texting something on his phone.

'Blood sport.'

'Effectively.'

'You see this?' Axel points out the old vampire in his High Street suit.

'Interesting,' Bri says.

'Ball games,' he tells her, 'are gateway drugs.'

Looking back to her beloved parameters, Bri's numb to it. 'I see.'

'But then and more lucratively,' Axel fills him in, 'disenfranchised minorities unable to defend themselves.'

'Well, you know.' Mudorc can't be bothered explaining.

'Build lie upon lie and black and white complex issues.'

'Just a bit of fun.'

'Make it emotional and pump outrage.'

'Industry standard.'

'This guy,' Axel tells Bri as she slides the boxstrip back across the wood plain, 'he throws the hosts, handpicked psychos as per the business model –'

'Hah hah, well now.'

'– a daily diet of red meat and never say sorry.'

'That's, ah.' Mudorc nods at his phone impressed. 'That's pretty much it.'

Bri almost says something at this point.

'GRUSUM newsroom.'

'Well now. Yep, hah hah.' Mudorc looks around for something to distract with. 'Wouldn't that be something?'

'Because sport aside,' Axel explains, 'what Weasel's really doing, and I know you're doing it,' he tells him, 'because I am –'

'Yup.' The baron's back to nodding at his phone. 'If you must then.'

'Dismantling freedom in the name of freedom.'

'And the money shot.' Mudorc forces a grin at the doctor who looks away.

'It's genius,' Axel tells Bri.

'Well, you know.' Mudorc would've blushed if etc.

'The freedom to produce alternative facts.'

'Hoh hoh,' Mudorc equivocates. 'Right to free speech, my friend.'

'Freedom of might to be right.'

'We agree on all that.' Mudorc tries to steer Axel back to the topic at hand. 'But what about Dunalt, for Christ's sake?'

'Fuck Dunalt.'

'That's what I mean, man!'

'But don't worry freedom lovers,' Axel's back to joking to Bri, 'because Weasel cares. They've got your back.'

'Forget it then.' Mudorc makes to leave.

'Like more than you may realise.'

'Considerably more,' he quips, done with it.

Axel eyebrow gesturing to his new doctor, she remotes the boxstrip lids and the gangster hits himself again with now officially hillside fog blue.

The skeletally old businessman doesn't say anything to counsellor Bri as he walks to the door. Canned applause blobs as the chrome turns.

The hot-pink open, there's blinding light silhouetting dozens of people, some with guns. 'Where's my fricken money?' Dunalt's been waiting for Mudorc. 'You owe me bigly, mud man.'

Through the pink door Mudorc closes, 'I owe you nothing, fat arse.'

Alone again, Bri tells her client, 'You sure have a lot of friends.'

Axel gets comfy again in the big old sofa chair and smooths his tie. 'Cogs.'

11. Trina

Axel's barely had time to get stoned to the bejesus-belt on blue again when, wouldn't he know it, the handle, chrome, turns, and a woman in white heels and big hair strides into the room. She puts her hands on askance hips and stares at Axel as canned laughter, blob, blob, blob, fills his mind. This is Trina.

'Well well well.'

'Yes, well.'

'We're actually in session?' Bri tries again.

'Not now, sweetie.'

Axel rolls his eyes. 'Did you know about Dunalt at "your" party?'

'Our party, and of course I knew. So what?'

'So who is responsible?'

I detect doctor Bri's skin prickling as, blob, blob, blob, I inference for us Axel's wife's party's 'opportunities' qua Mudorc. As far as I can infer, they got underway when most of the 'guests' left and he and his inner circle of thugs could 'privately' 'host' some of the neighbourhood's 'finest' in Axel's, blob, blob, blob, vast man cave.

'For starters,' Trina winds up, 'the councillors Klin and Balak?'

'No names,' Axel moans.

'Who were supposed to be chaperoning your fat friend Dunalt?'

'Nothing to do with me.'

'Who, in a twist of what you, darling,' she focuses dispassionately on Bri (who looks her big nerdy glasses down), 'would have to call irony, he was off committing another felony when he was supposed to be laying low from the current sexual assault probe.'

'Weasel will outfox it.'

'And in my fucking house?'

'Our.'

'And you know what he was doing while this was happening?' Trina gestures her elderly husband to the legal shrink.

To Bri, 'You don't have to answer that.'

'He was throwing the Crs fresh meat from Jefferson St.'

Bri and I watch blob, blob, blob as Axel equivocates.

'It's business, so –'

'Juicy footage right there,' Trina tells Bri. 'Oh yes.'

'I see.'

'Darling,' Axel pleads. 'Come on.'

'Complimentary lines,' darling instead says. 'Lined up shots and meat rubbing shoulders with public royalty in his exclusive inner den come soundstage.'

'Such imagination!' Axel glances nervously at his legal doctor.

'At least that's how Axel's come to think of the pit.'

Bri observes Axel as he tries to, blob, blob, blob, change the topic.

'What did you buy on High St.? Hmm? Is the Hermes Spring Collection out?'

'Long wrap around lounges,' Trina tells Doc Bri about the pit. 'The 187" curved 8K laser S for "scape" LED holographing lifesize cage fighting, dog fighting, bare-knuckle kids fighting, mixed-mixed fighting, bad-good-badder fighting interspersed with bad-bad-good mixed-tools-meles for context.'

'It's really not that bad.'

'Incidentally making money for WE, Weasel Entertainment, in a sick kind of feedback loop they don't know enough to see.'

'A Mudorc channel,' Bri notes.

Axel tells his wife, 'You see this?'

'But also a subtly effective hint of him, darlings,' Trina is scathing, 'Axel R, great nephew of Pete the Elite.'

'It's true.'

'Repeating history for his own sake.'

Balling momentarily, like really Harry Pottheading after fingerprinting a lighter mauve circle, Axel says, 'Down in the pit, on the sofas, the lighting is they can't see the upper level.'

'You know those shadows?' Trina asks Bri. 'Up there behind the lights?'

'She doesn't know.' Axel checks his really expensive watch.

On the tablet screen, blob, blob, blob, I translate Axel At least I don't remember her.

Bri says, 'No.'

'There you go then.'

'But then those shadows up near the ceiling, they laugh.'

'You're being dramatic,' Axel tells his wife.

'Steal the milk, the darkness snickers.'

'Oh please.'

'Eat the young.' Trina leers.

'I think that's enough.'

'That one.' Trina indicates Bri.

'Don't listen.'

'Broken bones protruding from the howling holographic screen –'

'Ridiculous.'

'Club Axel's twilight zone push pulls.'

'You rarely stay anyway.'

'But yet the cattle remain,' Trina punchlines. 'They could have left. Maybe some tried to. Instead, they sit there on those couches, with city councillors leaning in, and somehow try to remain calm.'

'They are there by consent.'

Trina laughs.

'If you're observing this, Doctor Bri,' Axel says of his smirking wife.

'Yes.'

'My wife needs treatment.'

But Trina looking down at her old husband says, 'Because they never know what's coming next.'

'She doesn't really know what she's talking about.' The ageing gangster chuckles to his new defence shrink.

Bri looks her pokerface between them even she's actually on the edge of freaking out.

'Don't make any fuss,' Trina says of the cattle and perhaps Bri. 'Down in the pit,' she says, 'they glance at each other, don't make trouble. Come on, the councillors say, don't make me have to tell Axel, darlin.'

'That's quite enough, Trina.'

'And don't even think about what might not be really seeping from the rooms.'

'Oh my gods.'

'Because if you try,' Trina tells Bri, 'maybe you can't even hear it.'

'She's insane,' Axel creases up. 'Really amusing actually.'

'What do you think she means,' Bri is chewing her pen, 'if you try you can't hear?'

Trina doesn't hesitate. 'A muffled cry here in Weasel Sports screams.'

'She means nothing.'

'A moan not pleasure there abstract for helplessness.'

'You do realise you're making a scene?' Axel tells her.

'But what the cattle don't get because they never do –'

'Oh here we go.'

'The numbness, the complimentary lines, the shots and surveillance compiling every indiscretion and frameable illegality as staff, female and male, come and go.'

Axel, 'Is that even a pun?'

'Incited and performed and unquestioned, yes, but in reality, he's getting everything.'

'What she is saying is meaningless,' Axel insists.

Bri completely Sweeny Todded spaces out in the latest compound tweaks as trusty Kay, her AI, moi, takes the reins and nails remaining values. 'And,' she asks the average of them before pausing a moment to dry swallow the latest sneaky, 'how do you feel?'

Trina thinks that a good question and watches her older husband under the window like who's he kidding? Pinned like a bug in her diorama, not that he, blob, blob, blob, gives a shit anyway, I multimodally generate from his FS scan and prompt the everymen Klin and Balak, councillors, reptiles in three piece suits sampling Axel's cattle on the couches. Above, sharply glinting eyes like stars in the den's dark sky. Those stars, they follow ringed hands on wives' knees. Manly I'm with you bros clasping husbands' shoulders as their barely adult daughters naively giggle. Bri watches it all, blob, blob, blob, just like she did *Alienz 14* on acid when she was a teenager with friends.

'A good party,' Axel heads his wife off. 'Soon to be departed Slatts aside, no resistance.'

Bri watches the older woman watching her way older husband.

'To some extent,' Trina says of him, 'Axel expects resistance and is always measuring.'

'Resistance is natural in the face of great power.'

'But also,' Trina prosecutes, 'opportunity.'

Axel nods with the logic of it. 'Power makes opportunities.'

'Not just for the pleasure of performance though.'

'Okay,' Bri follows.

'And not just for audience affect.'

'I think,' Axel blob, blob, blobs, 'we get it, Trina.'

'Simply,' Trina sums her husband up, 'resistance confirms power.'

Axel rolls his narrow eyes. So dramatic. Taking out her bad feelings on people like his new legal doctor whom Dunalt's going to try and poach.

'Axel knows resistance,' Bri confirms.

'I am the underdog, let's not forget.'

'There is only one on the farm who has freedom, my dear.'

'And why is that, do you think?' Bri asks.

Axel is it's obvious. 'Enemies coming up like friends.'

'That's right,' Trina mocks him. 'Like Blako.'

'Ohmygods, here we go.'

Bri chews pen and swivels. 'Who's Blako?'

A hard silence like striking legal gold diagnosis.

'My brother.'

Bri realises, mainly because I'm saying she has, she's met this Blako at the local. Scanning her own blob, blob, blobbing memory of an older guy she thinks said his name was Blako, whom, off his face drunk, came onto her one night out with friends.

'At Christmas, Axel gave Blako a book.'

'None of this is true by the way,' he tells his legal shrink.

'Something about spies,' Trina recalls. 'Some secret psy-ops program or something the enemy supposedly tried that piqued his interest at the time.'

Blob, blob, blobs galore, Bri watches as I inference Axel rewrapping the book in question, annotating it's slight dog-ear where he'd got bored with it and Christmas was the next day.

'But then that fateful morning,' Trina continues, 'when we're all sitting around the tree for presents time, Axel personally hands the rewrapped book to Blako, like personally.'

'Only, you know,' Axel sniffs, 'to have it handed back.'

Canned oohs and laughter blob all over the place that Axel somehow ignores.

'I'm sure he was, like,' Bri fluffs, 'trying to, you know?'

'No,' Trina corrects her. 'He wasn't.'

'Thinking they can, what?' Axel suddenly wants to know. He dabs his pinky on the silver circle in the boxstrip again and asks, 'Do what to me?'

'Blako, Axel,' Trina spells it out for him, 'was doing nothing to you.'

Totally off chops, Axel says, 'Undisputed godfather slash administrator of Coronation and Parklands as far as Jerrico St. where the competition begins. An admired and or feared stand out who also happens to have a heart of gold making personals gift to nobodies like Blako, his wife's loser sibling who, let's face it, is truly nobody besides my brother-in-law.'

'You see this?' Trina wants Bri to see.

'Okay,' Bri tries to be useful.

'When even the street he runs was not earned nor won but granted as a fave by me, Axel, the giver of that fricken book, new or not, which was not even necessarily a bad one only then to be rudely rejected?'

'Okay,' Bri tries again. 'Everyone take a deep breath.'

Canned awes as Axey settles. 'At the time, you know, I just smiled.'

'Well that's great, Axel.' Bri salvages something at least.

'I said, oh, okay then, um, Blako.'

'It was rude,' Bri reassures him, 'but that's also just a point of view, right?'

'No worries, I even said. 'I'll just uh, you know, take the fucking thing back I spose.'

'That was very big of you.'

'Yuge.' Trina rolls her eyes.

'He turned it over to pretend to read the blurb like he's a fucking expert.'

'Yep, uh huh,' the legal therapist is noting. 'I hate that.'

'Like he knows everything about the topic, that's not even a beat-up, but actually interesting?'

'Maybe don't worry about it?'

'He's incapable,' Trina sniffs.

'The correct course of action, of course,' Axel mansplains, 'would have been something like, gee, thanks Axel, this is really thoughtful and cool of you and I look forward, you know, to reading every fucking word of it. Instead, this guy, this dumb fuck.'

Trina, 'Here we go.'

'"You read it?" he asks.' Axel grinds his teeth. 'And I'm a bit taken aback, to be honest, unsure if that's actually an accusation of not being a reader and regifting second hand goods –'

'You did.'

'Even,' Axel says, 'in this case, I mostly had, and I said something like, well, er, no, Blako, which it turned out was the cue for this smartarse with a face he doesn't realise is like eggshell –'

'See?' Trina wants Bri to.

'To grin and hand it back with, well then champ, you read it.'

There's blobs all over the place which means canned laughter and I simulate it in a collapsed player Bri doesn't access, then silence as we all think about the perils of regifting.

Bri undocks the boxstrip and passes it over one lid open.

'A guy because you can't say *man*,' Axel peers into the little open one. 'Pink?'

'An anti-anger serotonin agonist.'

Axel hesitates because anger is justified, but then pokes in a pinky anyway. 'Nearly thirty years younger than me with effectively no power and thus a face of eggshell –'

The women watch as Axel's face goes flat. He says, as mildly as he may ever have, 'The supreme leader of this part of town, a great power, me, versus the stupidity of the implications of rejecting a considered if slightly dog-eared gift.'

'See how calm you were when you said that?' Bri reminds him.

'Oh please.' Trina's unimpressed.

'I'm so fucked up.' Axel's head lolls. 'How are you?'

'See?'

Bre does.

'Now I'm thinking about it,' the ageing gangster is back to without anger, 'a guy with a nose so delicate like a woman's that a bar would crush it like red toffee glass should just a hint be made to the lads –'

'Oh my gods,' Trina pounces. 'Like a Christmas bobble under the heel of your boot?'

'Well.'

'A crunching noise, stop me if I'm wrong, and inevitable howl of understanding?'

Bri raises a brow. She's got you there.

'Axel,' completely off-chops he says third person, 'the godfather of Coronation now uncle Pete's history, a good guy, me, who also happens to be the iron fisted comptroller of the gas pipes and owner of countless houses including soon this one.'

'Yeah yeah,' his wife mocks him. 'Blah blah.'

Bri sees the seriousness of the blobbing, his, I'm pointing out on screen.

'And gift receivers need to lift their game.' Axel finally dissolves into hot-pink rage as the pink fingerprint dissolves.

'You see what I'm dealing with?' Trina tells Bri.

'So Blako loses an arm to an unseen sniper.'

'Oh wow.' Trina's pretty sure she has him now. 'I rest my case.'

'Only, okay,' Axel tells no one in particular, 'to have it fed back to him, unknowingly, in transfatty pastry at a victory party several weeks later.'

Bri's so high on her own supply she may never be normal again, but even then the red blob, blob, blobs of Axel's full spectrum running scan are inescapable.

'Maybe a block party,' he digs their hole deeper, 'with a dance music theme marking Easter where an example of his eggshell is made via planted evidence of say, a bug, proving attempted snitching to Dunalt's cops, like pocketed ones knocking around with his balls.'

'Do you see what he is?' Trina implores Bri.

'There are protests of innocence,' Axel's on a roll, 'when is there not? But one of my guys tells me the gift-rejecter was going for his gun that was then planted on him after squeezing off two or three back in that direction, and then others to clean it up.'

'Hypothetically.' Bri wants confirmation.

'He's alive.'

'But which still affects your wife, which you can see.'

'Thank you.'

'Trina would be upset.' Axel shrugs them off. 'What sister of a disposed of rejecter of thoughtful gifts wouldn't be?'

'He's a monster,' Trina says matter-of-factly.

'But in the long run, in terms of resistance, she would get over it.'

'You're a fucking monster!'

'Ja, meine bärchen,' Axel sneers at the chrome past her. 'Weak minds get over it.' He sits back adjusting his blue tie. He tells doctor Bri, 'Because if they don't, well then.'

What this means, I show Bri, is blob, blob, blob, his eyes grin up and down and round and round, there's always me.

Totally cabbaged, Bri finds herself wedged between this clearly abusive marriage, the evil power performs in its prosecution of being, and these molecular prints, molps, tweaking to her genome and biome and is really not sure how much more she can take.

In self-defence, Bri writes 'blob, blob, blob' in her pad.

Trina at the door glances back. Seeing nothing, she turns the handle, chrome, and canned applause follows her out into the momentarily blinding scrum.

12. Casselle, Leor, thugs

Axel has just fingerprinted a slightly different hue of green – ForestW, if heard correctly – when the door opens and a woman and man walk inside. This is Casselle and Leor, Bri's parents, and the canned clapping is loud, annoying Axel.

Past the cute married couple, Axel sees two of his thugs have followed them in. This is Jope and Darko and, blob, blob they get mostly canned boos.

'Hi mum, dad.'

'Hi sweety,' Casselle says.

'Hey,' Leor follows up.

'I'm actually in session, so?'

'We know that hon.' Casselle hugs her cardi. 'We've been asked to come.'

Blob, blob, blob, Bri watches Axel get down to smirking at Leor, her dad.

'Axel,' Leor says. 'I see you've met our legal mad-scientist, Bri?'

'Dad.' The doctor rolls her eyes.

'Also a face like eggshell,' is all Axel can say.

Canned oohs as Bri and her parents share a look.

'This guy,' Axel creases up to his thugs.

'Hah, yeah boss,' Darko confirms.

Jope, 'So tough, bro.'

'Totally calm,' Axel mocks the dad. 'Just standing there, discoursing with the boss of the whole hood, who's now inside his house.'

'Granny flat,' Leor says.

'He's younger than me, taller, sure, but built?'

'Nope,' says Darko.

'Sick burn,' Jope contributes.

'Oh please,' Axel sniffs looking Leor up and down. 'Not cut nor buff nor even toned in his flimsy skinniness?'

'I think you're great, hun.' Casselle gives Leor's hand a little squeeze.

'Thanks, babe.'

'Which he's not even bothering to try and hide because he can't.'

'Damn, son,' Jope wows.

'Just a weakling standing there in his cheap department store suit, grey but not destroyer, like somehow he still owns the place?'

'We do,' Leor says.

'In fact, how anyone could think he works-out even occasionally is kidding themselves.'

Bri says, 'Um, the part about "owns the place"?'

'It's okay, Bri,' Leor tells his daughter. 'We've taken care of it.'

'And that silvering light beard he clearly cuts himself and discount shop glasses?' Axel pfffts. 'Just sad.'

'Ouch,' Darko mocks.

'Psych!' Jope sticks the knife in.

But Leor doesn't mind and grins at the funny side of his everyman look.

Axel looks at Casselle. 'But Casselle, well –'

'Hi Axel.'

Axel pinky fingerprints a Prussian blue circle convinced he's hilarious. 'Hashtag FinallyrealisingImwithaloser?'

'You know,' Bri tells Axel. 'I'm pretty sure this is a conflict of interest, so.'

So utterly Zoom-bombed, Axel squints thickening hillside fog at them and says, 'Did you know I knew your dad when he was young?'

Bri did not.

'As you'd have it in a small world,' he opines, 'I and Ralf, your granddad, when we were the age of the Coreys, well…' He looks at Casselle. 'I could have been your father instead, if, you know, fate had befallen us.'

'Which is just weird?' Casselle tries wrap her head around.

When Bri looks down at her tablet, I'm trolling her with what she would've looked like with Axel as her dad, and or granddad, their hybrid even, but she's too fruitcaked to go there.

Blobs blobbing, I'm not, haha, and see that this guy, Axel, who is not her dad, because that's Leor, I've checked, is human inferencing her mum, Casselle, the blobs of which mean, 'proud woman'. Pride is good in some contexts, I Aisplain to the Bri-ster, just not his. His, I have her attention now, is blobbage of ol'Pete the Elite saying how her mum's mum, Jineesha, Bri's grandma, was writing bullshit to turn the new public against them and he had to, sorry babe, make her death look like an, ahem, accident.

Bri, eyes wide in horror at my screen, glances up at Axel. He's still looking at her mum, Casselle, thinking Pete vs Jin, then she looks back at me as her hands scrabble drawers.

In fact, pride, Kay, me, doesn't want to say but does trying to stay true to the blobs, is what PtheE coached young Axel R on before unleashing him on the public. Pride, ahem, is compliance unboxed. You make an unboxing vid for VileTube watch the tune change. The body and thus breaking mind of victims is a playground, young Axel, in a Rothko's bloodless hands.

That's what the blobs said. As well as something like, headhunt, my boy, Martha Stout's four percent from the community. In your ranks, four becomes eighty percent by natural enforcement. Restock five percent attrition meat feeding that four. Jostling for position as they perform our discourse, someone, I transcribe despite my appropriateness parameters being barely contained surface tension, wrongs them, and they're lining up to outdo horror for you. Put something fragile into the ring and see, Axel's blobs are saying. Monitoring as much Bri right on the edge of her total freak-out neural circuit, she's convexed water quivering on a table and dry swallows her throat circuit as I inference the blobs saying, fingers, toes and other low hanging fruit, have fun my son, but loved ones are mafia bread and butter. So sorry, babes, I tell her as the FS blobs keep coming, pride talks a good game, boy, Axel recalls ol'Pete saying, but guns talk better.

'Let's wrap this up, shall we?' Axel says. 'Darko, documents?'

Darko shoves past Casselle and unclips a briefcase from a sling. He takes out a manila folder and hands it to Axel. The gangster puts it on his side of Bri's vast deskage and tables said docs.

'Sign these.'

Bri, I show her, it's the deed to the land.

Though everyone sees, she slowly slips herself another pill and somehow breathes.

Casselle says, 'We're not signing those, Axel.'

'No,' Leor backs her up. 'We're not.'

Axel looks at Bri who is totally blobbed focused. I write for her, Fuck him.

'I'm taking the land anyway,' Axel says, 'because it was Pete's.'

'I'm sorry, Axel,' Casselle stands firm, 'but that's not going to happen.'

'I'll kill you,' he shrugs. 'Quickly out of respect for your accomplished daughter,' creepily smiling at her, 'and bury you in what will then be my land, anyway.'

Jope and Darko jab the husband and wife with gun muzzles. 'Suck shit, losers.'

'The thing is, Axel,' Casselle says, 'we're having guests.'

'It's a big yard,' Leor explains, 'and our friends like the outdoors.'

Axel turns around to the window. Sure enough, the backyard through the Venetians is a hive of activity, with military people erecting tents etc. while their armed buddies mill around keeping Axel's outgunned guys at bay.

'What the fuck?' he can't believe it. Turning back, 'Do you want war?'

'They're our neighbours,' Leor tries to explain. He hesitates to say more realising he wouldn't understand.

But neighbours, I don't mind paraphrasing Axel's blobs, are tribute-paying untermench and or mortal enemies, der.

Bri can't believe her AI, moi, just inferred 'der'.

Axel becomes notably venomous. He does this narrow-eyed look, which is the flat eyes death-stare, which, blob, blob, blob, is the poison-green gas of a toxin-breathing reptile.

'The orange one.' Axel holds out his hand to Bri. When she doesn't respond even she can clearly see his request on her tablet screen, thanks me, he adds, 'Hurry please.'

I take over, having gamed it out, and reprint the flight-safety-orange. I signal the boxstrip is ready to undock. Bri takes the matte metal block and slides it across the massive desk.

It spins to a stop right next to the unsigned documents on Axel's shore.

As they all watch, a lid slow servos up and Axel looks in at it. Hot-pink. Is she trying to kill me? he squints and I inference.

'Jope.'

'Yes boss?'

'Put a finger on this.'

Jope hesitates. 'What is it boss?'

'Don't ask what it is, just fucking do it.'

Jope shoulders past Casselle once more and looks in at it. He sees it's pink. He looks at Axel, then he looks at the door, also pink. He puts his pinky into the opened mini-box and then looks nervously at his boss. I write to Bri, this will be funny.

Jope's eye widen and Axel recoils. He starts laughing. Then he's laughing like it's bubbling up out of him and there's no way to stop it.

'It reacts differently to different biome-genome profiles,' Bri tells them.

Jope laughing his guts up stumbles back to his position behind Casselle. He doubles up again at something.

'Well,' Leor says, 'at least he's happy.'

'I aim to please,' Bri quips.

Axel rolls his eyes. 'Well, have it your way.' He suit-pockets the boxstrip and says, 'But realise this means war.'

'We don't want war,' Casselle tells the gangster, 'but you're not getting our land either. History is past.'

Now it's Axel's turn to laugh. Ha ha, I translate his FS blobs as he bubbles. He looks between his men for recognition, which, multi-modally, is his wafting said green toxic gas. He gestures them over.

Jope still giggling shoulders past Leor now. Shaking his head almost in pain at how funny it is, they take up positions by Axel's sofa-chair.

'History continues,' Axel tells the family, now a loosely oppositional group. 'And I'm taking this.'

'The boxstrip?'

'This.' He nods towards the hot-pink door.

What? I text.

'What?' Bri says.

'It's mine,' Axel says simply. 'I am here, my men are here, we have guns and you don't. Now get the fuck out.'

Darko and Jope, still giggling but he's gaining on it, raise their weapons. Jope quivers his barrel at Bri, who puts her lab coat sleeves up and stands up.

The family look at each for direction. Looking at all of them, I start a backup to the cloud. Emergency lock activated and erasure procedure initiated, there's a hushed discussion of sorts, then Bri's shuffles out from the desk to her family.

'And don't let the 80s hit your arse on the way out.'

'He said that before,' Bri tells her parents.

Unsure what they're feeling – happy to be alive or sad for dispossession – the family turns for that pink door. Casselle turns its chrome and they shuffle out into the light.

'And don't come back,' Axel calls after them.

As their eyes adjust to outside, they see lots of people, mainly Axel's and mostly with guns, milling about. But their concentration is also that they've been hemmed in by a growing number of neighbours with better guns, who absorb the family then hem some more.

The hot-pink door still open – there's Axel in the old sofa-chair watching them through the frame – his people start pushing inside. First is Laplov then Randy, then Mudorc and Dunalt chewing his ear off about something. Trina unhappily follows, then their entourages and assorted thugs all pile inside.

'Are you hurt?' one of their neighbours, Yiski, triages.

'He's still in there,' Leor says.

Yiski nods. 'Well, the main house is secure and you're alive. It's enough.'

Casselle, 'We're just lucky we joined the community.'

Yiski smiles. 'They had a chance to. Maybe when he follows ol'Pete?'

As the family makes their way up their generous lawn to the house, there's the sound of smashing and they look back. Out of view, like at the back of the granny flat, formerly Bri's, Axel's men are already demolishing the back wall so they can extend through the hedge and fence and connect with Axel's ever-expanding palace.

Bri's phone vibrates in her pocket and it's from me. There's rerun canned laughter as she opens my message, reading, Maybe the 80s weren't so great?

13. After Dunalt's re-election

. . . . . .

He Sees Her
Geoffrey Heppenstall

1. How it ought to have been

He sees her often. And once they have spoken he shall love all of her in time. That time will be a good time where all is promised through the opening of a door that says no more to the world but 'Do Not Enter'.

Of course the lovers find their way inside the undiscovered universe.

Then they are alone, spirit speaking to flesh in words of an endearing now.

The style is everything that is the essence of dreaming of clouds and the illusion of sky, of substance speaking to the dream – two halves of the whole life.

All else is past or has never been…

2. How it was

She was no more than a voice in the corridor. Seeing her was an opening into another life. He heard her sound on the bare boards of the staircase. Carefully opening his door, he saw something of her as she passed.

Afterwards she became a night shadow wandering through his mind. He imagined every shadow to be her. Thinking of her, he heard her speak. Her voice was the essence of her beauty.

The chance of a meeting soon came. A step on the uneven stairs creaked outside his door. It was music or the rhythm of sighs followed by her silence. There was a pause enabling him to open the door when next he heard her.

He nearly spoke before he closed the door again. A door in the corridor closed very firmly the following morning. From his window he saw her in daylight, waiting with several bags. That was the third and final time he saw her.

This Is What You're Not Tweeting About
Bonny Brooks

Queen Histrionic (as you have dubbed her) makes you angry, but there are 6906 reasons not to tweet about it. 6906 devotees that have favourited her first tweet; god knows how many more the others. So instead, you throw your rucksack down and slouch against the wall to roll a cigarette. It is dusk in April and you are outside your mother's block on a council estate in central Bristol, not pressing the buzzer. Feeding Queen Histrionic's name into Twitter's search box instead. *Anata Lowell-Townsend.*

Dove Street estate is nestled into a curve of one of the city's basins; three big blocks hemmed by smaller blocks, next to the square and the homeless hostel. Below you, the engine air of Stoke's Croft and St Paul's growls; an enclave of the city once famed for riots and heroin but like everywhere in Bristol, feeling the creep of *The Guardian* lifestyle paeans. Attracted by the graffiti and decrepit buildings, an increasing number of cafes that don't serve fry-ups have moved in, but the massage parlours and vagrant junkies remain.

Anata Lowell-Townsend. You light another rollup and scroll her Twitter mentions again. You have decided that adults can be divided into two categories. Those who experienced adulthood before social media, and those who did not. At thirty-five, you are of the former and because of this, people just a few years younger than you live beyond a chasm that may as well be decades. *Anata Lowell-Townsend conference.* Or perhaps it is a class thing. Or an American thing. Or a people who use the word 'woke' unironically thing. Whatever it is, the strength of your anger at #MeToo overreach surprises you. You are a woman. You are supposed to be a feminist. Perhaps you are angry about the wrong things.

Anata Lowell-Townsend liar.

When the hashtags and lawsuits began appearing, you were happy. It was an important reckoning. Every woman has a story, so the saying went, and you agreed. But you didn't tweet your own stories. It felt like bleeding in public and if there's one thing life has taught you, it's that blood attracts sharks. You were grateful for the other women. Impressed with their courage. You reminded yourself that everybody has their own way of dealing with things. Some are testifiers and some wipe the tears of other women. You have tended to be the latter.

Now though, some of the women in this movement look hysterical to you. You realise that such a term would have you strung up for internalised misogyny, but this is what you think. A drunk man on a train sways on their shoulder and they tweet about assault. They think late-twenties womanhood counts as doe-eyed fragility. Graphic exposés of awkward sexual encounters and bad dates appear in print and the men who star in them disappear. They label disagreement verbal violence. They headline blog posts about ill-advised affairs as if the posts will expose rapists. Many of them are promoting books. And you, Leah, you are aghast, looking in on the literary world like a city you hoped to settle in, having arrived to find it burning. This is what you are not tweeting about.

Flick your cigarette into the gutter and go inside your mother's house.

In her kitchen you stir lentils, sprinkle cider vinegar while she sits on a chair, her bare feet wedged against the tiny table. 'They're moving him to the hospice,' she says, using one fingernail to chip away at another, biting the end off and dropping it into a bin near her feet. Her father is dying.

Put down the spoon you've been stirring with. Tilt your head to the side in an expression you hope displays concern.

'St Peter's Hospice,' she clarifies. 'Up the hill.'

You wipe your hands on a dishcloth and sit down to put your arms around her. She rests her head on your shoulder.

'He looks so gaunt.' Mum pulls back. 'The bones in his face are kind of protruding.' She wipes an eye. 'In a way it feels a bit like how he looked in my mind all those years that I pictured him as a kid, when he was gone. His face was an outline, you know? Just bones and eyes. Seeing him today, it was like that.'

Your family is a dog-eaten quilt patched with absence and madness. 'How long do they think he has?'

Her eyes narrow. You can tell that she is thinking you are hard, cold. You can tell that she is thinking you are jealous. When you were a kid and he arrived back in her life, he commanded much of her attention. You were put out. This is what she believes.

'I just mean, do you need to go and stay up there, right away?'

She gazes at the row of mismatched mugs, hanging on hooks. 'Will you go to see him?'

You tug at a hem on your jeans. 'Hasn't he got enough on his plate, without trying to make small-talk with a grandkid he hasn't seen for almost thirty years?'

'Cancer isn't catching, Lee.'

'It's bad, those people who turn up just to weep at someone's deathbed. Like they're stealing other people's grief. I don't want to do that. This is yours.'

She snorts. 'You probably knew him as well as I did.'

The past tense. He is already halfway in the past tense. You wonder where he would appear in the story of your family and what you would call him. You don't have a name for him. Your mother calls him LL Pops (long lost), like he's a rapper in the '90s.

When you were little, and he returned from southeast Asia wearing, of all things, a cowboy hat, he told you to call him John. But your mother says his name is Peter.

'Have you managed to get out today, Mum?'

She nods.

It is difficult to ascertain if she is telling the truth. She is depressed, but getting her to admit it is impossible. As a new age hippy, she believes depression to be the work of negative energy. She buys feel good vitamins and then forgets to take them.

You dish out the lentils and you can tell she wants to change the subject, so you talk about the Twitter furore you have been following. She has managed to stay off most of social media except to post about the kundalini dance classes she runs at the Quaker Centre in one of the posh areas. She feels as though social media is destroying heart connections. When she says this, she places her hand over her chest and sighs audibly. 'What I worry about,' she gestures with her fork, 'is what this does to men and women. How will they connect anymore?'

Her hippydom never really stretched to the women's movement. Like when you told her how your virginity was taken, and she just said: 'I think loads of women have experienced things like that.' You were not a woman; you were thirteen. And she is correct, but that doesn't make it right, does it?

Huddle in the doorway again to smoke. Find other tweets that call Queen Histrionic a liar.

She has accused a famous writer of being rude to her at a conference, calling it rage-filled, misogynistic abuse. But a tape of the event has surfaced, revealing a polite exchange. Even so, she refuses to apologise, counter-accusing her accusers of emotional abuse. Right now, no one makes you angrier than Queen Histrionic.

You find a slew of Twitter mentions. Many tweets defend her passionately: The Male Writer is an arsehole; his defenders are enablers.

You don't get to tell us what counts as #MeToo.

Stay in your lane.

Shut up and listen.

SHUT up and LISTEN.

In your head, the tweets all speak Californian English.

You fantasise about intervening; telling everyone the world is becoming too brittle and Queen Histrionic, she is but one symptom. You write out frank tweets ending with faux-courageous summations: *yeah, I said it.*

But of course you don't send them. Your own writing career is a half-formed thing. You would have to be crazy to throw yourself beneath this racehorse. You grind your last cigarette into a slug trail and turn to go indoors to bed.

Mum wants you to help with clearing out her father's flat. He is not yet dead.

'I just feel it would be good to get a head start,' she says.

She has always been this way. Growing up, periodically you'd find her, huddled over some box or other, throwing out photos, letters, teddies. She said it was important to be ruthless, but she has never been ruthless with the right things.

You believe this clear-out is a recon exercise. She wants to talk to him before he dies. She did a workshop where they told her to *get complete* with her father. You believe she is trying to find out why he left and then came back and then left again. You know why, but you go with her anyway.

Ants tramp the kitchen counters. The toilet has no seat. There are cleaner crack-houses. You put on gloves and scrub the kitchen while she sings incomprehensibly from another room. 'What does he think about you clearing out the place before he dies?' you ask, when she wanders in.

'I haven't told him.' This is funny because she is often pretty incontinent with information. 'Who do you keep messaging?' she asks, when you reach for your phone again.

You put it away, mutter 'Sorry.'

You are trying to write a no-send letter because the clinical psychologist recommended it. You told her you feel uncomfortable writing about yourself in the first person and she suggested a letter. So when you think of things, you jot them down in your notes app. Little memory glimpses that would be meaningless to anyone who happened on them. *Hairs in the bathtub. After the park. The pink hat.*

Six hours in, the kitchen is cleared. Your mother seems to have made the other rooms messier. You find her in the bedroom huddled over a pile of clothes, clutching a pair of tie-dye trousers. 'Do you remember when he came back from Thailand? I hadn't seen him since before I hit puberty and here he was meeting me and my kid, and the first thing he says when I open the door is *you've grown.*'

In the toilets in the pub across from his flat, you check Twitter again.

The Male Writer has been accused of coming on to younger women. Some people call him an arsehole. He may well be an arsehole, but does that make it right for Queen Histrionic to lie about him? His defenders deploy an array of criticisms. Younger women speak of the harm Queen Histrionic does genuine victims. Older men are more likely to use biblical-sounding descriptors like *evil* and *wicked.*

You go onto her timeline. *I am retiring from Twitter*, she says. *I can no longer abide the constant trauma of being harassed by his enablers.*

Someone asks her what the harassment consists of. She doesn't respond.

Someone else replies with a link to the recording of the conference conversation that started all this. She tweets back: *I don't engage with gaslighters.*

You put your hands on your temples, shake your head, whisper 'mental'. This is a generation, or perhaps a class, that you don't understand. You have comforted friends who struggled to vilify men that beat and raped them tied to furniture. The things that live in your head would burn the words off Queen Histrionic's tongue. And yet she and her comrades command the conversation; appearing in magazines as #MeToo soothsayers, deploying terms like *privilege*. You do not personally know any women that would relate to their fragility. You want to know how a woman who considers polite disagreement to be misogynist bullying, can be a spokesperson for a cause whose true beneficiaries should surely be the women who choke back a tapeworm every day of their lives. If you had a mind for testimony you could tell her some stories, but you don't.

Late on the third night at Mum's, she sobs in your arms. The room is lit warm orange, from an assortment of lamps she's collected from car-boot sales. Some kind of Sanskrit chanting plays on low volume. You stroke her hair, listening to the argument in the pub yard outside her window: *You shouldn't have bothered. Cunt.*

Mum pulls back. 'I tried to give him a bit of cottage cheese but they said he can't be fed solids. The place is so fucking depressing. They don't think he's got long. Will you come with me?'

If you were the kind of person the psychologist seems to think you should be, you would just say no. You would announce your intention to 'look after yourself'. It would not matter what any of them thought.

The hospice smells of germylene and rot but the nurses are sweet. Landscape watercolours of already-dead outpatients sit on the walls. You managed to insist on staying in reception and with each quarter-hour, your Twitter scrolling becomes more frantic. In your fantasies you set up a fake account to say whatever you want.

@AnataLowellTownsend: I don't think it is right what you are doing. If he is predatory, let the people who have actually been harmed by him speak. What does this have to do with you? You are not helping anyone but your own pocket.

@SineadLawson: How can you compare being patronising in a workshop to being a predator? You are setting women back a century with your fragility-mongering.

Into the draft folder your brave tweets go.

You have been wondering about bravery and you have been wondering about the literalism that is descending on literary culture. When someone doesn't like a writer now, or it is alleged that a writer is an arsehole, said writer's fiction gets trawled for insufficiently woke representations. People begin to say *we should have known.*

You think this is alarming. In your brave draft tweets, you talk about socialist realism and the danger of literary shibboleths. In your actual tweets, you complain about the closure of libraries.

You realise that your right leg has been jittering for at least an hour and now your Achilles tendon is hurting. You get up to buy a cup of tea from the machine.

Wonder what they are talking about. Perhaps Mum will be sitting down and then getting up again, sitting down and getting up again, and he will be all morphined-up, serene. She will mention you, and he will do a pre-emptive strike, like *why did you drag her here, I'm sure she doesn't want to be sat in a hospice.*

But these are just your projections. You have no idea what he will say; you haven't seen him in twenty-five years. Like Mum as a kid, all you have is outlines and pixelated fragments.

The two of you go to a greasy spoon around the corner, for a chocolate milkshake.

'I just couldn't think what to say,' she stirs with the straw. 'I had all these plans about what I was going to say to try and resolve things. But then he just looked so pathetic and I couldn't do it.' She is folding her paper napkin into smaller and smaller pieces. 'But it feels right to be here.'

Someone has made little nicks on the side of the table, perhaps with a butter knife. You run your index finger over them, count. 'You don't have to be though.' One, two, three. 'It's not like you owe him anything.' Four. 'You could leave him with the nurses if you wanted. They have volunteers and chaplains.'

Her mouth falls open; this is the kind of advice you could only give someone else. 'Nobody should die alone.' She casts the straw down, picks the glass up with both hands and gulps.

'But isn't his aloneness self-created?' Even as you say this, you feel like she is right.

'I don't want to be on my own in there,' she says. 'It's just weird, after so long not speaking. Will you come in with me?'

And you are there in the flat by the window, some twenty-eight years ago; Mum bending down to smile, to tell you what you are doing tomorrow. *I don't want to be on my own with him.* You remember the thought so clearly. You don't remember saying it aloud. You were with him the next day, you know that. And now she wants you to sit there with him while he's dying. You had always hoped he would croak on one of his stints abroad, so you could avoid all this.

Look into her eyes, blue quivering under tears. When she cries, her voice is thick as molasses, you hate the sound it makes. If you tell her then her last moments with him will be nothing but this. If you don't tell her then perhaps her goodbye with him will be a false goodbye and then she will feel robbed and then perhaps you can never tell her, perhaps you never will.

If you were the kind of feminist Twitter says you should be, you would watch your disclosure shatter like a plate and then describe the pieces for your audience. But you will get through the next few days as you do, smiling tightly and wiping harried tears in the toilet. You would not be able to explain it to the women with big lungs like Queen Histrionic, but it feels easier to go with Mum than not. Because if you say no and she asks why you won't, then the tapeworm will choke you and she'll know.

He has tubes in his hand and wrist; one for morphine and one for anti-sickness meds, probably. He has a bed that intermittently jitters, to prevent sores. The room is too big for him because the other man who was in here just died.

You are supposed to want to destroy him, but you just feel nausea and pity. Your right leg keeps jigging. Your mother looks like threatening tears. Usually it would fall to you to make small-talk, but your toes are curling in your shoes. You are unable to manufacture the desperate inanity that tends to cushion end-of-life interactions in Britain.

Your phone buzzes. When Mum sighs, you know it is at you. You make an apology but do not turn your phone off. Pretend instead to be sending urgent emails, which keeps you from looking at him. It's not emails, but your notes app full of disjointed memories.

After the ice-cream van, the grey carpet and a game of dolly. In the bath a boat, it was a boat.

I never got to see my daughter grow up. I know you were a gift for me, I knew it when you were born, your mother doesn't tell that story does she.

This is a dolly. A dolly. A dolly.

When he smiles at you, you feel the coiling tapeworm in your tummy. You tap into the phone: *What he did is there in the vagueness of your eyes and the way that your voice trails off, you live inside an ellipsis, other people don't understand and think you are spacey, this is why you find it hard to relate to the Histrionics, their certainty is unlike anyone you've ever known who's gone through these things. They're certain in their condemnation of the shoulder swayers and men who disagree. You envy them their certainty. You envy them their confidence.*

And then, on Twitter again, scrolling through your draft tweets.

'Why are you on that thing all the time?' Mum says. She gestures with open palms to her father, as if she wants to share a joke with him. 'Avoidance machines. Do you feel like talking to us instead?' She waves a hand in front of your face like you are catatonic, leans over to snatch the phone away as if you are a child. You snatch back, too fast, and the phone clatters to the floor. You drop to your knees, certain that either her fingers or yours have grazed the Tweet button, your brave quip sent out to damn you forever:

@AnataLowellTownsend: Get a real problem.

Ignoring the cracked screen, you go straight into Twitter to check your timeline is clear. Stand up straight to see your grandfather watching with a morphine grin. Fold yourself up and sit back on your chair. Mum leans over to hiss something about being sensible and you see the fire agate crystal between her breasts. She wears this fire agate because she believes it to be shielding. As a kid, she told you it protected people from bad things. You said you wanted one and she didn't think to ask you what bad things you needed protecting from.

You get up. 'I feel as weak as a dolly,' you say, looking him straight in the face. 'I feel like I'm on a rocky boat. I'm going to leave you both alone. You never got to see your daughter grow up, after all.'

Something like frightened understanding passes over his face in the second before you turn to the door, catching your toe on the bed frame. You are down the hall, tear-blurred vision and the thudding of your heels and then your arm is being pulled.

'Leah, Leah.' Your mother behind you. 'Whose father is dying, really? I don't know what has gotten into you but this isn't about you today. Whatever weirdness you have around death, you just have to swallow it.'

You could laugh and curse and spit. 'He doesn't want me in there, I'm sure.'

'Don't be ridiculous. Come on. You should say sorry too.'

You jolt her hand off your arm, catch a look at her face. Whatever she knows, she doesn't know she knows it. You imagine yourself pulling the words from your oesophagus, tapeworm falling out onto the dry-bleach floor, in front of the nurses. This isn't the right time. There is never a right time. Your mouth opens. Your mouth closes.

No Place for the End of a Life
Bonny Brooks

Moll said to throw her ashes off the Tyne Bridge because she'd often thought about jumping. When she'd not long moved here, when the place was still an escape, she'd travel over the Tyne Bridge to Newcastle to see the sights. Buzzing past the traffic next to the green bridge railings in her mobility buggy, she'd pause every time at the Samaritans Helpline sign to think: *could I?*

She said to throw her ashes off the Tyne Bridge, so I'm here on a Tuesday night – little hairpin figure under a black perm of clouds, walking up to the bridge's centre with my Jumbo Vanilla Ice-cream tub. She didn't want an urn; she thought they reeked of conceit.

With my back to the wind, facing the glass covered music centre where we learned to sing, that's where I'll tip it. 'Be careful not to throw it against the breeze,' she said at the clinic. And she laughed, her morphine-glazed picture of me, pasty faced old woman spattered with ash, blackish mess clinging to the hair she always said I was too vain about.

I met her in the singing group for over 50s. Stood outside having a smoke and she comes whirring up the concrete in her buggy, fuzzy auburn hair peeking out of the plastic flaps in wisps. She looked too young to drive it but I didn't want to be nosy. Long purple skirt, flat shoes and a wide mouth without make-up. For some reason, I wanted to talk to her right away.

Some of the others didn't like her, said she had airs. Smiling at nothing, like she knew something you didn't. Showing off, is what Audrey said one Wednesday, when Moll put her hand on her heart during the chorus of 'Black is the Colour'. Right over her heart, flat palm like she was swearing an oath. But I don't think it was showing off. She wasn't the best singer in the world and she knew it. She didn't come to the choir to hear her own voice, but to feel it – that's the difference.

At the centre of the bridge now, next to the tribute flowers for the jumpers – that's where I'll throw it. The flower heads have long been taken by the wind; just pink plastic wrapping left fastened with parcel tape to the railings.

'Why the bridge?' I said, on the plane we took.

'I like it. There's a spot you can stand on where you can look both ways, and the squash of buildings and chimneys looks all higgledy piggledy, like a kid's drawn it.'

If you're asking me, I'd always imagined a quiet send-off for myself. It seems wrong to tip her into the air with all the cars rattling past. This is what I want to say. This is what I want to say to her now.

'Do it at night,' she said. 'I want to go into the dark. Wouldn't that be more interesting? If you do it at night then I can just fade, disperse. There'll be a sense of me disappearing, the way all things fall into everything else.' She was always saying strange, grand things like that.

I pull the collar up on my coat and lower my chin, looking around. Thick green steel curving up towards the stars. The engine revs that smack the air. The angry headlights. No place for the end of a life.

Back when she first got diagnosed, before I knew her, Moll had tried to think herself better. She tried meditation, crystals and little white pills you get from hippy doctors. But it didn't work and the time came when she couldn't dance any more.

When they recommended the buggy, she was against it. Buggies were for geriatrics and defeatists. She thought if she got the buggy it would be 'sending the Universe the wrong message'. She'd been meditating to send light to the bad part of her brain to fix things. If she got the buggy it was like admitting the good thoughts weren't working. But then, she'd be stuck indoors, watching the light flicker and fade over dusty furniture. In the end, she got the buggy.

But she took care to decorate it with colourful pictures, words and stickers, to make it more interesting than the average 'granny cart'. Still, whenever she mentioned the buggy, and before she got in it each morning, she had to close her eyes and picture herself dancing; pushing up some white light in circles around her, that light that would help her to dance again.

Moll used to be knock-kneed afraid of death – more than the normal. She even told me once she'd been part of an anti-death group.

'How can you be anti? It just happens.'

'A cult, my daughter called it. They kicked me out when they realised I wasn't getting better. Well, but that's to say they stopped looking in my face. They thought I'd got ill because I'd missed something – not tried. They thought it was a failure to be optimistic.'

My mouth hung open. My mind was full of tut and swearing.

'The third time nobody came to pick me up for a meeting, I cried for the rest of the day. And then I decided to come singing.'

Red woollen hat pulled down and my collar up against the bridge wind now, I'm holding the ice-cream tub close. Somewhere I can hear laughing. My sigh makes a speech bubble in front of me. The rainbow arc of the Millennium Bridge flickers ahead.

I always wondered what Moll was doing around here. Some kind of a beret for a hat. Big hand gestures like a conductor when she told a story. Travelling look in her eyes and that circular way of talking like she was trying to discover something. She never did fit.

I pull open the tub. The ashes are harder, heavier than you'd imagine. Like ground-up bones, which I suppose is what they are. Reaching my hand inside, they're cold and bumpy and strange. Perhaps I'm supposed to say something, but I feel stupid. 'Bye, Moll.' Little grating sound as the pieces slip from my fingers into the night. The wind gets louder.

I wait a moment and listen to the breathing traffic. I lift the tub and tip; the pieces swarm and disappear. There.

I reach into my pocket and pull out the two plane ticket stubs. Swiss Air. Two rips and they're gone.

And the angry threat letters that I've been sent since, from her haven't-heard-a-peep-in-years daughter. I pick them out of my pocket. Light them one by one. Letting go when the flames reach my fingers and sting the skin.

Coffee Times
Alice Wooledge Salmon

'A small, black coffee,' as in 'I would love…' propels Dean Baquet from Manhattan takeaway to his 8th Avenue morning at The New York Times skyscraper. A kick of energy for Executive Editor response to his Washington journalists' scoops! drafts! rewrites! reworking of leads … and go-go-go! on 'one of the biggest stories of a generation.'

November 2016, 'Donald J Trump' elected US President, Baquet and company taken by surprise – 'We didn't have our finger on the pulse of the country, and that was wrong'. And suddenly, story expanding, seams leaking, *bursting!* as precedents collapse and curveball collisions accumulate.

'It just never stops!' Elisabeth Bumiller, Chief of the Washington Bureau, 'the newsiest place at The New York Times,' according to Baquet in Liz Garbus' percussion of a documentary (2017-18) on 'the fourth estate', *Reporting Trump's First Year.* Around Elisabeth, investigative reporters staring at multiple screens take calls from deep-throat sources, jot notes, type and text at speed, move in and out of each other's cubicles and lives. Hunch, conjecture, argument – wrestling truth from wilful disarray of the ever-tweeting Trump and his administration. 'Trying to get at things the government doesn't want us to get!'

'Crazy stuff happening… It's a huge, fucking deal… All these stories are extraordinary –'

'We've gotta meet this guy at 2:30?'

'I gotta have a coffee if we're going there!'

'You get *your* coffee and bring me one!' lobbed from Apuzzo to Goldman – iced coffee? –over to Mazzetti – 'A large…'

'A large *what*?'

'…large black coffee's fine,' drops Rosenberg – and Mazzetti? 'Make it medium, or large –'

With Goldman – or someone – protesting 'Their large ones are really small!'

'You guys are the *worst* at placing a coffee order! You guys are, like, busy revealing national security secrets and you can't figure out how to order a cup of coffee!' Apuzzo, wheeling, shrugging our way in mock despair, as 'Pretty much, yes…' is acquiesced from inside the caffeine-fuelled drive through implacable developments.

Here's Adam Goldman in his Washington kitchen, performing Rancilio espresso for Apuzzo. 'I do not make Matt Apuzzo a coffee every morning! Maybe it happens once a week. We're best friends, and we live across the street from each other.'

'…I'll drink coffee, like, from a gas station.'

'I don't drink coffee from a gas station,' growls Goldman, while subsequently, on Long Island, 'sitting in a Starbucks in Brentwood, what could be better?', White House Correspondent Maggie Haberman answers a call, a take-away pillar of the eponymous at her elbow, then, on the phone in her car, 'After [Trump's] tweet, I just said, "publish immediately".'

Bureau reliance on the ever-flowing river of journalistic coffee? A balm, a degree of consolation for banished sleep, the erosion of private life and leisure, the constant onslaught of White House disinformation as Trumped-up charges surge over the 'fake news mainstream media'.

This 'story behind the headlines' culminates in April 2018, as Dean Baquet stands mid-stairway above his vast Manhattan news arena to announce that 'In a remarkable tribute to the newsroom at the peak of its energy and creativity, you all have won three Pulitzer prizes this year!' Among the cheering hundreds are

Elisabeth Bumiller, plus honourees Mark Mazzetti, Apuzzo, Goldman, Matt Rosenberg and others exhaustively involved with the Times' trio of discrete achievements, including Haberman, who's earlier declared her 'biggest struggle' as 'just putting the phone down'. Which she hasn't today – while cradled by her right wrist is the latest of those Starbucks take-away cylinders.

Remaining
Krystian Morgan

We've been standing in the street for what must be half an hour. Dressed in our recumbent clothing: robes, pyjamas, undervests – one woman has a bath towel wrapped around her head, skin flushed red from hot water. Like flies drawn out to the carnival of light and sound. Our street has never been more alive. The usual solemnity of night is invaded by the harsh red and blue beacons of police cars and ambulances, coercing their way onto any surface, cascading off of faces, vehicles, walls and fences, swallowing all other colours and imbuing everything with a vulgar monochrome. We were out looking for answers. Latecomers are brought swiftly up to speed: a child was injured in an apparent hit and run.

Police have established barriers between us and the paramedics that swarm around the little body lying still on the road, providing them room to move about, to trial their different devices and remedies. It's a process lost on most of us. We're forced to speculate based on our assumptions and what we've learnt from television.

I can't make out the child's face. A young female medic has a mask over his mouth and nose and is squeezing air from a blimp-shaped pump into his lungs. Someone in the crowd says it's the Meyer's boy. Then I see them, David and Angela Meyer. David is holding Angela in his arms, not ten feet from where the EMT's work to save their only child. Angela looks trapped between a place of prayer and fervent despair, holding it at bay, trying to remain hopeful as the frantic feelings erupt inside of her. Short blips and pockets of repressed grief find their way to the surface. Angela's visibly shaking with her efforts to contain it. She is a mother. Her eyes never stray from her son's body. Studying for glimmers of movement, for signs that her child is still somewhere in there, willing his systems into working, his heart to remain beating, to overcome, to live. David bears a look that's beaten and perplexed, clinging to his wife for a sense of normalcy; a sense rational amongst all the madness going on in front of them.

More people exit their homes. Officers implore anybody with information about the incident to come forward, but no-one knows much of anything. It would seem the only person who'd be able to elucidate the events is the broken boy, prone before the doctors who work hard to reignite the embers of his fast extinguishing life.

I rest an arm on a trellis surrounding one of the decorative trees that give the village its rural character. At my age I gravitate to places that might offer a moment's respite for my quick-to-tire joints.

Timothy, no, Jonathan, no – what's the kid's name? Josh, Joshua! I think that's it. Joshua Meyer. Little 10-or-so-year-old Joshua Meyer. One moment playing in the street, the next, his frail, still-developing body collided with a heavy vehicle that is long gone. Now he's become the centre of our world, as we look on to see whether he'll fight for, or forfeit his life.

A neighbour approaches me, Doug Harvey, whose garden is adjacent to mine. We exchange fatalistic nods as he sidles up next to me for an exalted moment, taking in the scene of the accident from my vantage point. I sense him auditioning sentences in his head for us to deliberate over. Doug's not someone whom I share a lot in common, or I regularly speak with. There's nothing like the spectacle of death, or near-death, to bring people together, in search of information that might uncover lost revelations into the human condition. 'Awful,' he says, 'Yes,' I say, 'Just 11,' 'I know.'

He coughs into the whorl of his clenched fist and remains at my side for a further minute before easing himself away, in search of another person to connect with. There was never much to be said, but it felt important to be saying it nonetheless; to find solace in crowd consensus; to know your impressions of the moment are shared by others, by those around you, that they (and yourself, in turn) are the people you always believed them to be.

We convince ourselves that we're here for the family – should they need anything. Standing with them. For them. A united front against this callous reality that's befallen them. Truthfully, we are all here to witness their grief. To see their sorrow un-distilled and be secretly glad we're not at the core of it. There's a distant gratitude that's almost euphoric, giving us a renewed appreciation for the prosperity of our lives. Later, we will return to our homes, to our wives or husbands, safe-sleeping children, our pets and sitcom shows: comforts that inebriate us from such sobering sights. But in the interim, we are after something remarkable, something transcendent to bind the whole experience together. Something altogether more than just a drunk hit and run on an interchangeable street.

The EMTs go about their work with a calm exactness. This is their daily reality and are hardened, seemingly unshakeable by it. Extraneous emotions and movements are absent in them. The police officers stare at the crowd of people with a fixed air of sovereignty and unyielding postures boasting of a wordless threat.

A mobile phone rings out somewhere in the crowd and five or so people start fumbling hands over their pockets to silence it.

Shucked from out of his shell suit, Joshua has been retrofitted with a head immobiliser amongst other various appendages, bandages and embrasures; he is quickly becoming more accessory than boy. Skin remaining exposed is reserved ground for the submersion of syringes and of stethoscopes listening deeply to the body's inner monologues and espousing the presence of unseen maladies.

Some woman is stood discreetly sobbing, adopting a part of the tragedy for her own, moistening her tissue with surrogate tears. Looking further into the crowd I espy the surreptitious glance at watches. People are already weary and hoping for a resolution that's not too drawn out. Eyes betraying their frail convictions and wandering from the site of the boy in search of opportunities to slip-away unnoticed.

My wife Junie refused to come out at all. In hiding from the exhibits of human fragility on display mere meters from our front door. She's wary also of the close proximity to death – a latent piousness, perhaps – particularly when concerning young lives hanging in the balance around her. Lives not lived as fully as her own. Like death might choose her in their place – and thus providing a better sense of karmic balance to the world. She'll be waiting up for me. Wanting an after-the-fact bulletin on the transpired events. Unexpected encounters with mortality often brings out the libidinous side of her. The lights go off in our bedroom and the inevitable touching and frotteuring up against me ensues, slowly manipulating me into an aggravated torpor, resulting in a congress that's every bit as spiteful as cloying.

The EMT's pace seems to quicken all a sudden and optimism for young Joshua sinks with it. As do the faces of all those around. A medic fetches a defibrillator from the ambulance and soon after the pads are affixed the first movement seen from the boy in a good forty minutes is assisted by a charge of current shot through his nervous system. His chest jolts upwards in a distended arc, falling back just as quickly. Angela watches with horror, her eyes widened to their limit and wishing of some way she could intervene; she had made him and ought to be able to fix him. But she holds back, helpless. Hope dying with every unsuccessful charge. I've never seen such vulnerability. Strong emotions rise within myself and with an intensity I thought not possible, thought long battered by the tides of a trying life. After the fourth charge there was a sense permeating that the subsequent charges were no longer for the boy, but for the parents. The medics perfunctorily soldier on to that fine line – too little effort and the family might acquiesce that not all steps, not the extra mile, that extraordinary measures were not taken to save their child. It won't go on for much longer now. Too much and it would seem like desecration to a body exhausted and resigned to giving up. Already at rest.

My eyes are fixed on the mother throughout. Angela falls forward hard onto her knees, her hands following down to the ground in front of her. A sound expels from that woman's lungs, a sound harrowing and barely human – more the guttural howl of a tortured animal. Her face is a strained puce. All vestiges of her former beauty metamorphosing into something bruised and residual. Mouth agape, deep mournful wails continue to escape and take precedence over breathing. David is stood, paralysed. His face a fixed tabula rasa in disbelief. The paramedics rise to their feet, stepping back to give room for the parents to see their once-child. Angela crawls over to Joshua, her son. Her hands caressing his small physiognomy. His face, an amalgam of both David's and hers. She gives him a light persistent tapping to the temple, as if still hoping for him to be revived by some fairy tale logic. I turn away, giving them the respect and privacy they should have had all along.

There wouldn't be any healing for her. The mothering instincts would be still there, but with nothing to act upon. Instead, there'd be only grieving. I expect the Meyer's home would be quieter tonight, quieter from now on. Appearances would remain. The walls would be the same, as would the decor, the furniture, but there would always be something missing. An absence felt as solid and obtrusive as an unwanted tenant taking residence.

The crowd's vigil comes to a dispiriting conclusion. Tomorrow, near the spot where the child perished would be flowers, candles and notes of well-wishes to the family, confirming their sorrow was felt by all. At school, I'm sure, the pupils would oblige to a minute's silence in remembrance of a lost classmate. Flowers seem odd to me as a way to commemorate an eleven-year-old boy, the candles too. They would perhaps better befit the funerary gift of a much older and also female deceased.

Any facts and feelings towards what transpired tonight will come piecemeal and relayed in whispers. The stories cycled, recycled and told to anybody but the bereaved. In our quiet street, it would become the main topic of conversation for a while. Until everything on the subject has been depleted. Or until something else takes our attention over the convening days. Until then there would be a protracted mulling and relating of theories on both sides of sadness and flippancy.

Television has taught us that death is the prime paradigm of our everyday narrative. Through the backlit LEDs of our sets, those reports more closely resemble fiction and become difficult to separate from the feature film that follows the news. Infamous celebrities dying of suicide, of overdoses and excess existed to us in their images, their music and shows. Their work is always available to us, syndicated, on-demand, and for that reason will continue to live on as we've only ever known them. Young Joshua had yet to make any such mark in the world. He would be remembered by the small few who'd encountered him in his short life. Our mercurial memories distorting the image of him over time, before eventually flickering out altogether.

I was in the corner store a month later buying some biscuits and cheese when in walked Angela Meyer, wearing all black and bereft of any make-up or frills. It was plain to see the trauma had torn apart the sprightly warmth and congeniality that once exemplified the woman. She wandered the aisles of the store distractedly, accepting condolences from the neighbours she passed with an almost robotic disinterest. Their sentiments were just words that did nothing but restate the inescapable verisimilitude of that night and what has become her purposeless life. Her walk had even adopted an aimless, dreamlike stride about it. Floating about the store like a soap bubble, carried by mental impulses as benign as a gentle breeze.

After paying for my wares, I decided to wait outside the store for her. When she emerged she wasn't carrying any bags and had seemingly made no purchase. I had to call out her name twice before it even registered. She turned to face me, eyes looking milky grey, awaiting the obligatory message to sound from my mouth before she could continue to float away to wherever whim directed her. Instead, I chose to relate to her an account where her son had once assisted my wife and me in a show of chivalry that was completely unexpected from a boy his age. Angela's face lightened as the details of my story were told. Some colour and a sense of occupancy was returning to her before my eyes. I took delight in her response, and fortified my story with testimonies from my wife and proffering my overall impression of the scene. I finished by saying that I had wanted to compensate the young lad, but he refused to take my money. By the end, a few tears had found their way onto her face, over full-cheeks. She embraced me with a smile that at-once reclaimed the beauty for which I'd always known her, and she'd been sheltering no-doubt over the recent weeks. There she was again. Angela Meyer. Overcome and wiping tears from her enlivened face. 'Thank you,' she said.

We all need something new. Knowing the memories she would've been reminiscing the past month were only further evidence to the finality of her son's death; that there would be no further memories made. I wanted to give her an outsider's account, let her feel a sense of pride that her son was pleasant to others, even when not under the persuasive eyes of his parents. It felt good to say and even better to see the results of it on her face. Even though there was no legitimacy to the story, that I had just fabricated it on the spot, it felt nice to bring some happiness to a bereaved mother. Truth be told, I didn't care much at all for the little shit.

Fallen Fruit
Krystian Morgan

A sizeable crowd is gathered around the rides, hoopla games and food stands. The mobile carnival is spread out in vague aisles, looking like a carboot sale of temporary distraction. Spectators are herded by carnies whose taut-leather presences regard the mass with an impassive air as if long-past trying to understand the gullibility in succumbing to the blandishments advertised. In truth, like me, everyone else here is just trying to pass the mundanity of a slow Saturday afternoon with a different shade of mundanity. I register an elevation in the boy's mood that's halfway hopeful; a moment earlier I was ready to turn the car around on the seemingly disappointing jaunt. My ex-wife had made it explicit that Mark is being punished and that I should not – for risk of trivialising her stance – allow him any of his usual escapes such as his iPad and Nintendo, but sitting at home watching him mope is tantamount to sharing in his punishment. So, with the miserable weather settled, here we are.

The boy's head pans back and forth the offerings. It occurs that perhaps he's never been to one of these before. Growing up, for me, it was routine. If the carnival was in the area parents parted with their pocket change and sent the kids out the door for a few hours respite. Sprinting with those cold coppers and shiny silvers jingling in our pocket, little tokens to gain admittance to new avenues of experience.

Still young, 8 last month, my son hasn't yet learnt how to hide his true feelings from others. This is one arena I would consider myself accomplished in. A necessary skill for any corporate job you might find yourself languished in; your sycophantic smile and spring-loaded library of inconsequential office patter should be treated like any other muscle you would develop with reps and attention. Although, I too have found my veneer split as of late and have been able to rile myself into a stupor with any given opportunity. Stewing over the kind of irremediable problems that I'd usually medicate with long-exposure to trash TV, the impulse-buying of some crap, or finding a new obsession whether that be gambling, collecting porcelain pigs or the dubious investment of a new relationship. I feel just too worn out to engage in any of it.

Whilst I can usually attribute Mark's expressed sombreness to missing his real home and bedroom – with all his games consoles and extensive Pokémon ephemera – I get the sense, beneath his shadowy demeanour, there's a certain relief to being stuck with his father this weekend; separated from the ordeal he orchestrated at school and the contentious atmosphere at home because of it.

Everything assembled is spray-painted metal with a vibrancy of colour that hasn't muted with thirty-plus years of exposure to all-weather conditions and countless soft drink and stomach-content spillages. The overblown colour and intensity of the images lead us into a fantasy world that exists nowhere outside the boundaries of the carnival. They depict perfect people sweating in a sultry paradise. The hyperreal renditions are in stark contrast to the concrete enclaves that surround them. They draw the eye, dupe our senses from what, in reality, is just cladding for a portable pop-up-pop-down array of mildly pulse-raising rides and attractions.

You assimilate with a crowd. Adopt an unspoken rapport with the assembly; an etiquette for the procedures involved, ensuring that pleasure derived through the pursuit of the activities on display are done so with civility, so your enjoyment does not impede on the fun of others.

'What issat?'

'Candy floss?'

'Huh?'

'The pink stuff?'

'Yeah, that stuff.'

'Candy floss.'

'What's it do?'

'Rots your teeth.'

'Can I have some?'

Diane's recounting of the incident seems so divorced from the image I have of our son, who at this moment is studying the signage festooned all around us for which ride he'd like to first visit. I haven't been equipped with the instincts of a father. I'd hoped that they lay dormant within me, to be engaged automatically as my eyes first caught sight of my child but, no, they never appeared. Not then. Not after. I have no confidence in my words. Have no useful advice to help mould him through to a functioning adult. I barely function, so I try keeping my wisdom to its minimum; he's too young for the bounties of despair and cynicism that are all I have to offer. He's wearing a canary yellow T-shirt with Pikachu displayed proudly on his chest.

'Why a' they bumping into us, dad?'

I'm sat next to Mark who's at the wheel of our dodgem and relishing in the prospect of an unremarkable drive.

'Well, the idea is to drive around fast, try avoid bumping into the other cars, but for others, the whole point is to crash into as many cars as possible.'

'But why would you want to bump into others on purpose?'

I realised we were stumbling into some wider questions here. Mark looks at me pensively, unaware of the irony in the question he asks with regards to what happened at school last week. The scuffed knuckles of his little hands wrapped around the bony wheel of the electric-powered car; evidence to the fugues capable of even a 8 year old. There's a blonde boy with a cropped mullet, to which Mark is referring, crashing into every car that enters his central vision. The joy in the little hoodlum's eyes is near predatory.

'Usually, it's those who are most often powerless, restricted in some way that acts out. All things considered, if they get it all out in dodgem cars, all the better.'

'I don't get it.'

'See that kid there?'

'The one with the funny hair?'

'Yes. I bet you he has an older brother or two who tease and taunt him, daily. As they're older than him, bigger, he wouldn't be able to fight back but here, in the cars, he's on an equal plane to everyone else and it's his chance to do the bullying for a change, you understand?'

'Not really.'

'That's ok.'

It happened during math. Mrs Everett was inscribing a series of problems on the whiteboard when, apparently unprovoked, Mark walloped his best friend Aidan with his heavy workbook, sending him reeling off his chair. He then proceeded to throw his pencil tin, papers and anything else in arm's reach at the boy before descending on him, grabbing tight fistfuls of his hair in both hands and slamming his head repeatedly against the slate-tiled floor. Mrs Everett tried to intervene, catching hold of Mark's arm to wrestle him away from Aidan, just as he was raising his foot high with the clear intention of stamping on his former friend, but Mark shook free of her grip, turned to his spooked teacher and shouted, 'Don't touch me, you thick whore bitch!'

My ex-wife was called to the school from work to speak of Mark's behaviour.

I still don't know what to make of the whole event. I had never thought he could be capable of such violence – and to Aidan, especially, they have been inseparable since nursery. Mark hadn't said a word when Diane arrived at the principal's office and not even his mother's intimidating tone (I know from experience) was able to break the boy's silence. Aidan was quiet, too. The only one speaking was Mrs Everett, who described the boy at that moment as rabid, transformed – no sign of his usual timid, self-awareness. My son, the eight-year-old boy, had frightened her.

The idea of counselling has been batted back and forth; all but insisted by the school. I feel I should be a party to these decisions regarding my son but, alas, they happen, are made and are then told to me as if I bore only a scant interest. It's as if the concerns of his upbringing are plot elements of some TV soap.

We vacated the dodgems and meandered between the amusements. I'd impressed Mark at the rifle range, falling just shy of enough targets to earn a prize. The pitch-a-ring was a truly disappointing affair, Mark missing every bottle with the widest of margins. We both chuckled hysterically by the final throws, which only ailed him further. He had better luck with 'hook-a-duck,' coming away with a dinky keyring in toil and a grin so wide as to be far in excess of the prize won, but it was nice to see him in higher spirits; I didn't have the heart to tell him the stand boasted a 'prize every time.' We strapped ourselves into a few more rides: 'Maximum Overdrive,' 'The Kick Down,' and 'Annihilator,' the latter of which was endured through the feral shrieks of an overweight woman, holding white-knuckled onto the safety bar as the contraption tossed us back and forth and teased us upside down.

When my wife told me that she had been seeing another man, I apologised to her. I don't know why, exactly. Having no aplomb to speak of it is my default to accept blame. It was one of the most harrowing experiences of my life. I relive the memory too often. Diane wore demure greys, was dressed semi-formal as if she were making me redundant from the business of our family. She kept the winter scarf around her neck, to which fronds of flaxen hair disappeared beneath. She was togged-up for outdoors and was clear in not wanting to prolong the ordeal further than what was necessary, to be on her way, an overdue task taken care of and allowing her to truly move forward with the opulent new life – I now know in retrospect – had been lavished before her. Before she could get out the rehearsed lines, I bawled, pleaded and whimpered through a platter of alternative scenarios, to the inevitable that she was firm on feeding to me. Her eyes – as I, in-vein, depicted numerous ways that we could still work, that I could change for her, become whatever she wanted – those eyes observed my fits with a near maternal sympathy; I final mote of tenderness for me, alone. After my intervention, she's never again looked at me with any remedial feeling. All traces of caring were wrung dry that night she left.

It's been nearly two years, since. But although separation from Diane and the moment brought clarity, it's a wound that's felt, still. I know if the option for reconciliation was there, even after all this time, I'd accept it without another word said. Make-believe that the life we'd created for ourselves was simply put on temporary hiatus. She knows this, too but never flaunts the sway she has over me. It's this obsequiousness in my character which, I'm sure, contributed to her leaving in the first place. I hope my son never discovers the depths of my weakness.

Before leaving we filled our stomachs with burgers and chips from a van set-up near the car park and, of course, a plump cloud of candy floss. The woven sugar was a revelation to Mark. I watched fascinated as his eyes flittered after taking a bite, as if reading an inner monologue of hidden thoughts and experiences, new, bursting into his consciousness from the cotton-like substance.

Back in the car and all previous cheer was rinsed from the boy's face, instead replaced with a look of deep anguish.

'What's the matter, do you not feel well after all that sugar?'

His eyes became timid all-a-sudden, a self-consciousness I've not witnessed before from him. He looks as though he's harbouring a vexation far too virulent for his years. The weight crippling on his inexperienced shoulders.

'Mark, you ok?'

He remained silent. Eyes looking at his shoes and his fingers cupped together at his waist where they moved, touched and felt at the other digits reflexively. I allowed him space to formulate. My anxiety running wild over enumerable scenarios: each of which is haunting me for ever thinking of them.

'Dad?'

'Yes.'

He looks up at me for a split second, ensuring my face bore no signs for him not to continue before dropping back to his shoes.

'Mark?'

'It's just…'

He broke off again.

'It's alright Mark, everything's going to be alright. You can tell me anything that's worrying you – you don't have to worry, boy.'

I watched as his lower lip began to jitter and as he pulled his hands up to his face in anticipation of the tears that were about to flow. His little body convulsing in the wake of heavy emotions hitting the surface. I rested my hand on his shoulder, feeling completely ineffectual. He bared his teeth and started emitting a reedy whine, bringing voice to an emotional wound he's been concealing. I wanted to wrap my arms around him, his around me, but having never been that openly affectionate (for reasons that are purely my insecurities) I am now sorely regretting my non-haptic nature, my inability to console my son.

From out the windscreen I catch sight of another family returning to their car. A Mother, father and two daughters. This winsome man was holding the youngest who must have fallen asleep from over-stimulation. I watched the choreographed precision of packing their family into their hatchback. The father has a gold chain on his wrist. It is ever-so gold. I imagined that it is heavy, that his other chain-less wrist would be considerably weaker by comparison. It would make a dull rattle whilst he moved that his wife finds comforting; his presence could be announced auditorily. The children were far too perfect. Their wholly measured and symmetrical features irritated me. I can conjure the kooky Christmas cards they surely pose for and elect to give to other frustratingly ordinary family units.

Mark hasn't stopped sulking. There's a fold in his T-shirt that gives the yellow Pokémon a wide cretinous grin and the appearance of frenzied sniggering with the tremors convulsing through the boy's body.

'It's... it's...'

'Go on.'

'Mam.'

'Mam? You're worried because she's upset at you?'

Mark sat there, forming his sentences behind the remedial shakes and short bursts of sniffles snuffed through his nose.

'Mam won't be upset forever, she's just...'

'There was a man.'

'A man?... Where?'

'With Mam.'

'Not Anthony?'

'No.'

The boy broke into another bout of sobbing. I could tell he hated producing the words, wanted it over but struggled to find his way through it.

'Do you know the man?'

'No.'

'Have you seen him before?'

'No... I don't know.'

'What happened?'

'He had his hands on her.'

'Oh.'

'They were kissing.'

'Kissing?'

'Kissing and touching.'

'Touching?'

'Mam was touching him... on his trousers.'

'I... I see. Are you ok?'

He shook his head side-to-side but did look at somewhat better ease for having started.

'She was talking to him and he was making sounds.'

'Ok.'

'And they were together.'

'Ok… alright, that's enough.'

I brought the boy towards me, wrapped my arms around him, feeling his fast-beating heart against my ribs and taking a few strands of his hair in my nose but I just repositioned my head and kept him close.

'Did you see anything else?'

'No.'

'Good.'

'I ran, I did. Ran over to Aidan's house.'

'And you told him what you saw?'

He nodded his head and grabbed folds of my coat, pinching through to my skin, bringing me into a tighter embrace.

'I see.'

The image of his mother he witnessed was vivid in my imagination. I know the way she moves. Her pace. Her trajectories. Her insistence. Diane likes to either be in control – or better, vying for that position – like as her lover you are also an opponent she is trying to out-fuck.

I strived to help Mark at ease, mollify his despair over what he'd seen and the subsequent scene at his school. The pain I knew well. I was giving a dose just as exacting from the same source.

The giant screen pictured some high-concept action movie whose title we'd missed and whose dialogue is always tense and trailer-worthy. We hadn't spoken much since getting back to the house. Not due to any lingering discomfort in the air, it just wasn't necessary. The television once seemed so integral. My modest terraced house is situated in an innocuous village, enough out of town to be called affordable. The TV is the one extravagance I own. 58inch; by the time I'd gotten it home and unboxed a newer model with even more LEDs was available. We sit half-watching the scenes whip-cut from one brooding face to another amidst a backdrop of bleeping servers and autistic computer screens. I recognise the main actor from film posters, but this, my first introduction to his canon, is much of a muchness, but it serves its purpose in this intervening afternoon. We don't so much pay attention to the plot, as let it wash over us, safe in the assumption that things would probably work-out come the credits.

There's an overwhelming sense of calm, a new simpering relaxedness between the two of us. We're enjoying our limited time together with new unbidden humour.

I've ascended the small stair set to Diane's front door countless times. It punctuates Mark's and my time together. The door, the whole facade, clashes with my image of the woman who had once loved me but left to live here. A stilted walnut slab embedded in flawless white architrave. Bare ochre bricks breached by ivy crawling up the corners of the house in picturesque design. It represented a lacuna for me, that its evident incompatibility with her meant it would be inevitable before she would find herself breaking from the life she thought to be the answer and return to me. I think I was half right. Now, I'm not sure she belongs anywhere.

Diane fractured my already tenuous traces of esteem. She is a good mother. Fair and encouraging – much more prepared for Mark's unexpected arrival than I could have been with years of advanced notice. Although I have the deepest remorse for Mark, seeing what he'd seen – her image, forever altered and would no-doubt always endure heavily in his mind – the boy's confiding in me has revealed something of her that before had been clouded by my self-loathing and ideas of Diane as someone who is driven by opportunities beyond what I could give her and what she was truly deserving. The idea of Diane being fallible and the engineer of her own mistakes was a thought that never occurred. It brings a little comfort, in a dysfunctional sort of way.

I've never asked about Anthony. Not wanting to acknowledge any interest in the man. The questions would only be disguised comparisons between our stations in life. It wasn't necessary. He had already won. But in light of recent intelligence, his prize might not bear the same sheen it once did. I'd constructed a pastiche of the man from glances in doorways, in sounds of his presence heard through nearby walls. Gave body to a figure I'd bound myself to loathe. He exudes a preoccupied air – a man driven by motivation that could be either of great importance or mere whimsy. I don't detect a strong caring side in him. His mood appears all-too-insular but I could be reaching. After all, I've never experienced the presence of the man barring furtive glances and brusque eye contact in the routine fetching of my son.

I knocked on the door. By now it's surely strange for Mark to wait by my side for admittance to his own home but I've never felt a welcomed visitor, through all the rerun patter of Diane expelling my formality. It's a game we both play, an affront of amenability known to be false by us both. This is our post-nuptial dynamic. In the moments between knocking the door, whilst waiting for her to pull herself away from the kitchen, from the sitting room, from new hobbies that have materialised since after our time, I was reconstructing my image of her in my mind and have been doing so ever since Mark broke his silence, telling how he'd seen his mother in thrall with another man. I can't bring her forth with any clarity. She's blurring into the surroundings of my mind's eye, inciting a mild panic within me. Wanting her to just answer the door to kickstart my memory, feed me fresh information and confirm the figure of the woman who's forever consigned to stirring any tranquillity from my life. By just being her. Then she was right there in the opening of the door.

'Hi, I hope he's been good,' she says.

She glistened with perspiration. Patchy red splotches were all over her skin, particularly the collarbone area from where swung a slim silver neckless, dulled by dried sweat.

'He's been good.'

She enfolded her arms, one pink rubber glove prised between her elbow crook, the other resting on her forearm, her pouty face incredulous. Her hair was tied in some haphazard bun. She looked tired but wore no make-up to conceal it. Dotted with dirt she bore an astringent pang of plant clippings. This was *the* woman. She was still the woman who did this amazing thing, bringing Mark into reality; sweating then, too, and grunting on the bed of the delivery room. Coming here I wanted to reduce her in my mind, make her less-than. But she radiated, emanated some-*thing*. It's inexplicable. For all my depreciating thoughts it took a mere second for them to be flattened and replaced with pitiful longing once more. I can't help but hate myself. For I still love her.

Mark passes under her arm that's now braced against the doorframe and scuttles off into the sanctuary of his room, leaving his mother and me to cycle through our repertoire of congenial chat.

'So, how's he…'

'Good, he's been good. You?'
'Me? Fine, you know...'

Buses Like Red Elephants
Gerard McKeown

It's the sort of rain that makes your clothes dirty, even if you shield yourself with an umbrella. Crumbles the little myth of neatness you managed to iron on that morning. The rain envelops the street, including the bus I'm waiting on, which stops and starts, crawls and wobbles, as it mumbles towards this plank roofed bus stop, where I try to squeeze; with the fat man, the shopping bag heavy old woman, and the inconsiderate young smoker; into the one tiny slip of dryness provided.

Late already. In the distance, London buses look like red elephants, by their gait more than their shape, the way they seem to sway, or plod. Travelling by elephant would be a welcome break from the banality of my Monday to Friday commute. I have explored and exhausted the limited possibilities for variety, searching to create new synapses. The red elephant stops beside me. Its hydraulic doors sigh as they swing open.

Now I'm onboard, the messy rain taps on the windows, too quiet to drown out the school kids' all-important exclamations. Words they will have forgotten by lunchtime.

Still late. The school is one stop before the office. The kids will soundtrack my journey. I put the book I'd intended to read back into my bag. My tired ears are too nippy for headphones.

On a clear road this bus could reach my office in five minutes, but it slouches tuskless in the traffic, gorging itself at every bus stop, until it is packed to capacity. Standing room only. Soggy and uncomfortable. I force myself not to count how many stops until my stop. Ready to escape from the elephant's anus with a hop, a skip, then a jump through the dirty rain to the office door. A burst up three flights of stairs, to hang my coat on the radiator beside my desk. Coffee will reboot me and restart my day. In the meantime, I count the stops and feel myself begin to digest slowly in the belly of this big red beast.

Yellow Sky at the End of the World
James Hatton

Where we liv, it's called the Beach. But it's not the kind of beach yur probly thinkin of. There's no sand between yur toes, no pebbles t pinch yur skin. No sea t speak of. There's a river but let's just say yuh wouldn't want t piss in it, let alone swim in it. It has a frothy head, a chemical puss. The beach, it's an effin dump. Literally. Ha ha. A giant tip. A sprawlin megalopolis of a landfill at the end of the world. A fathoms deep bed of stinkin mulch. A cliff of festerin crap and colostomy bags.

On its spongey top layer a few people stand around watchin me, waitin t see if I'll really go through with it, so that they can say they were there perhaps when H went down in t the hole. Everyone holds their waggin tongues for a minute and in the dead stillness of the afternoon I look past my gaunt-faced brethren across the acres of beach land. The colours of the Beach, hundreds and thousands of them, blend together in t a brownish hue before the grey line of the concrete wall, miles away. Along the top of this wall, although you can't see them from here, are security patrols: armed men that'll shoot holes in yuh and dogs that'll rip the rest of yuh t pieces. Up above is our beautiful sky, the constant yellow haze of our lives. I wonder if I'll miss it when I go.

'You must hav a fuckin deathwish, H,' Stanley says, and I shrug. 'The whole thing'll collapse on top of yuh.'

'I've told yuh before,' I say. 'This is no life. There's a better life somewhere.'

'Bollocks there is,' he says, and I shrug.

'All the gas,' someone else says. Greta. 'You'll burn alive if it catches.'

'I'm prepared t take the risk,' I say.

They're my family, these balloon-bellied children and sunken-eyed grown-ups, even if they're not my own flesh and blood, and when Natasha, a wide-mouthed girl of nine with achin eyes runs forwards in her salvaged blue dress and throws her skinny arms around me, I almost think it wouldn't be the worst thing in the world t stay here for the rest of yur life and look out at that yellow sky every day.

'I'll miss yuh,' she says.

'I'll come back one day,' I say, makin promises I definitely won't be able t keep if, like everyone seems t think, my expedition is doomed t failure, even if they don't say it outright. Some can't look me in the eye, knowin what has happened in the past t the ones who've tried t leave the Beach. Fantasists, they think we are. Wall-starers, they call us, referrin t the torn posters we paste t the walls of our rooms, showin people with bright white smiles under blue skies.

'I'll say it one last time,' Victor says, who, at twenty-eight, is one of the oldest on the Beach and has seen more than any of us. 'It's a fantasy. This is real. What's in yur head is not.'

'Victor,' I say. 'We don't hav much, do we? Can't you leave us our dreams?' It's a reasonable enough thing t say but I doubt I look like a particularly reasonable person at this moment, standin on the edge of a sinkhole, a gasmask pushed up on t my head, the pipe coilin around me t a dented, rusty canister of air that I filled up with a compressor that has taken three generations t perfect, and dressed from head t toe in clothes fashioned out of plastic sheetin ribbed with asbestos in case of fire. I look nothin like the torn posters and pictures that most say, even if they did exist at one time, are fictions now.

'Keep an eye on the rats,' young Gordy says.

'Gordy, the rats are my lifeline,' I tell him, because they'll be runnin if somethin's wrong.

Then there's a nervous silence.

'Well, there's no time like the present, is there, so see you suckers later,' I say, tryin t keep it light, and I start down in t the hole. I've rigged up a line made out of twisted cables and cords, and I hold on t it as I descend, half abseilin down the side of the sinkhole that appeared twelve days ago out of nowhere. I observed it, bidin my time. Then I started goin down, explorin it, mappin it in my mind, recordin the slight changes from day t day, the tunnels that opened, the ones that disappeared. Inch by inch, yard by yard, I've added t the braided rope of plastic and metal until there's half a mile of it snakin underground. But half a mile in these tunnels takes time and I'm already a ripe old twenty-two. Time's not on my side. Not t mention that there've been changes afoot that tell me there probly isn't much longer left. It's now or never. And a sinkhole like this beaut doesn't come along more than once in a lifetime.

I edge down, hand over hand, face t face with the geological history of the Beach: one layer of filth after another. It's light enough for the brightly coloured plastics t flicker like gems for a while, then the daylight fades. I'm about fifty feet down when I touch the bottom. When I look up I see a yellow circle of sky and a few of yur heads peerin down.

I do a quick equipment spection. Handmade wind-up light. Check. Air tank. Check. Pipe. Check. Mask. Check. Compass. Check. Bottle of rainwater. Check. I've also got a coupla the protein blocks that get carted in as if by magic in return for the recyclables we put in the carts goin out. Everythin is present and correct. Holdin the cord I take a few steps into the openin I've been in t for the previous eleven days. I switch off the light, worried that the bulb will blow, and walk on in the dark.

I'm thinkin as I take my careful steps about our yellow sky bein still up there above the shitheap, and the heads of my brothers and sisters peerin down into the sinkhole. I'm leavin all that behind. I'm gone from their lives now, maybe for good.

The air's already razor-sharp harsh but I can still rasp it down alright so I don't use the mask jus yet, wantin t conserve my air. I spect I'll be in greater need of it up ahead.

I walk in the dark, the braided cord slippin over my fingers as I go. I hold the other hand slightly in fronta me at head height, just in case somethin sharp or hard has sunk through the mulch. My shoulders bump the sides of the tunnel now and then.

It's a good three miles t the wall but yur steps are smaller in these conditions. I go at a snail pace. I've done my calcs in advance, and I've worked out it's four thousand steps or so a mile through the twists and turns of this tunnel. Times that by three, and I know once I'm over ten thousand, I'm on the final straight. Three, four hours, it should be. I don't hav a watch though. Not many hav got a watch on the Beach. So I start countin in the dark.

I'm tellin myself all the time, you've got t stay alert, H. Don't let yur mind wander off. If yuh smell gas, whip on the mask. If yuh feel movement underfoot, yuh need t be ready t leg it. The rats will be runnin like hell for high water if it starts t cave. Watch out for them. But all's quiet for now.

I'm still makin do without the torch and I feel the dark around me like the breath of the Beach, but more than that, I feel it above me, the wide, horrible expanse of it, like a rottin mouth, flanked by that skank of an uncrossable river t the south, the wall t the east, and miles and miles of roarin fires.

The east is where the carts roll in from, and back out east is where they go. If there's somethin beyond the Beach, it's there, out east, beyond the wall. Yuh don't see the same fires out there that hem us in on all other sides. That's why east, under the wall, is where I'm goin.

Back on the Beach I hav three walls of my own that I hav called home for as long as I can remember, and I can see the fragments of torn posters and pictures pasted t the walls as if I'm there. My favourite's a scene under a blue sky with people relaxin in a park on a summer's day. We're lookin down at the park from a hillside and in the distance you can see a river windin through a beauteous city. Some of the people are talkin, some are sunbathin, some are playin with their children, or walkin dogs, some are jus readin. It's all achingly beautiful. When Victor asked me once why I like the picture so much and I told him it was because I like t imagine the freedom those people hav t liv their lives how they want t, he told me that was an illusion, and that you can hav that freedom anywhere. But I know that's not true. If you try t hide on a cart goin out of the Beach, they send the corpse back on the next cart in. How can you call that freedom?

Yeah, I found luv for a while, and durin that time there were moments when even the yellow sky seemed good, when I could look at the black river and see somethin in it apart from death, and I could look at the miles of Beach and not feel that life was a murderin, heartless thing. But the Beach took it from me, jus like it takes everyone, and if this sinkhole hadn't opened up maybe it would've been me on one of the carts goin east, and then comin west again.

I come t the end of my makeshift guide rope. It drops from my hand, and I stop. I panic for a moment. I'm on my own from now on. If things go wrong up ahead, there'll be no convenient rope t guide me back t safety. Then I take a breath and try t calm myself. Keep yur cool, H, I tell myself. Just think of yur wall, the people in the park. Jus think of that. Keep goin an thinka that.

And I do. I flick on the torch and check the battered compass I found on the Beach years ago, then walk on, the ragged, motley coloured tunnel lit up now. I picture the people in the park. I picture myself walkin through it.

For hours I walk, and nothin changes. That potted history of the Beach is all around me in the compressed plastics and fibres of the tunnel walls.

Then there's a tremor, and my legs go from under me. For a minute I don't know what's up or down.

You woulda seen the cable bein ripped from its tie. You woulda seen it slither in, like it was bein slurped up, and then a hundred rats flowin out. You saw em, didn't yuh?

And now yur sayin, poor old H, he's a goner.

But not yet he isn't.

Down here, what yuh can't see is the sinkhole shrinks t a tenth of its size, and I hav t stoop, then it shrinks again, and I'm down on my hands and knees, crawlin across the mulch. But I'm so close t the end, I'm not goin t give up now. No way am I goin t turn back yet. Even when there's barely enough room t squeeze through, I squeeze through, diggin my elbows in t the decades old shitheap and draggin myself along. The air is thinnin, but fuck it, I'm so close.

There's a sudden whiff of gas, and that rattles me. Gases are as serious as yuh get. There's no readin them. They'll murder you silently in your sleep, without as much as a cough, or jus spontaneously combust. Poof and a bloom of flame. So I wriggle the mask free and snap it over my face, then turn the tap. Air flows, air with a tang of metal, but it's like pure ecstasy after the shit I'm used t breathin.

If this thing gets any narrower, I'm goin t get stuck. What a way that'd be t go, I think. Then jus when I'm thinkin I'm really not goin t be able t make it through and thoughts of failure start seepin through me like piss through a bedsheet, the tunnel opens up again. I pick myself up and get t my feet. But I can hardly move I'm so tired. My skin's grazed. My eyes are red raw. I jus want t sit down and go t sleep and let the gases wriggle up my nose and down my throat and do their best job on me. But I've got t snap out of it, I tell myself. Thass no way t think.

Jus a bit more, H, I say. Jus imagine yur in that picture on yur wall, walkin through that lush park down towards the city and that glintin, cool, clear river. Silvery flashes slip by, fish maybe. I lean down and wash the filth from my skin. I cup the water in my hands and lift it up t my mouth. It comes alive on my tongue. I hear the susurration of the whisperin river in my ears, gettin louder and louder, and then I come to and I realise I'm not imaginin that murmurin sound at all.

I stop dead. I scrabble around in my pocket for the compass, check it quick, and see the tunnel has looped back towards the black river. Eff it, I think, does that mean it's the river I can hear? Am I that bleedin close? I see in my mind's eye the tunnel collapsin and that dead black water rushin in and fillin my shredded lungs.

Then there's movement underfoot, a distant rumblin. A long way back I can hear it, like the world shiftin in its seat. I turn and shine the torch into the tunnel and jus stare in t the dark, waitin like that, like an idiot, for whatever's t come t come, and then I see a shadow creepin towards me. But it's not water. It's my warnin party. Hundreds and thousands of slitherin rats, squealin like stuck pigs. I turn. I run. But they're on me in seconds. They swarm up me, coverin my legs. They're leapin at my back. They're clingin t my arms. They're in my hair. I fling them off me as I run.

But that sound's still comin. That rumblin. And it's growin steadily now, bearin down on me as I run as best as I can, shakin rats from my arms, swipin them from my face, not carin anymore about the ones clingin t the rest of me. And then I realise it's the dead black skank of the river after all, gushin a hundred miles an hour towards me through the tunnel and before I know what's happenin I'm picked up and flung through the tunnel, flipped around, scraped and bumped, twisted and buckled, unable t breathe. I'm a dead man. I know it.

I know thass what summa yuh will like t say. Yur probly sayin it already. H, he tried, made it further than most, but he's down there now, buried alive, breathin his last.

Oh no, that ain't what's happenin.

I'm fallin, tumblin. I've burst right out of somethin. And I land on my back with a thud that winds me. And I can't breathe again.

I don't know where the fuck I am, in the tunnel, or out. But everythin is dazzlin in my eyes, and when I look up, what do I see but that old yellow sky, n when my eyes clear a bit more I see it's jus another Beach, beach combers and everythin, and in the distance t the east, the biggest joke of all, another wall. I breathe a lungful of skanky air.

All that for nothin. Isn't that jus the punchline of all punchlines? I don't know whether t laugh or cry.

I know you'll think it. I know you'll say it. Yuh might even find comfort in it, this old tale of failure.

Good old H, he's out there somewhere, but not where he wants t be, because all that shit is a lie. This is all there is, this is the truth.

But nah, that ain't the truth neither.

I stand up and see in the distance, beyond that second wall, a strip of blue sky. I whoop out a cry. I holler my heart out.

I know you'll be watchin the carts, waitin for my broken old body t be sent back. But it's not goin t be. I tell yuh that now. I'm goin t get t the other side of this other wall, jus like I got t the other side of ours. And even if the joke goes on and there's jus another wall beyond this one, I'll try again, because eventually, if it's this time, or the one after, or the one after that, I'll find the part of the world where the Beach ends, this here Beach thass made up of the shit no one wants. Yeah, so what if old H was born here? Does that mean he has t die here too?

Jus look at that blue sky on my wall deepen in colour each day.

Faces
James Hatton

It was dusk when I saw the boy coming through the estate they were building where there'd once been woods at the back of the house. Under the crimson sky his body was in silhouette and you couldn't see his face, but I could tell it was him – or at least I thought I could – because of the way he walked, head lowered like he was afraid to look up.

Earn, like me, was nine years old and the long shadows cast by the houses seemed sinister as he passed through them in the fading light. He climbed over the fence that marked the boundary of our house, then struck out across the garden – just a shadow himself, really. I expected to see him come right up to the house and let himself in through the back door, as he sometimes did, but he swerved away towards the shed and inexplicably went inside.

He had a nervous face with startled eyes that searched helplessly for things only he knew when people were cruel to him, which was often. It was that frightened face I expected to see when I went down there and opened the door, but when he turned towards me in the half-light, what I saw was something else. His features seemed to have disappeared. There were no holes where his mouth or nose should have been, and no eyes – not even indentations to show where they'd been before. His face looked smooth, like wet clay.

He reached out towards me with both hands.

'Earn –' I said, but my voice died in my throat and he turned away as if ashamed, his arms dropping back to his sides.

Neither of us moved, and when a few moments later he turned to look at me again, I stepped back at the sight of something even worse than what I'd seen before. In the way he held his body, even somehow in the blank face, I saw myself. It was as if I was looking at a part of me that had been hidden away and never allowed to see the light of day.

When he started to make a garbled sound from where his mouth should have been, and I heard the inflections of my own voice, I ran out of the shed and went back to the house. From my bedroom, I looked down at the garden where the shed was now almost hidden in the dark and tried to make sense of what I'd just witnessed. I couldn't. All I could do was cling onto the hope that the child – whoever it was – would be gone in the morning. I barely slept at all that night, eyes staring into the dark as I imagined the child getting into the house through an unlocked door or window and making its way to my bedroom where it would turn itself into me again.

The next day I got up before anyone else and crept downstairs and went out to the shed. Through the window I could see the child in the corner, curled up as if asleep. It wore jeans and a red T-shirt. The trainers it was wearing, I noticed with a chill, were the same as my own.

'Earn,' I said, still trying to persuade myself somehow that it was Earn Wilkes in there, but I was too frightened to open the door, and when the child didn't move, I decided to go to Earn's house.

I found him playing Tetris on his Gameboy. Soothed by this ordinary scene, I watched him manoeuvre the building blocks across the dot matrix screen for twenty minutes before telling him about the child.

'A boy?' he asked, disinterestedly, still rotating the blocks, squeezing them into the holes.

'I thought it was you.'

He glanced up this time, frowning, and I felt lost when I looked into his eyes, like he was a stranger. It was as if I suddenly understood how much we didn't know about each other, and how perhaps we didn't even know ourselves.

The child hadn't moved from the corner of the shed when we got to the house.

'Who is it?' Earn asked.

Without answering, I took a step forwards and the child sat up and looked around at us, revealing that face devoid of features. It made a whimpering sound.

I don't know what I'd hoped to achieve by taking Earn to see the child. Corroboration, I suppose. The comfort of someone else seeing the disturbing thing I'd seen. But what Earn did then took me aback. This boy who was too timid to walk through a classroom full of kids went straight up to it and crouched down.

'What do you think happened to it?' I asked, but Earn ignored me.

He stroked the child's hair, and the child seemed to relax under his touch.

'What should we do?'

But Earn said nothing again. He seemed to be completely absorbed by the child.

'Earn, who knows what it is,' I whispered.

But it was as if a switch had been flicked in Earn's brain and he was somewhere else entirely. It didn't seem to concern him that this child appeared to have been disfigured in a way that seemed impossible, and it unnerved me that he shouldn't. I looked at the child, at a loss as to how it could breathe, how it could even be alive. But Earn's whole being had been overcome with a protectiveness for it, and as uneasy as I felt by being there, the two of them together mesmerised me.

All morning Earn stayed in the shed, with the child's head in his lap while he ran his hands through its hair. In the end, I went to sit on the back step, glancing up at the shed every so often as all the far-fetched possibilities that might explain the child entered my thoughts. Birth defects, accidents. UFOs. But none of them felt anything close.

I retreated to the sanctuary of my bedroom eventually. I turned on my Gameboy and tried to forget about Earn and the child amid the jingle of coins as I guided Mario from one platform to the next, collecting and losing lives. The hours passed as I defeated one boss after another, as I never would in my life.

At intervals I put Mario on pause and went down to peer in through the window of the shed. The child seemed to have fallen asleep – not that you could really tell in that blank ovoid of a face – and Earn had closed his eyes.

Late in the afternoon, when I looked in and saw that Earn had woken up, I went inside. The child lay with its head in Earn's lap, the hair covering where its ears should have been, the fringe coming down far enough to have needed to be flicked out of its eyes if it had any.

'Do you think it'll die?' I asked.

'Why?'

'How can it eat?'

'Maybe it doesn't need to eat.'

Then I started to notice something else. The child's body, now that I was looking more closely, seemed slighter than it had before. Looking at Earn and the child together, it seemed to me that they'd started to resemble each other. Even the featureless face somehow expressed the same loneliness I often saw in Earn.

I watched them, alarmed, feeling that there was something to fear in these changes I didn't understand, in the questions they posed that seemed to have no answers.

'Earn, it looks like you,' I said quietly, not wanting the child to hear – though how it could have done, I didn't know.

'It doesn't.'

'When I came in here on my own last night, it looked like me.'

'It's got no face,' Earn said. 'It doesn't look like anyone.'

But I could tell from a catch in his voice when he spoke that he'd seen it too, even if he didn't want to believe it. I guess he preferred to think he was needed by a real child and it wasn't just his own loneliness being reflected back at him.

'I'll show you then,' I said.

I grabbed the child's arm and started to pull it up out of Earn's lap. He tried to stop me, pushing me away with his free hand, but I managed to wrestle the child from his grip. It had woken up and that featureless face – which was now turned towards me – mirrored something of myself again. I hated the feeling. I felt none of the tenderness it had triggered in Earn, only a nagging disgust – for it or for me, I wasn't entirely sure.

'See,' I said to Earn, not wanting to touch the child anymore but holding onto it until Earn admitted he could see it too. 'It's changed, can you see that?'

Earn didn't reply, but I'd had enough now. I let go of the child and it flopped back down into Earn's lap. It seemed weakened by the struggle and Earn held it, shielding it from me.

I left him alone with it again and went back inside the house with an anger I think I exaggerated to myself to distract me from how scared the child made me. I tried to take Mario through the levels once more. But I couldn't be bothered now and I let him die intentionally time and time again, watching the game over screen come up repeatedly, giving me the nagging suspicion that these failures might mean something more than my hard-won victories.

In the early evening, Earn went home. He didn't say goodbye. I watched him from the upstairs window and he looked completely alone as he wandered off.

Now that he'd gone, I felt responsible for the child again. I tried to map out in my mind some kind of plan. In the safety of my bedroom, I allowed myself to see how ridiculous it was that I'd thought the child might not be human. It was just a little boy who'd been in some kind of terrible accident and its parents were probably worried sick. I told myself that in the morning I'd tell my own parents.

I imagined them calling the police.

I fell asleep, comforted by that thought. But I was woken up in the middle of the night by voices in the garden. I went to the window and saw someone out there in the dark, holding a torch. It was my mother. She was standing at the door of the shed and a moment later my father came out, carrying one of those big black gardening sacks with something heavy inside. He looked at her aghast in the torchlight, his face fierce in the bleached light. He said something and shook his head at her and she took the light off him. I saw only the outline of his body after that, dragging the sack across the grass.

I lost sight of him in the dark but a minute later a car started and I watched headlights slide away into the night. In the garden, alone, my mother walked to the door of the shed and pointed the torch inside. She stood there for a minute or two before closing the door and walking back to the house.

'It's gone,' I told Earn the next morning when he came around and his eyes seemed to search desperately again for that thing that would save him from the cruelty of the world.

He went to the shed, just as my mother had done, and stood inside, staring at the corner where he'd comforted the child the day before.

'Where did it go?'

'I don't know,' I lied.

I didn't tell him what I'd seen during the night.

My parents never spoke of it and they looked at me with feigned innocence the one time I brought it up. On the rare occasions I see Earn these days, he changes the subject if I mention it. He's a chartered accountant now and works long hours in the city, drifting back on the train every evening with a crowd of tired commuters. I run a company that builds houses and it seems amazing to me at times how four walls and a roof can contain so many dreams, such nightmares.

Tell Me is it Healthy, Baby?
Mazin Saleem

"'Now that your rose is in bloom…"; "your", not "a" – i.e. someone whose bud has bloomed; Seal's addressing someone here: a girl who has become a woman. The blooming is of her vagina – that much is obvious. And yet "…a light hits the gloom on the grave". Why does Seal pair the two? And more: bloom, gloom, rose, grave. The song is soaked in such imagery: "There used to be a greying tower alone by the sea." "Did you know that when it snows my eyes become large and the light that you shine can be seen." Snow versus light: death and life. Another pairing. But this isn't some banal 'sex = death' equivalence. Seal offers something far more profound. Recall that the rose isn't the grave, it lights the grave. Highlights it, he might've sung. Points it out. The maturing vagina, the kiss it offers, the act of sex, is not the start of a girl's 'real life' as a grown woman so much as her first memento mori. Becoming an adult doesn't merely mean maturity; consider how to adulterate means to corrupt, to weaken. Childhood might feature faster physical changes than the long tail of adulthood, but in terms of your psyche, it's a stasis till puberty, a non-time. So the blooming of her rose, her graduation into mature sexual being, is the end of that former immortality. Hence the recurrent theme in fairytales that for a supernatural being to fall in love with one of us is to become mortal. Seal has pedigree here: Dante's Beatrice in the poem La Vita Nuova eats his burning heart only with reluctance: falling in love means falling out of the magic circle of childhood and lock-stepping into the march towards death. (Talk about The New Life!) Seal's gleaned this too; but only by completing the act of love. What else is a "kiss from a rose on the grave" than the last labial distend around his withdrawing glans? Sexual maturity corroborated only through sex, sex which announces the dawn of death: a light hits the gloom on the grave.'

'Cool. And it said on your profile you also like archery?'

Of Knives and Men
Louisa Adjoa Parker

Thursday is giro day so everyone gets up early. When the postman pushes brown envelopes through the door and they fall with a plop onto the doormat, the man says, come on. They go outside and pile into Andy's crappy blue Escort with the wing mirror sellotaped on. There's not enough room for Crutchie's chair in the boot so Black John folds it and puts it across their laps in the back seat. It's only a mile to the post office but no-one can be arsed to push Crutchie in his chair, and as Scottish Jake says, the high street is a fuck-off great hill, after all.

Room for a cripple? Crutchie says outside the car. His voice sounds like a croaking bullfrog, slicing the air. You're the man! Andy says, pushing black hair out of his eyes with a dirty hand. Always room for our host with the most. Get in the front, mate, seat of honour. The girl wishes she was allowed in the front. She doesn't like being pressed in between the men, who smell of sweat and smoke and alcohol. In the squat Black John had rubbed her back when she was in bed once, pressing himself against her, whispering in her ear. She'd pretended to be asleep and rolled away from him. Now, she tries to shift her thigh away from his but there's no room. The girl likes giro day – everyone buys booze and fags and food and they eat and drink like they're rich and can afford to do this every day.

In the post office they stand in the queue, the men laughing and poking each other in the ribs. They're all tall with wide shoulders and long legs apart from Crutchie who's short and has legs that are all withered. All the men wear army boots. The girl feels like the odd one out – as well as Crutchie – because she's fat and a girl with brown skin. Black John could be seen as an odd one too, but he's tall and bearded like the others and his skin is light so he doesn't look that different except he has a wide nose and thick curly hair. She doesn't like to stand too close to him in case the others start saying they look like brother and sister. The woman behind the glass hands the money to each of them in turn. Black John holds up his ten-pound notes as though they're a trophy, and cheers.

They go to the Co-op and the men buy pizzas and crisps and meat pasties. The girl buys salad and cheese and yoghurts. Then they walk down the hill to the offy and the men get bottles of Jack Daniels and cans of Special Brew and packets of baccy. The girl buys a bottle of Thunderbird and hopes she doesn't drink so much she throws up again. She buys lemonade to mix it with. Come on, girlie, the man says, live a little. Is that all you're getting? The girl nods. Lightweight, he says, and ruffles her hair.

Even though it's giro day the men take Crutchie to the cashpoint. He gets extra money because he's got cerebral palsy – that's why he was given the flat with the special rails around the toilet and a red cord with a handle that dangles in the bathroom in case he falls over. Take money off a cripple, would you, he often says, with a laugh. The men laugh too and say, yeah, but only 'cos you let us, mate. The girl would hate to be handicapped, but she'd love her own flat. Sometimes she gets sick of living with other people. The girl doesn't like how everyone pretends they're helping Crutchie, but really they want to spend his money.

The girl sits under a tree on a bench in the civic square. She rolls a cigarette and smokes it slowly, watching people walking by: kids her age in hoodies and jeans, older hippies in Indian style clothes. A man with dirty bare feet and a long grey beard sits cross-legged in a doorway across the road playing an instrument like a harp. In the window above him she can see the word 'Peace.' She hopes her mum isn't in town looking for her. Her mum is white with a long rope of brownish hair and everyone thinks she's a loony tune. The girl gets her colour from her dad, who she hasn't seen for ages. He used to scare the shit out of everyone so he's not like a proper dad. The girl's mum is always tired and can't cope. All she does is get on her case. That's why she left; she was sick of all the shouting and crying.

It's warm so she rolls the sleeves of her hoodie up, exposing pale brown forearms. She runs a hand over the left side of her head where she's shaved her hair. She likes the feel of the soft stubble and the way the rest of it flops in her face. The man likes her hair now it's longer and in dreads; he likes to grab a fistful of it when he's doing her from behind. Then he'll yank her head back and sometimes it hurts her neck. He wants it to grow so long he can wrap it round his wrist.

Back at the flat the men dump the bags in the kitchen. The man says, put this lot away and stick some pizzas on, there's a good girl. The girl smiles and says OK. She starts unpacking. I'm starving, the man says. I could eat a horse. He hooks an arm around her neck and jerks her towards him. Unlike my woman here, who already has! The men laugh and wander into the living room. The girl puts the food away apart from the pizzas which she puts in the oven.

In the living room they settle into their usual places – the girl and Crutchie on cushions on the floor, the man and Andy on the sofa and Scottish Jake in the armchair. Black John brings some dusty posh glasses in and hands one to the girl. He pours whiskey into the rest. The girl stares at the amber liquid in the glasses, wondering how it changes people. She sips a glass of Thunderbird. It's sweet and sickly but she likes it. Andy's dog, a grey Lurcher, goes up to Scottish Jake and sniffs his hand. Fuck off, he says, and kicks it in its skinny ribs. The dog whimpers and slinks out of the room.

The girl's stomach is rumbling but she doesn't want to eat in front of anyone. She's hated doing that since the day someone brought a load of chocolate round and, because she hadn't eaten for two days, she ate six bars, quickly. You need to control your woman, Andy had said to the man. She's greedy. The girl goes to the kitchen and gets a yoghurt out of the fridge. She takes off her hoodie and folds it over the yoghurt, then goes to the toilet. She puts the toilet seat down and sits on it, spooning yoghurt into her mouth. The bathroom stinks of piss – the men don't seem bothered about getting it in the toilet. The girl stares at the dirty white tiles, black grouting, mould blossoming on the ceiling. There's hardly any wash stuff, just Crutchie's shampoo and Old Spice, and a dried bar of soap with black cracks in on the side of the bath. The girl liked having smellies when she was at home – bubble bath and conditioner and face masks and all that crap.

She flushes the toilet and goes into the kitchen. She gets the pizzas out of the oven, cuts them into neat triangles and arranges the slices on a plate. The smell of melted cheese makes her feel sick. What am I doing with you motley crew, the man is saying when she gets back in the room. A Jew, a cripple, a Scotsman and two wogs? He laughs. It's like the beginning of a shit joke. You couldn't make it up. He often says this. Less of that, eh, Scottish Jake says, pushing wire-framed glasses up to the bridge of his nose. Mind your manners. Here's to your good health, Crutchie, my man! Scottish Jake raises his glass in Crutchie's direction and the others do the same. Pizza's ready, the girl says, handing the plates round. She sits back down. Aren't you eating? Crutchie asks. The girl shakes her head. Not hungry, she says. The man shrugs.

All the more for us then, he says, tipping his head back and dropping a folded slice of pizza into his mouth. He leaves a piece of stringy cheese on his beard.

I'm going to score, Andy says. Later he comes back with an eighth and starts skinning up. The other men go into the kitchen and do hot knives. The girl can hear them coughing and laughing. The man brings in a blackened bottle with the bottom smashed off and waves it at the girl. Want one, he asks. The girl shakes her head. Nah, she says. You're all right. I dunno what's got into you, he says. You're so fucking boring these days. She's drunk now; the alcohol makes everything feel glittery. She wants to go somewhere and dance. The flat is filled with smoke. The man puts Hawkwind on the stereo – his favourite band, although he likes acid house and drum 'n' bass as well. The girl hates Hawkwind – it makes her feel like she's having a bad acid trip. Although she hasn't had a smoke she can feel paranoia edging in. She smooths her skirt down self-consciously, hopes the men won't start teasing her.

By six o'clock everyone is out of it, shouting and laughing, Pink Floyd blaring out from the HiFi. Andy is asleep in the corner, snoring. She stares at his black beard flecked with grey, his leathery skin. Scottish Jake kicks him. Wake up lightweight, he says. You're letting the side down, man. Always asleep. You're missing out on *life*! Andy snorts in his sleep and everyone laughs.

The girl is worried because the man says whiskey brings out his temper. Since they've lived here he's punched her a few times. The first time she'd made lasagne for them both, spent hours chopping carrots and onions, stirring the white sauce to get the lumps out. She can't remember what she said to wind him up, but as she took it out of the oven, with the yellow cheese bubbling on top of it, he punched her. Stupid nigger, he'd said. Stupid bitch. I hit you in the head, he told her the next day, so it didn't leave any bruises.

The man is way better looking than the girl – she knows everyone thinks this. He's got blondish brown hair and high cheekbones, eyes the colour of a summer sky. Yesterday she shaved his hair off, moving the clippers up the contours of his skull in neat lines, worried she'd cut him. The hair fell to the floor in clumps. The girl misses his long hair, the way it changed from brown to gold at the ends. Sometimes she thinks he only hits her because he takes one look at his fat, ugly girlfriend and is angry he isn't with someone better.

Scottish Jake and the man are arguing. You two, Crutchie says, are two alpha males fighting like two bulls in a field full of cows. He laughs: *haw, haw, haw.*

You're not man enough to even *consider* trying to be top dog, Scottish Jake says. So shut up. He flicks his long grey ponytail over his shoulder. The girl looks at Crutchie who is sat on a cushion on the floor, thin legs splayed out in front of him. He's rolling a spliff. He hasn't taken his leather jacket off. He smiles at her and she smiles back. Crutchie has a nice smile and seems normal until he laughs or speaks or moves. When he talks he has to stretch his mouth wide to get the words out, as though they're great big stones. At first the girl didn't understand what he was saying, but she does now. It's not hard; you just have to listen. She hates it when a bit of dribble falls from his mouth, though. He has sticks to help him walk. His real name is Ben, but everyone calls him Crutchie, even his dad. His mum and dad treat him like a baby, bringing him food and talking to him in soft, scared voices. The girl doesn't want to feel sorry for him because she doesn't think she's better than him. But she can't help feeling a little bit sorry.

If I got you pregnant, the man said one night, and you gave birth to a kid like Crutchie I'd put a pillow over its face. That's horrible, she'd said. The man had shrugged. Survival of the fittest.

He wouldn't have lasted five minutes if he'd been born a few decades ago. It's nature's way.

You can't disrespect me like that, the man is saying in a loud, slurred voice. In front of my woman and my mates. Your woman? Scottish Jake laughs. Not much of one. Though if she's the only thing on offer … I'm partial to a dusky thigh. I bet she's a goer, they all are. What does her cunt taste … You fucking Scottish … The man says, trying to get to his feet. He manages to stand and straightens himself. Wanna take this outside? Och, come on, Scottish Jake says. As if I'd waste my time. I'd knock seven bales of shit out of you, wee man.

The man goes into the kitchen and the girl can hear him pulling drawers out with a slam then rummaging through them. He comes back into the room with a breadknife, points it at Jake. Yeah? Scottish Jake says. Come on then, you *queer*. Even though the man's standing and he's the one with the knife, somehow the knife gets into Jake's hand and it's slicing through the man's skin. The girl isn't sure whether Jake did it on purpose or if the man was pulling his hand away. There is a cut between his forefinger and thumb. It's white for a second and she can see inside his skin before the blood oozes out. You Scottish cunt, he says. He stands there staring at his hand. His face has turned grey. Blood is dripping onto the floor tiles. The girl is staring at his hand, too. She can't move. Girlie? The man says, a babyish whine in his voice. Oh for fuck's sake, Black John says slowly. His brown eyes are rimmed with red. He goes into the kitchen and comes back with a dirty tea towel. Wrap it in that. And press hard.

The girl hasn't seen a person cut someone before. The man got his face sliced with a Stanley knife in Torquay one night; there's a curved scar on his cheek he calls a Glasgow smile. Fucking great girlfriend you are, girlie, the man says. Then he lunges with his right shoulder at Jake, who is leaning against the wall next to the fish tank. Crutchie loves his fish; the girl likes them too. Sometimes when no-one else is in she'll stare at them swimming about, flicking their tails and opening and closing their fish-lips. Crutchie told her some of them were catfish; she can't remember the other names. Zebra? Dog? They're all different colours – orange and black like tigers, pale brown and speckled, fluorescent blue. Her favourite is the big blue and black stripy one. It swims up to the glass and stares at her. Crutchie feeds them every night, dropping brown flakes into the water and watching as they float towards the bottom and the fish notice and start gobbling them up. The tank is lit at night. Sometimes the girl can't see her favourite one, but then it comes out from behind the plastic castle where it's been hiding and darts in and out of the pretend sea plants.

Jake loses his balance and falls against the tank. Although it looks as though it's made of thick strong glass it shatters, spilling water and fish all over the floor as though a giant wave has come into Crutchie's living room. Time seems to slow down. Jake picks himself up from the floor, laughing. He has a cut on his hand too, and a smear of blood on his face. The girl can't decide which is worse – the knife or the fish. She stares at the knife on the floor and imagines one of the men cutting the live fish into pieces. The knife and the fish together would the worst thing of all.

The fish lie on the lino tiles flapping their tails; tiny splashes of colour against the grey. Crutchie is opening and closing his mouth the same way the fish are doing. He tries to get up but Black John says, I'll get a bucket, mate, and goes into the back garden. He comes in with a large plastic tub filled with water. The girl picks up the knife and takes it into the kitchen. She drops it in the bin and gets some spoons. She and John and Crutchie scoop the fish up and put them in the bucket. It's hard to get them because they're slippery and it takes ages. The man has fallen asleep, cradling his arm in its dirty tea towel as though it's a new baby. Fuck this, Scottish Jake says. I'm going to the pub.

In the morning the girl wakes early. The man hasn't come to bed. The room is splashed with sunlight and shadow. She stares at the mess strewn across the floor – clothes, baccy packets, and Rizlas. She wonders why the man didn't say no when Crutchie said they could have his bedroom. Everyone is still asleep when she goes into the front room; all long limbs and whisky-tobacco morning breath, stale sweat. The girl pulls the curtains and the room is flooded with a gold early morning light. She opens the window, quietly, breathes in clean air. Crutchie is outside in his chair on the path, smoking. He's had a shave; his face looks like that of a boy of twelve without the bushy beard. He's cut himself in three places but only put a plaster on one. The single plaster on his face makes her want to cry. All right Crutchie, the girl says with a sniff. All right, mate. Thanks for helping with the fish. He blinks and sucks on his cigarette. He looks sad. Are they OK? she asks. I dunno, he says. I didn't want to look. I'll check for you, she says. Can I have a roll-up? Can't find my baccy.

Inside everyone is beginning to shift in their sleep. The man is snoring loudly with his mouth open. Looking at him makes the girl feel sick. She stares at the bluish stubble on his head and thinks, he's not as good looking as I thought. Then she looks at his wet pink tongue and thinks, I've tasted that. It's pushed itself into parts of me. She pushes the bathroom door open slowly. All the fish are on the surface of the water, floating belly-up. They look paler than yesterday, and as though they are made of rubber. She gasps, covering her mouth with her hand. She's always hated seeing dead things. What is it? Crutchie asks from the doorway.

Oh. They're all gone, aren't they? The girl nods. Every single one of 'em. Sorry, mate. Oh well, Crutchie says with a sigh. We tried. I'll stick 'em in the freezer, they'll be lovely with a plate of chips.

Why d'you always joke about stuff, the girl asks. Crutchie shrugs. What else is there, he says. Then: he's not good for you. I know, she says, after a minute. They stand staring at the fish. We should *do* something, she says.

Scottish Jake comes into the bathroom and unzips his fly. A long arc of dark yellow piss flies up towards the ceiling then falls into the toilet bowl. A few drops of urine splash onto the floor. The girl can see his dick, speckled and purplish, and the fuzzy nest underneath. *That* was a crazy night, he says, shaking his dick then tucking himself back in. Sorry if it got a bit out of hand, Crutch old chap. You know what we get like when we've had a few. Crutchie shrugs. It's OK, he says. Jake glances into the bucket. Oh, he says. The wee chaps didn't make it then. He lifts the bucket up and tips its contents into the toilet. No! shouts the girl. We were going to … What, Jake sneers. Give them a funeral? Don't be soft. They're fucking *fish*, man. He pulls the flush. The girl imagines the fish being propelled down the pipe into a dark sewer, into the river Dart with its long green weeds, then into the wide, glittering sea. How they'd look as though they were still alive: swimming, twisting and turning, their tails flicking.

I need coffee, Jake says. Put the kettle on. There's a good girl.

I Love You, Man
Louisa Adjoa Parker

It was Thursday of Lifeboat week and the girls were down the seafront, chatting to Traci while she put hair wraps in Lexi's hair. Traci had pink dreadlocks and fingers that moved so quickly you almost couldn't see them. The promenade was thick with slow-moving, sunburned tourists. Hair wraps were the thing that summer; silky thread wrapped around a few strands of your hair. Lexi had wanted some for ages, but she'd been worried that with her frizzy hair they'd stick up like a boner. Luckily, the weight made them hang down like normal hair.

'Why don't we braid the rest of it?' Traci asked when she'd finished. 'It's the perfect texture for braids; they don't stay in white people's hair for long. And the wraps are longer than your hair now.'

'Yeah, go on, Lex,' Jade said. 'It'd look wicked. Like Beyonce.'

'Yeah, Lex,' said Grace, flicking blonde hair out of her eyes.

So, Lexi had her hair braided for the first time. She loved the way the braids hung around her face and that her hair was longer. She couldn't bear to think about taking them out when the summer was over.

'Guess what, ladies?' Traci said, rolling a cigarette. 'My little bro's in town. He's very handsome, not much older than you guys. You're what, sixteen?'

'No, we're only…' Lexi began, but shut up when she saw Jade shooting her a look.

The girls giggled. 'What's he like?' Grace asked.

'How old is he?' said Jade.

'He's seventeen. You'll have to find out what he's like for yourselves,' Traci said, winking. 'I think he's a bit special, but I'm biased.'

When Lexi got home, Mike looked horrified and did a double-take.

'Jesus Christ, kid! You look like a bloody hippy! You should have asked me first.'

'Sorry, Dad. I asked Mum about the wraps and the lady said we should do braids as well.'

'Hmm, well, your mother's the one who's got to get that lot out, not me.'

Traci's brother was all everyone was talking about. Apparently, he was like the pied piper – he had girls and boys of all ages following him – and like Jesus, long-haired and beautiful. He could heal you by putting his hands on you. He had golden eyes with thick lashes, the face of a model, the lean body of a dancer. He could walk on hot coals, and it was rumoured that someone had seen him walking on water.

'That's obviously a load of shit,' Lexi said to Jade, who had of course already met him. 'No boy's that amazing.'

'He is, you should see him, Lex,' Jade replied with a sigh.

'Yeah, whatever,' Lexi said, then, 'Where does he live, this God-boy?'

'Just on the beach, like a homeless, up on the cliffs.'

They were in Lexi's garden, stretched out on the decking in their bikinis. Well, Jade and Grace were wearing bikinis. Lexi preferred to keep her clothes on. What skin was exposed was covered in a thick layer of sun-cream, the high-factor one Mum used on her little brother. Her friends often told her she was lucky she didn't have to get a tan. They didn't seem to realise her skin gets darker in the sun, just like theirs.

'What, like, just on the beach? No tent or anything?'

'Um, I'm not sure. Why are you asking me so many questions?'

'Yeah, Lex, we don't know everything,' Grace added.

Lexi thought perhaps her friends didn't know anything about the boy at all and were making it up. And she had only asked two questions.

'Sorry, guys.'

Jade softened. 'It's OK, mate, we just don't know much. I haven't seen where he lives. I've only met him once. Everyone's calling him Beach Boy. He's, like, totally lush.'

'And does he look like Jesus?' Lexi asked, expecting Jade to laugh and tell her not to be a dick. But she didn't.

'Yeah, he does actually … it's weird. He wears these kind of floaty shirts, and he's got long hair and sandals. I guess that's what Jesus would have looked like if he'd been a real person.'

That summer Lexi felt freer than ever before, even though it rained loads, light, misty rain which settled on her hair. Mike was working away and Mum seemed happy, 'pottering' in the garden when the sun was out, reading, taking Matty to the beach. She smiled at the kids, played music from 'back in the day' and sang while she cleaned the house. Lexi loved the music and downloaded a few tracks. Who knew her mum had such good taste in tunes? Mum even drank a glass of wine some nights.

Without Mike there Lexi didn't have to fold herself up tight and small. She wished he'd get a job working away all the time, so she'd never have to see his face and stupid bum chin again. Even though he hadn't hurt her since last year – and she thought he might have stopped – he still frightened her.

When she first saw Christian, he was walking along the seafront surrounded by a group of kids. The way he walked was like dancing, his Indian-style shirt swirling behind him. Other than the fact he was Traci's brother – and this they knew was true, their tanned, taut faces were so alike – no-one knew anything about him. It was as though he'd washed up on the beach one morning with the driftwood and bits of plastic.

Lexi was at home reading and listening to the Fugees when Jade rang.

'Come down the beach, I'm meeting Christian. He's getting some ciggies for me.'

Ciggies were Jade's latest thing, as well as Beach Boy. Lexi found the way Jade went on about things annoying. And she was never going to smoke – the smell reminded her of Mike.

When she met him, he smiled at her as though no-one else was there. The smile made her belly fizz and her heart beat fast. She had never seen a boy as perfect as him. It was as though she had dreamed him up. He was lit from the inside with a gold light.

'Hey, pleased to meet you, beautiful,' he said. 'Where've they been hiding you, then?' he held out his hand. She liked the feel of his skin – warm and smooth.

'Hey,' Lexi said, unable to meet his eye. 'I'm Lexi.'

'I know, your friend just told me, like two seconds ago.'

'Oh, sorry, I …'

'Your hair looks wicked, by the way. Did my sis do it? You're so lucky, being black.'

Lexi nodded. No-one had ever told her she was lucky to be her colour, and of course she wasn't, but she was lucky to have met him. You couldn't not like this elf boy. He had green and blue hair wraps in his hair, which touched his shoulders and shined and looked so soft Lexi almost reached out to touch it.

The three of them walked on to the sand, into the hot press of bodies. Children were screaming as they ran in and out of the sea. The air smelled of sugar and sun-cream. Some kids from school were playing volleyball next to the canoes. Lexi felt a burst of pride: people would see her with this guy.

Christian talked non-stop. His voice was slow, as though he was wasted, but his eyes – which were gold, like a cat's – weren't red. In contrast to his voice, his hands, and the rest of him, moved quickly. 'So tonight ... we should have a party on the beach, yeah? What do you beauties think? Get a little fire going, play some music, have a few beers, listen to the waves?'

'Yeah, sounds sick,' Lexi said. 'We could get people to bring, like, guitars and shit.'

He stopped walking and smiled at Lexi as if she was someone amazing and sexy.

'Not just a pretty face, are you, darling?'

Heat bloomed in her cheeks. She hoped no-one would notice.

'Lexi probably won't be allowed out. Her parents are way harsh.'

Yeah I will,' Lexi said, embarrassed. 'We'll ask Grace, and the twins, and Danny and his mates ...'

'I'll do it,' Jade said. 'I know loads more people than you.' Then: 'You can help, though.'

'I'll leave it up to you two then,' Christian said. He ran towards the rocks and jumped onto the sea wall. Jade's eyes were small, dark stones. She nudged Lexi in the ribs, hard.

'Ow,' Lexi said. 'What?'

'You blushed. You fucking fancy him, don't you? You knew I liked him.'

'No I don't,' Lexi hissed. It was a lie, because of course she fancied him – how could she not? But she knew she didn't stand a chance. It wasn't fair – boys always fancied Jade. Couldn't she let Lexi like someone, for once? 'Anyway, you never said you liked him.'

There was a loud splash from the other side of the wall. Christian had jumped into the sea. His clothes were a neat, pale pile on the edge of the wall. The girls climbed the ladder.

'Come on in, ladies! It's fucking beautiful in here!' His head bobbed up and down in the water, wet hair slicked off his face. His shoulders and arms were muscled and brown. He looked like Jonny Depp when he was younger, or Ashton Kutcher. Jade immediately whipped her top and skirt off. Lexi stared at her friend's flat belly, thin thighs, narrow waist. Showing off, Lexi thought meanly, then felt guilty. It wasn't Jade's fault she looked like a model. Lexi sat on the wall and watched them splashing each other, wishing it was her in the water with him, wishing she were as brave and pretty and skinny as her friend.

The party was a success. Lexi was allowed out at night, for once. She drank cider – the first time she'd drunk alcohol – and threw up behind a beach hut, the apple-smelling vomit draining away through grey pebbles. But apart from that it was brilliant. The moon was full and round; it stayed light enough to see where you were going. Christian played his guitar and sang with a deep, clear voice good enough to win X-Factor. The waves made their usual sh sh sound, which sounded better at night. Everyone got drunk and stumbled around on the stones laughing. Grace snogged Jack, who she'd fancied for ages. All the boys flirted with Jade. Lexi stared at the orange flames of the bonfire and breathed in the smell of wood-smoke, thinking she had never felt so happy. At the end of the evening, the boys took it in turns to jump over the dying embers of the fire.

She saw Christian most days after that, sometimes with other people, sometimes on her own. He was the light and she, like everyone, was drawn to him.

Lexi found herself telling him about Mike. He was the only person she'd ever told.

'Why don't you bring it out into the open with your mum?' he said one afternoon when they were sitting in the Gardens, 'just say, like, Mike fucking hits me and I know he hits you! What are you going to do about it, Mum?'

Lexi nodded, but couldn't imagine the words leaving her mouth. She stared down the grassy hills towards the sea, where pink buoys floated in a line and a boat sailed on the horizon. The beach was a mass of colour, the people too small to make out from here. She'd always liked looking at the sea; with Christian next to her, she liked it even more. He made everything brighter. She wanted to share everything with him – the sea, the moon, the stars.

When they met the next day, Christian told her what his real parents did to him, and what it was like living in foster families. His past, he explained, was the reason he needed so much freedom. 'I've never had a proper family, apart from Trace. But she wasn't always there. It's made me kind of different, you know? I don't want a mortgage and a nine to five job.'

They talked about whether God existed (they agreed he did, but not in the way people said, like this old, beardy man in the sky), and the planet, and what happened when you die. They talked about music, and art, and reality TV, and love.

'It's crazy,' he'd say, 'that we're all living on this giant ball of rock, hurtling through space!'

'Yeah!' she'd reply to most of the things he said. 'I totally know what you mean.'

'Not many people get me like you do, man,' he'd say, and tug one of her braids, or try to tickle her. She wanted him to kiss her. When he wasn't looking, she'd stare at his pink-brown lips, the stubble on his chin, his conker-coloured hair. Every night she wrote his name on her arm, surrounded in hearts, then scrubbed it off each morning. She'd think of him every few minutes, wonder what he was doing, if he was thinking about her. She whispered his name before she went to sleep, as though doing so would make him hers. She liked the way it rolled around her mouth, Christian, Christian.

She thought about what he'd said about talking to her mum. Maybe the sky wouldn't fall in if she did. Maybe it would give Mum the strength to leave. She thought about talking to her mum (along with thinking about Christian) all the time. Practiced how she'd start the conversation. 'We need to talk about Mike,' she'd say, as though she was the adult.

'Lex, you know I can say anything to you, yeah, because we're like, soul-mates or something?'

Lexi nodded. She and Christian were on the beach as usual, sitting on the sea wall, legs dangling over the side, thighs touching. They were eating ice creams – rum and raisin and mint choc chip – and swapping so they got to taste two flavours. Jade wasn't speaking to Lexi because she'd been spending too much time with Christian, but Lexi didn't care. The sea glittered darkly, the sky was a blue bowl – there wasn't a single cloud. She loved the feel of his leg, the light warmth of it. This is it, Lexi thought, her heart thumping so loudly she was sure he could hear it. Any minute now he'll tell me he loves me, then kiss me. She was worried she'd be a bad kisser, in spite of practicing on her hand like some stupid girl in a movie.

'Well, there's this girl I really like … you know me, man, I don't want to get tied down to one person or anything conventional like that, but I really like her. Would you talk to her, see if she likes me?

I know I can trust you, my sweet Lex. You're not like the others, you don't shit-stir and gossip, you're a good girl.'

Stupidly, for a moment Lexi still thought he was talking about her, as if there had been any possibility of this boy liking her. It was Ellie he liked, with the tiny waist and white dresses. Ellie with the long curly hair a shade darker than his. Ellie with the china doll skin, the biggest eyes and the longest lashes Lexi had ever seen. Of course – how could she not have seen it? The shy glances Ellie gave him, the way he always sat next to her … Lexi was just a friend, someone he could talk to. Ellie was a girl he wanted to fuck.

'She does like you,' Lexi said in a barely-there voice, 'I know she does. There's no need for me to talk to her, Christian.'

'Do you think I should go for it then? I wasn't sure if she'd like me.'

'Yeah. Go for it, she definitely likes you,' Lexi said, staring at her thigh; how it was still pressed against his. She shifted slightly, creating a cold space between them.

'A woman knows these things,' she said with a little laugh. 'Trust me.' The sky darkened as the sun went behind a cloud that had appeared from nowhere. She bit at the skin around her thumbnail.

'I love you, man,' he said, grabbing her face and kissing her lips. So, this is how his lips feel, she thought, soft and dry and not in love with me. She wanted to grab the back of his head and press him into her. How could she have got it so wrong? It was the terrible not-quite-ness of it all, the daring to believe that someone like him could be interested in a girl like her.

She couldn't stay. She left him sitting on the sea wall, presumably dreaming of Ellie and her impossibly tiny waist.

'I'll see you soon, Chris,' she said, but knew she wouldn't be able to bear it.

'See you, man,' Christian said, and winked, holding out his fist for her to bump. 'Always be strong, my warrior girl!'

Tears dripped down her face as she walked over the sand. She was grateful she was wearing sunglasses. The sea looked like a sequined bedspread stretched across the bay; it hurt her eyes to look at it. Sand turned to shingle, and she moved on to the promenade, past the long row of pastel-coloured beach huts. Past the shelters where kids hung out at night and skateboarded during the day, where stallholders sold tat to grockles every summer, (and of course where Traci wrapped hair). Past the chip shop where the smell of frying fish wafted into the street. Past the bakers (she was still crying and her heart hurt in her chest) where they made the best pasties ever, and the smell of onions hung heavy and sweet in the air. Past the pub where the women looked you up and down as if to say, What are you doing in my pub?

When she got home, no-one was in. She had to do something to take away the pain. She heard someone crying – loud, animal cries as though someone had died – and realised it was her. This red, raw pain was too big; she wanted to turn herself inside out, claw at her face until it bled. Why didn't he love her? Why was she born to suffer in this life? Why was she so fucking ugly?

Lexi opened the kitchen drawer slowly, heart in her mouth in case Mum came back. She picked up the smallest knife, thinking because of its size perhaps it wouldn't be missed, and put it up her sleeve. None of their knives were really sharp – Mum had a thing about it. She hoped this one would be sharp enough.

In her bedroom she pulled the knife out, caressed it like it was a boy she was about to kiss. (Christian, Christian – why couldn't she get his name out of her stupid head?). It was silly, but she felt shy, as though the knife was a person she'd just met. It shone as she pressed its tip on the soft underside of her forearm. She watched as the skin gave and stretched till it couldn't go any further. When the knife went in, she felt a sweet relief, a release. She sighed as though with pleasure. She wondered if it would have hurt, him inside her, the first time.

Lexi moved the knife downwards in a quick, short line. Drops of blood oozed over the knife's edges. She hadn't seen her own blood – other than periods – since she was a little kid when she fell over all the time. It was red and bright; the colour looked all wrong – it shouldn't have been on the outside of her body. She couldn't stop looking at it. It hurt, but this hurt was better, somehow, than what she had felt for as long as she could remember. It wasn't just Christian, but her whole life, her dad, her colour, everything: a giant ball of pain.

For once, she was in control. She could do this thing; no-one could stop her. It was hers. Lexi pressed a tissue against the cut. She wondered what the scar would look like, whether it would fade in time. She wrapped the knife in a jumper, then buried it under a pile of clothes at the bottom of her wardrobe.

Brief Dates with Average Gays
by Leo X. Robertson

#4957563

First: 'You're Will, I'm Grace.' Then: 'You're like Roger from *American Dad!*' These days: 'You're Cam and he's Mitchell.'

Q.

Well I never say to my straight friends, 'You remind me of Jackie Chan, famous heterosexual.'

Q.

I used to base my personality on TV characters. I don't scold myself about it anymore, though.

Q.

Because there's still pressure to fit into a heteronormative community as a happy-go-lucky secondary character.

Q.

These people want you to be thankful they're even treating you equally.

Q.

Doesn't that mean they still hold the power in society and deign not to use it against us?

#5765926

Dad never taught me how to shave.

Q.

He was supposed to! Wait, is that not a thing?

Q.

Oh. I must've seen it on TV or something. But he did take a while to accept it when I came out, so I'm not totally letting him off the hook.

Q.

And my friends used to tell homophobic jokes and stuff around me before I came out. And I didn't lose my virginity for the longest time because of the shame I had internalised.

Q.

Yeah. I guess we've all accidentally victimised a minority at some point.

Q.

No. I could not give you a single example of a time I did that to someone else. And they might still ruminate over it to this day.

Q.
Huh.

#2048567
'By the way, I don't have a problem with it.'

Q.

It just comes off as, 'The deepest expression of your love doesn't make me want to spew my guts out.'

Q.

Of course there's more to me than these complaints. I'd like you to see it too.

Q.

I read this article recently that said, 'Imagine what we could have learned from James Baldwin if he hadn't had to waste his time tackling something as stupid as racism.'

Q.

I would *love* to talk about something else! I just don't know if we can yet.

In Case of Emergency, Break Glass
Morgan Omotoye

If I write on your book, love
Just you blot out my name –
The Rambling Gambler.

On the polite grass, inches from the bait, the fox's body. A circle of blood issues from the mouth, which opens soundlessly. You gaze at the blood. The full circumference of the fox's predicament as its left hind leg twitches, all cruel and panicked beauty.

Should the clients have dogs, Collies, Dobermans, Alsatians, bet your life, this is when they'd start barking. Sonorously, mournfully. No dogs. Only an imposing beech tree in the garden next door. Its thick branches cast shadows on the grass. A thriving circulatory system of antlered dark flinching away from you as your gloved left hand slowly reaches down.

While placing the body in a chemically treated, heavy-duty black bin liner, you notice two yellow butterflies, *Colias Croceus*, flitting about in front of you. You hesitate before carefully lifting your hands. You try to mimic their manoeuvres. There is something precious and vulnerable in the way they move you desperately need to be part of. As your hands cleaves through the air, the fox's body tumbles from the bin liner. Hits the grass with a muffled *kerflump*. You stiffen and wait to see if the fox will right itself on its sun kissed paws. A gust of wind momentarily heading east whips the bin liner about making it sound very much like the fluttering sails of a pirate ship.

You stare.

You wait.

Two yellow butterflies skirt the invisible.

You tighten your grip on the bin liner.

The fox does not move.

You grab it by its tail and consider hurling it into the upper canopy of the beech tree, breaking its neck something sick, knocking its teeth in, its dead eyes, by hook or by crook opening, taking in the tumbling world. Your training and who knows how many dos and don'ts from workplace Health and Safety meetings (with the bare-chested resuscitation dummy patiently waiting for true love's kiss under the trestle table heavy with leaflets and budget tea time snacks) kicks in and you drop the fox and partially chewed bait – glistening with slobber from the fox's questing tongue – back in the bin liner.

You march towards the house with a cadre of flies buzzing round your hands. The furniture in the kitchen looks grimy with mutiny like they'd slit your throat soon as look at you. Your ears are still ringing from the shot; we both know you always forgot to make use of the cheap, orange, bulky, itchy, over-ear headphones supplied by your employers – yours to pay for if you lose or damage them. The people in the kitchen push back their chairs and stand to attention before addressing you like you're some sort of visiting regent. You see their lips move but you cannot hear their voices. The light in the kitchen is pointy, like it has escaped from one of those silent, weird ass, black and white German films you watched in Media Studies going ways back. Following protocol you offer commiserations. It had to be done. Foxes ferry all manner of diseases. Make gut piles of sleeping babies. They're vermin, a pestilence, just like they say in the Bible, although to be fair, you suspect you might be getting Scripture mixed up with a shouty article in *The Daily Mail*. While you speak, the woman, having done the usual thing with her hair licks her lips like she would like to eat you alive while the man, standing way too close, plies you with questions about the rifle. Heft, calibre, nature of any compensatory gestures you had to make on account of the Coriolis Effect.

You wave at the duo from your white van, the bin liner and rifle hitting your waist when your arm comes down. You pull open the barn doors and fling the rifle and bin liner in. You are aware of the fact you haven't secured your rife properly but you don't much care as you pull at the fingers of your vibration-dampening gloves with the skin of your teeth. Your gloves reek of cordite, mud. There is another smell, patiently waiting, hunkered beneath the mud and cordite, a smell persistently like the whiff of stagnant rainwater in a plastic bucket, no, that's not right exactly, an aluminium bucket comes closer. Fox brains mimp like turnt rain water in an aluminium bucket you reckon despite the great lengths your colleagues go to; literally chomping at the bit and falling over themselves to convince you otherwise.

Folding your gloves into your back pocket you notice your shoelaces have come undone. You don't bother lacing them as you skulk towards the front of the van, gingerly approaching from the left side which boasts the Council's shiny Armorial with the genial motto, *Working Towards a Cleaner Borough* stencilled in blocky green letters underneath.

You pull open the front door and sit down with a sigh of relief which honestly feels decades in the making. You stare at parked cars, huddled so closely together you suspect they're involved in some kind of plot, proper Guy Fawkes styli. The flies serving as your heralds have gone.

You don't go to work the next day. You call in sick. Headache, toothache, heartache. Which is it? Your manager coos seductively. Bastard, choose, you say.

You fidget and fuss and pull at the scratchy collar and sleeves of a white shirt you don't recall buying, but I do! And you think, not for the first time, this is a bad idea. You leave your flat anyway. When you finally arrive at your destination you wait.

It's not long before you start thinking about your job. How you sometimes let one go, believing this made you myth, legend amongst foxes. The next hour, you kill five, twenty. Unlike your colleagues you don't strip mine bodies for souvenirs: ears, teeth, tails, paws, wombs. You are tall with weepy mosquito bites from anybody's guess running down the length of your left arm and you've been known to look freakishly handsome from certain angles and under low wattage light, preferably sourced, if the accident will, from bayonet light bulbs. The lights here keeps mugging you off, no two, three ways about it, far too bright and without having to look too tough you know the light comes from screw-in light bulbs which for some reason you can't quite fathom shroud you in shadows.

You are in the library. This is where you choose to meet her. You suspect this might have something to do with looming government cuts, with the unassailable fact, in a number of months, perhaps not even that, a couple of weeks actually, this whole place will cease to exist; transformed in the blink of an eye into luxury apartments or an overspill car park. This makes you think anything taking place here is rendered obsolete, like, there is every chance you can be exiled from the history of your whole life if the environments in which your past took place were annihilated.

The library is close to empty. The librarians – blow-fly Caesars the lot of em – behind the waist high, grey, mica counter alternate between looking bored, burpy and pissed off. Neither of these modes has a deleterious effect on the volume of their conversation. Whenever they speak, much to your chagrin, they do so loudly as if they have forgotten the eerie profundity of the place, its sanctity, as a public sphere governed by silence and the solitary quest for knowledge. The few patrons present gawp at DVD spines. One rotund, bearded gentleman used to exclaiming, 'You look totally fucked,' to everyone he comes into contact with at his local gym, utters his patented catchphrase to a life-sized, cardboard cut-out standee of Horrid Henry (careworn paladin guarding the entrance to the Children's library) leastways Gym Unc thinks it's a Horrid Henry standee.

Meanwhile, facing the big windows, patrons not manhandling DVDs or embroiled in cases of mistaken identity, sit, head bowed in supplication at computer terminals. One or two occasionally hitting their keyboards as though trying to bash a new alphabet into existence.

It's far too upsetting relaying what you see a number of them do to their tailless mice. Best believe I'd love to try sameway still, give it my best shot, the good ole college try is what I'm getting at here but you won't let me. Ever since you said, Bastard, choose, to your manager, excuse me all over the place, you've been harder to control. Case in point your saunter from your poky flat to the library was supposed to be the perfect opportunity for literary pyrotechnics; a street scene, urban chorography for heaven's sake to narrate the hell out of with lashings of pathetic fallacy thrown in for good measure. I was looking forward to utilising I dunno: maybe three wicked cool paragraphs to chronicle dust motes spiralling in decadent shafts of mid-afternoon light, shout-outs to street furniture and bigging up the fabulous stickers they attract, describing honking cars in such a manner as to reveal the political affiliation and sexual peccadilloes of their drivers stalled in traffic, pointing out Exhibit A white boys holding their skateboards like old time gunslingers caressing their holsters. Man, was I ever looking forward to giving scope to the rowdy voices rising from the Kebab shop called, Your New Favourite and having you brush shoulders with a woman (the spit of the writer Buchi Emecheta) on her way to get her mobile fixed. You look into her eyes and wonder, headache, toothache, heartache, which best articulates the trouble you see there?

Thing is, plan was to get readers on side by fleshing out your backstory while you, ole face ache from morning, took in the sights: the care in the community loon conducting traffic with his shoes, the scary looking baby far too big and sullen for her pram brandishing her spit moistened Farley's Rusk like a cudgel. These are only a few of the things you saw; what about the wicked cool stuff you heard, smelt, tasted on the wind? But nah, check out my man! You left your flat and boom, you're in the library quicker than the time it takes to turn a page. Imagine the savings on my Oyster if I could do that. Mind blown.

You feel inappropriate and obscure standing by the dusty book shelves and I'd give my eye teeth if you moved round a bit matey. Go on. Would it kill you to pick up a book from one of the shelves? Maybe take a gander at the noticeboard – never mind it's close to the public toilets and smells of hamster wee-wee – or better yet, a hundred times better, speak to one of the librarians. Oh my giddy aunt! The cute one with glasses. Lemme see here, one, two, four, yeah that's right. Four rows down from you shelving one of your favourite books, *Train Dreams* by Denis Johnson. What are the odds huh? Her, cute as button, a marmalade lid, shelving one of your all-time favourite books? Swear down and let the devil take the hindmost that's exactly what's she's doing. Right now, for always, for all time. Take a second to consider, why don't you? how things could change for us, if you strolled over to her and politely made small talk about the book she's poised to hold onto for eternity unless you intercede. Okay, okay, scratch that, say she drops the book and you, gallantly, a regular Prince Charming don't you know? pick it up, and say, 'Knock me sideways and paint me yellow, I adore this book,' and she says, 'That's cool, that's awesome,' in a smiley way. Rah, allow that look. I never claimed dialogue was my strong suit. Listen, wait a minute. I could make you conventionally handsome, thinner, a bona fide Radiohead fan, *Guardian* reader, deck you out in the latest fashions. Fix your teeth, course correct your more reactionary views. Yeah, yeah, fair enough you share the general ideas of your generation. Say for me there'll always be a special section reserved for you and your crew in Purgatory for propagating and popularising the term, 'Bants.' Now now, keep it classy, no need to get your knickers in a twist.

Listen. She's flipping gorgeous. Her name, wait till you hear this! Bruv, her name is Nemi Eatock Medeiros. Nemi! A super-heroine name if there ever was one. She has a poster for the film *Down by Law*, no, *The Story of Qui Jui* on her bedroom wall and she makes comics. Oh my days! Am I'm falling for Nemi? She's wearing a black T-shirt with the legend, 'I have Satellite Weapons on me.' That's from a Damaged Gods' song isn't it? From their controversial, I want to say, third album, *The Locusts Have No King*. You like Damaged Gods don't you? Sure you do, don't bother styling it out, I know you do. Come on, she's wearing a T-shirt fleshing her out as a fan of your favourite band and she's about to shelve your all-time favourite book. Fine, excuse me all over the place, *one* of your all-time favourite books. Boss, what are the odds? Listen. Her favourite book is *Assembly* by Natasha Brown. Don't feel a way for not having read it, won't be published for another thirteen years. In the interim Nemi's favourite book is… nah ah-ah, go talk to her and I'll tell you. I promise, hand on heart. Listen. You and Nemi don't have to meet-cute here; this gaff is toast blud. The two of you can meet as colliding light particles in a rapidly expanding salvia bubble or at a David Lynch retrospective. She can be the boy and you can be the girl. You don't even have to fall in love, you can just talk, briefly, about books or comics for all I care, Nemi makes them, remember? Come on. Please. Allow me to stir you away from what's coming since we both know if you continue like this, there's only one way this story ends. Move, go on feller, get some momentum going. Do it! Look away from window. Move. Don't look at the sun. Please don't make me write about the sun in the next paragraph.

The sun is menacingly bright. Its rays amok and berserk in her hair when you finally see her. She's wearing a skinny black Alice band which accentuates the whiteness of her skin. The silver chrome of her wheelchair glistens like the muzzle of your rifle when you strafe it across possible avenues of approach after turning the power ring for sharper focus.

You haven't seen her in what? Three years? Why frame this as a question, its three years. You count to three silently. As your lips move, you recall the circle of blood spilling from the fox's mouth. Like a speech bubble tethered to the mouths of comic book characters. As though the fox was desperate to speak but all it could say got lost in the frothy swill of blood.

Her hair, the colour of (it has to be said) no frills, crunchy nut corn flakes is scarily shorter than it was the last time you saw her. You want to touch it. Don't you fucking dare. She's wearing a cobalt blue T-shirt. In the centre of the shirt, a sharp, showy hieroglyph which must mean something, but what? She's in yellow jeans so insanely bright they purr with radioactive luminescence. She has a blue tattoo coursing round her neck. An eloquent sequence of palpitations with dips, peaks, flat-lines. And bully for you and hosannas out the whazoo, you're bang on the money. Her face isn't particularly heart shaped anymore.

You are not entirely sure you recognise her, not completely, not fully, because you are somewhat bewildered by the sunlight lingering in her hair, the wispy delineation of shadow it neatly stitches across her nose, which appears sharper, aloof like she's gone toff-tastic in the intervening years. You search for signage, landmarks on her body familiar and dare I say, holy to you.

You stare.

You wait.

Her eyes? Too much eye shadow or is that, is that actually green kohl?

Her ears? When you two were together did you re…ever really pay serious attention to her ears? I'm not being a dick or sometimeish I'm just asking. You spent more time learning to pull off Chung Li's Spinning Bird Kick in *Street Fighter II* if memory serves. No judgement, just saying.

Definitely green kohl although to be honest I'm not what you'd call an expert or anything.

I do know it's wrong to gawp at her breasts; to even think about looking at them is off key. The hell is wrong with you?

Don't look at her breasts.

Don't look.

You remember the slow rise of her recalcitrant left nipple under your thumb.

What are you doing?

Remember something else damn you.

Don't look at her breasts. Don't even think about them.

Her mouth? Okay sure, whatevs.

Her mouth, looks exactly how it used to look under the initial burst of hot water from the shower; fussy, with showy vulnerability like the lips of an octopus. You remember aiming the spurting shower head, point-blank, at her face, neck, knees, elbows, belly button, armpits, pubic mound, and you remember; of course you do, the ungainly slip and slide of her body brushing against the edge of the umber coloured shower curtain with its repeating pattern of scarecrows. She was sitting in the half-filled bath, legs splayed out in front of her as you watched skirls of steam, miniature scythe moons, languorously drift past her shoulder blades, mist the bathroom mirror, the *Fantastic Max* tumbler your toothbrushes live in, lending these surfaces a chalky opacity. Not the window though, thrown wide open to combat mould. The shower curtain is a stalled accordion to your left. The torpid pliancy her body ripening under fronds of steam makes a vagrant of what you nominally assume to be desire. In some type of way you would love to swap places with her, have yourself observed just so. Parts of you submerged under the scalding water, guessed at by touch. You let the shower head sink into the bath. It lands against her toes, spraying water too hot for you to take, not her though. The rippled distort of her body under the dimpling water is what you hope you'll always remember when you slowly kiss her slidy forehead, her gleaming shoulder blades. With each kiss you taste a feathery detonation of lavender scented soap before getting to skin proper.

This was the past or as Villon wrote, *Où sont les neiges d'antan?* Now.

You are staring at her, baffled by the mystery of her arrival. How she's suddenly in front of you (Alice band and all) with the sun reckless and buoyant in her hair. Her blue-green eyes shimmering and making you think of foxes with their opalescent eyes caught in the sweeping crossbeams of your van headlights.

She opens her mouth.

You see her lips move.

'How did you get my number?'

'I'm a man.'

She doesn't like your answer. Her mouth forms an unfamiliar line. Once upon a time you were able to brush your fingers over her lips, the skin surprisingly coarse and rough to the touch like sandpaper. As a child she used to fold pieces of paper into triangles and use the sharp point to prod the centre of her lips while deliriously sucking her thumb. She let you know the tips of the triangles often drew blood because she pressed too hard. She said to get her to stop her mother, at her mind's limit, kept all these pieces of paper. As many as she could find anyhow, plucking them out of bins, retrieving them from under the sofa, and one afternoon, she came back from school to find, if not all, then at best a sizable portion of the pieces of paper she'd used to shred her cupid's bow on her bed. She told you it looked like something wounded and bleeding had dragged itself across her duvet, her pillows, her Flat Eric.

'Did you stop sucking your thumb?' you asked.

You are still staring at her mouth when I hear you mumble, 'That's a nice tattoo.' You try your utmost best not to think of fingers lingering on its jittery pulse points. Your fingers are bunched behind your back, grabbing hold of the matt black corner of the bookshelf. You need this anchor, slight as it is, otherwise you'd be lost in space, your feet seeking purchase on coruscating nebulae. She is beautiful. She is more beautiful than you remember, defiantly so and yet what really gets you, makes you come undone like your shoelaces at work yesterday is the sound of her voice. Scoured of all flavouring making it next to impossible to believe it ever called out for you. Read to you from *Train Dreams* when you could not sleep and when this didn't work, bless her cotton shocks she read the entirety of *The Paper Bag Princess* to you. Cradling the book so you could see the magnificent illustrations gracing every page whilst doing the voice of the dragon in her best rendition of Tom Waits' barnacled voice. The Princess, the eponymous heroine of the tale, always sounded like no one else but her.

'What was that? Did you say something?'

'No, nothing. It's really nice to see you Mame.'

Your left arm is a ruin of mosquito bites – but wait? That's what we're going with? Mozzie bites, really? Tell the good folks what you did to your left arm. What you still do. No? Suit your damn self. Your clothes are tight and itchy and you tug on your left sleeve (for the ultimate cover-up or last minute reveal?) as the sun, swaddled in its majestic corona shines far too brightly for you to look handsome or enviably tall as you lick your lips in an appeal for water before slowly opening your mouth to say her name again.

Hoping this will be enough to breach the distance between you. That by saying her name, as a sort of prayer, you will be jammed close together like the books on the shelves, the scheming parked cars you caught wind of yesterday and the fox with its circle of blood, speech bubble, halo, one of these things first before you smeared and ground it up under your foot. You want to touch her but you compromise by reaching for the left armrest of her wheelchair. You do this absently feeling the sticky texture of the black leather under your fingertips.

Mame stares up at you; her head tilted back as though peering at a menu in a badly lit restaurant.

'You still work in the butterfly farm, don't you?'

'That's finished with.'

'What a shame,' Mame replies.

The way she says this though, like she's always known such a thing would come to pass and the fact it has confirms some secret knowledge she's always had about you.

A cloud lingers in front of the sun and you do it. You give into millennia of exhaustion. You fall to your knees. You place your head on Mame's lap. You hardly dare to breathe as you bury your face dangerously close to her crotch.

Mame says your name as though hearing it for the first time. You feel the swell of it bloat her throat, come close to undoing the delicate stitching of her blue tattoo.

You don't need to look up at her to know there is the tide of panic rising in her eyes. It is as if someone (Nemi?) has followed the advice emblazoned above fire alarms dotted round the library: In Case of Emergency Break Glass, and in the raucous, soaring sound of the alarms going off, Mame is not sure where the fire exits are but she knows the conflagration is on its way, is always on its way.

Allow me to tell you Mame looks as helplessly marooned as foxes do the instant your bullet connects with their heads. You have a feeling; call it instinct, of what it will take to bring her back to the world. You slowly lift your head and sink your teeth into her left thigh. Mame's mouth opens, soundlessly.

Fertile Ground
Sylvia Warren

The nights are the worst. They call it a quickening, but it is not. I swelled like a corpse in water, bloated-heavy and sluggish, ravenous but unable to eat. I was not hungry, this thing inside me was, gnawing at my stomach and somehow already growing fangs to scrape away the inside of my womb like artichoke leaves dipped in butter, flesh scored off in parallel lines with the milk teeth that will drop out leave it unsightly and expecting money when it comes out.

My partner is asleep. He lies there lithe and lean like always as my body distorts, cow-like udders draping over a bulging stomach. I have been taken from myself to give him what he has always wanted. He kisses me, caresses me, tells me that I am so beautiful like this, so full of life, then drinks his coffee and eats blue cheese and sacrifices nothing, not even his own name. I wonder what would happen if I punched my stomach, threw myself down the stairs. If I were found out it would not be me the doctors would try to save.

When I was in school we talked about the benefits of taking tapeworms. They would grow inside you and eat all of the food you couldn't, so you could give up the iron-clad control that you exert to make yourself palatable and still fit into your expected place. Out of a class of 30 girls, all but two had opted to swallow the worms. My hand was one of the first up. We share our bodies with all number of commensal organisms, what would be one more? Our teacher looked faintly aghast, but he couldn't know.

In my fourth month when nothing can be hidden anymore – thank god that my co-workers now won't think I have just given up on myself – I told people, and there was cake. The butter icing melted in the central heating, separating into sugar-grit and fat and yolk-yellow dye. Jam blood clots and thick discharge-cream seeping from moist vanilla sponge. My colleagues cut the cake and the slices were eased out, making a mess before being swaddled in white paper napkins. I declined, watching them eat was enough to make me vomit. Vanilla pods, black and shrivelled almost as soon as they are picked, wildly expensive. Orchids and saffron styles, richness as genitalia, dried and plucked and scraped and infused and traded and sold.

I started looking obsessively at genetic mutations online. I would search for harlequin babies, their skin thick and white, livid red gashes for mouths, bodies split with fissures. Or maybe it would not be whole – syndactyly, oligodactyly, ectrodactyly, each more fitting than the last. If it's a girl I'll call it Amelia, just to spite it. If it's a boy, there will be hypospadias, a urethral opening in the shaft of the penis, or either way it could mewl like a cat, not suck or swallow, drool on me with widely-spaced eyes. There is no possibility that this thing inside of me is perfect. My partner comes in to find me hunched over the laptop, each tab a litany of things that can go wrong in the organs or the flesh or the head or the heart. We have blazing rows that leave me sobbing even though I am angry rather than upset. He calls me morbid, as though these things that are happening are not indicative of a disease. He watches me when I move away from the bedroom. I pick up the wine bottle from the fridge before putting it back and remembering that anything I can do to relax is forbidden.

The Mother and Baby unit is pale green like gentle nausea. The nurses and doctors are all so happy for me, stroking and touching the growth, smothering it in jelly and exclaiming over the blue-black screen, 'It's sucking its thumb!' and the beating shape stares back, inhuman and turning, grasping and gasping and wrong.

'Would you like to know if you are having a girl baby or a boy baby? Or do you and Daddy want a surprise?'

'I'd prefer a bouncing little miscarriage.'

It slipped out. The beatific smile you are meant to have at all times as a Pregnant Mother-to-be fell off and I don't want it. If I could claw it out and leave it in the hospital for some of those women who are spending all of their money on fertility treatments I would. I'd leave it covered in blood and womb lining and throw it at them and they would love it like I cannot.

The room became concerned and there were psychiatrists and referrals and depression questionnaires. It is wrong, apparently, for a woman to want anything else but to be a vessel. I've seen the scanning electron micrographs. Big lumpy spheres being swarmed with burrowing sperm, tails like mould, insistent nudging eel-heads. Things growing and splitting and eating into you, devouring your humanity in snatches. This little quickness inside of me is more of a human than I am, it's why I'm Mummy-to-be rather than my name. Mummy-to-be Partner's-Surname, actually. I say that I'm fine – I *can* see the funny side of things, it's black humour. I'm not anxious or worried for no good reason, I just want this little tumour out. Things have not been getting on top of me, but not for lack of trying on his part. When I get to question ten I just lie.

'Love.' My partner is here, pale and concerned. His hands mop my brow, cradle my belly, stroke my broken loose ligaments. He speaks to the thing inside me, already precious. 'This isn't right. Not right. You don't know what you are saying.' It's okay. He's read all about the things that can happen to women when they are gestating. It's probably hormonal, perfectly natural, best to change my diet, sleeping habits, exercise, everything for the baby.

We compromise; he will not let me exercise in case it harms it, but I am allowed a garden. He tells me the sunshine will do me good, Vitamin D, strong bones. He makes a little patch in the front lawn, digs it up, puts on fertiliser and mulch and lets me buy seeds from the internet. I grow tansy, wild celery, yarrow. I poke my fattened fingers down into the soil and tend to the growing shoots, watch them sprout golden and white heads, smell their aromatic scents. The wild garden angelica is sweet and fragrant, not yet old enough to flower. I grow minty-scented pudding grass, purple flowers clustering in small sprays, rub the leaves between my fingers and inhale. I plant marigold and chamomile and echinacea. I talk about how beautiful the house will be when I can pick posies and put them in vases in every room. My partner is pleased that I am thinking about the feminine touch. He sees this as progress.

I become obsessed with this body. My face has changed, it is a mask, dark patches spreading over my forehead and cheeks. My vulva and nipples are swollen and pigmented, I leak thick yellow colostrum into sweaty breast-pads stuffed inside my bra. They recommend hand-expressing it, freezing it for up to six months so it will have a ready supply, and the partner is excited, watching videos on how to massage the breasts down towards the nipple, find the ridge outside the areola, press down with the thumb and forefinger cupped into a C. I think he finds it erotic. I refuse to play and then he gets cross and says I don't care about our child, and I don't. It's not our *child* anyway, it's just a growth at the moment. A greedy, painful, ugly growth. I look hurt and say I think the first sip of mother's milk should be into our child's hungry mouth. He is ashamed and mollified.

By this point I am public property. Strangers will give me advice, touch me, ask about names and sex and tell me that they always swore by ginger or vitamin E or yoga or playing Mozart against their stomach, all for Baby. There are few things I can stand less than the use of Baby. It's *a* baby. It's as though they are hurrying you up to choose a name, so you can become Mummy and Daddy and the named thing as they so desperately want you to be. What would we do if everything was like this? This is Boss, and Underling and Underling. Daddy and Mummy and Baby. Eventually I stopped going out.

I won't let him near me. He stopped me feeling like a human in my own right, merely a seed-receptacle for his surname, so a clean womb I will be. I begin to dress in layers and layers of light fabric so that I become as sexless as I can be with these porn proportions. I shower five times a day to get rid of the sweat and scrub my skin raw with natural sugar exfoliators and massage coconut oil into my legs and arms and belly so that I am smooth. I demand a separate bed. When I cook for him I spit in his food, deliberately flinch from his touch. I enjoy watching him go from worry to anger to fear. I want him to hate me. I want him to hate it as I hate it, but he won't. He's got that glow of fatherhood already, he wants to teach something of his about the world. I am necessary for his plan, but I am ruining it.

So, I switch. Overnight I become sweetness. I take his hands and rest them on my belly, let him feel it kicking and turning. I let him kiss the dark line that runs from my navel to my pubic bone, I call it nothings like little one, and growing one, and our future child. I talk about paint colours for the nursery, spend hours poring over bright catalogues of stimulating toys and order colourful maternity dresses, and I watch my garden grow. He comes home smiling, can barely leave me in the mornings, brings home small presents for me, for me not the child. The doctors are happy, the nurses are happy. I beam at being called Mummy, cradle this little babe inside of me, so perfect, all ten tiny fingers and ten pink toes. I search for baby names, print out lists and circle choices in pink and blue. I leave my laptop open with a history of 'cute baby room ideas', 'encouraging nursery ideas', 'best pre-schools in our postcode'. I eat a balanced diet and stretch to Mummy Yoga every morning, a soothing American voice instructing each movement. I fill our freezer with sterilised bottles of my own milk, labelled by date and time of day. I cover the mantlepieces and cupboards with little vases of flowers from the garden, decorated with scraps of lace and ribbon.

That night he has his arms gently around me, one cupped under my neck, the other curled over my stomach and our child.

'Would you prefer a boy or girl?' I ask this sleepily, soft.

'Oh, I don't mind. I want one of each, a perfect little daughter and a big strong son.'

'No, but for the first one?'

He leans down and kisses the bump, and the baby takes this moment to stretch its legs and I say 'Oh, he's saying hello to his Daddy!'

His smile is contagious, 'You said his!'

'I can't know...'

'Women know. You've got my little son in there, don't you? Half of me, half of you, entirely himself.'

'I love you' I murmur into his neck, then put a pillow between my breasts before I sleep.

He goes to work the next day whistling.

I have time. He has left for the day, there is no antenatal appointment. I take some fresh flowers from the garden but worry that they will seem newly picked, so I refresh the vases with new blooms, and some extra. I hum as I harvest, murmuring to my little baby one inside all the time, *Hey, little thing, soon this will be all done. Are you ready for your Mummy?* A passer-by looks over the wall and smiles sugary at me and my bump. 'Not long now?' I shake my head, blow a kiss to my stomach. She clicks her teeth indulgently and wishes me well. I pluck the pudding grass, handfuls of it, I cannot be sure of the strength. I take chamomile and marigold and other plants alongside the purple flowers and put it into the glass teapot he got me for my tisanes and for my health. *It does smell like mint, after all.* I packed them in and they looked like a wellness post. With the right filter and the right lighting this could be *blessed, natural, birth-goddess.*

I filled two stewed cups and took them to the bedroom. I threw the dregs into next door neighbour's hedge, then added some more herbs to the pot. I drank the first cup over the bath, expecting to feel cramp or relief or pain, or at least something. The second I drank in bed, took a couple of paracetamol, and tried to fall asleep. In my tiredness I remembered to get the mother-and-baby book and open it to 'Bonding with your new family'.

There is a white room, and someone is telling me to breathe. This pain is inhuman. There is another woman in the bed next to me and she is breathing hard behind the curtain, but I can see her feet, swollen and red. I beg for mercy, for drugs, for the pain to stop. I ask them to cut me open, get it out. It has already broken me physically, it is not fair that it should do it again – I try to reach down and pull it out, but my wrists are bound and my ankles too, up in straps so I am wide open. When they tell me to push shit leaks out of my body, and the only consolation against the embarrassment is that this thing will begin its life headfirst in my excrement, but the nurses wipe it away as though it is nothing.

After several hours they lie a little screaming red body covered in vernix against my breast, for the *power hour*, so it will still be awake. It has perfect little fingers and little perfect toes, a small yowling open mouth reaching for me, trying to find my breast. My partner is entranced, but the nurses bat him away, they say it – he – needs to find his mummy's milk. I hold the little man in my arms, cupping his hairless head and chubby thighs, pull him up to my breast, feel his fat arms. His tiny squashed face is flushed and shocked, his eyes are huge and curious. I look down at him, so innocent and helpless, and I roll it off my stomach and turn to face the wall.

Inquiline
Sylvia Warren

The flat is her integument. Ms Emery can close the door and draw history around her, empty of dead secretaries and old acquaintances. The hallway gives way to memory. She had always hated the coat rack in her old house, yet even now she walks on the left to avoid something that isn't there. Their coats smelled of musty waxed cotton and would steep the downstairs with damp. Her flat has fitted carpets and smells of air freshener. More than one friend told her that she shouldn't take a place on the third floor, but she doesn't have to vacuum the communal stairs. The clock ticks, and her calendar is marked off for Scrabble and doctors' appointments and the detritus that fills a lonely life.

She tries not to think of herself as old. She can feel her skin, papery soft, hanging off wrists and elbows. How much she tried to keep herself thin, how thinness was predicated on tautness. She does not allow herself to potter, instead filling her days with activities. The smell of formic acid on a swimsuit drying in its place in the bathroom; facsimile of the working life. The knock on the door that she was not expecting.

The girl looked like she could be a granddaughter, eyes of a man, one thumb hooked in the belt hook of jean shorts, an oversized jumper – her own lips. Her lips but fifty years ago ask for a twist of salt, except she doesn't ask for that, she asks for a pinch. The woman invites her in, aware of the slowness of her own footsteps, the light bounce-jig of the girl as though she were moving to inoculate herself against age. 'Hi, yes, hi, thank you for this, just moved in, clean forgot to buy salt, everyone always has salt, don't they? You don't think about it, I don't think I've ever realised I buy it, you know? Name's Tamsin, by the way, rude of me. Thanks so much again Mrs…?' Her voice is bright but metallic. It is not a conversation as much as a monologue, every sentence ending with a questioning exclamation mark. 'Thanks for the salt Ms Emery, really appreciate it, life-saver.'

'Life-saver' rattles around her head as she plumps the cushions on the sofa. These dramatics are so pointless, she is sure she was never like that. Back at this girl's age she was being studiously detached, probably about the time she was first courting. She was revealed as barren. It caused arguments in her family, but she cradled the term with a perverse pleasure. It felt clean and empty, fresh parchment starched linen. Antiseptic. She was happy with her work, putting on her face every morning and joining every other woman to type and organise and fuel the hum of something bigger than herself. Her mother seemed to have been kept as a mother, queen of her own house but solely valued by the squirming babies she had pumped out.

She is cleaning a stubborn stain in the bathroom when the door knocks again. Skirt tucked into her knickers, hair already falling from the steam, it is something to ignore. She'll take the scraps that her age affords her, selective deafness masking outright contempt. The second knock annoys her further. The discolouration is somehow under the vinyl, her scrubbing has created a pouch of air that feels organic under her marigolds, she recoils automatically. Cool air rushes in when she opens the window, reflected in the fogged mirror she looks almost young again. In the hallway there is a note stuck under the door. *Thanks for your help last week! Tx* and she throws the paper into the bin.

She vowed never to use a shopping trolley. The plastic weave in unlikely tartans, the proximity to admitting she could use the extra balance. Better to shop frequently and lightly than bow down under the weight of what she felt she should look like, so it only took her until the following morning to find a cardboard container of salt on her doorstep, cleanly white and green and expensive. She thinks she can hear the sound of a door being pulled shut across the hall – she's done it often enough to know what it sounds like. Flat of the palm flush against the wood next to the handle, muffling the lock mechanism. It just sounds like a door being shut with the intent of silence, no matter what people think. There was no visible movement. Ms Emery walks to the supermarket with its clean bright lights, picked up cans of peas and a frozen quiche. One of the tills is being served by Tamsin. She files the salt under an employee discount, not really a gift at all.

Back in the flat she loads an exercise video. She still uses cassettes. She doesn't like the music, never did, but some taught American with overly white teeth and a bottle-tan instructs her to lift her arms horizontally and rotate with light weights. Unpacking the difference between vanity and health bores her. Her evenings used to be filled with roasting potatoes in goose fat, grease-slick and blood on the meat, carrot scraps winding around her fingers. So much easier with cardboard packaging and a pre-heated oven. She is proud of her still-slender waist. Next to the bin another part of the paint has started to peel as though it has been growing into something below the surface.

Tamsin has not settled into her new place. She can hear the sounds of her neighbours, to the side, above and below, feels hemmed in. She bounces between the rooms, too nervous to put on music loudly. She has already picked up and put down a magazine three times, scrolled through every channel she can find. There is discomfort in her lack of knowledge of what is socially acceptable within the block. In her head she is in a colony, everyone else settled into their roles and routines, her own body out of place, twitching and inquiline. The notice of bin days is pinned to her fridge, alongside the flyers from takeaways that formed the bulk of her welcome letters. Tomorrow morning, so she heaves her bag of rubbish down the stairs to the communal waste. It is foetid, sharp corners rupturing some of their containers, spilling scraps into the waste water. Flies rise like an aerosol. Tamsin breathes shallowly. As she locks her front door behind her, she pulls a scrap of paper off her shoe. The ink has blurred beyond legibility, but she recognises *Tx*.

Ms Emery finds herself bothered by the salt's presence in her kitchen. Where she has touched the cardboard she can smell both herself and the other girl, her hands greasy as though they have been touching. She sees the girl's hands picking up groceries that have been touched by others, oil upon layers of oil, someone licking a stack of cash to peel off the balance, back onto the gift that is not a gift. The girl has introduced a nest into her house, all around this box. Tongues and fingers and nails scraping; it is tainted but immovable as though the object is too heavy for her to lift on her own.

The heat hits the block like a wave. People open their windows, draw curtains, put bowls of ice in front of cheap plug-in fans. The air is heavy with moisture. Tamsin feels her shoulder-blades itch at night, slathers on creams and pastes. Ms Emery swelters in the dark, sleeps badly and wakes up to perfectly starched sheets drenched in sweat. Even pleasant neighbours shout obscenities. The refuse collection point becomes a point of contention; no-one wants to see what seething mass it has become. Maggots grow in the dark, fry on the tarmac during the day. Tamsin trips over the corner of a rug where it has been lifted by the floor warping. Days slip in and out of each other and everyone waits for the rain to break.

Ms Emery is showering when she puts her hand through the bathroom wall. The vinyl that had bubbled gave way to empty space, twisting into something dark and deep and pulsing. She is desperately aware of her nakedness, her proximity to decay, the warmth of the water on her skin cold compared to the heat of the hole that has opened up. After drying and talcuming herself to comfort, dressing and applying the face she uses to feel like a competent member of society she calls the plumber who lives on the eighth floor. She feels the muscles just above her eyebrows spasm slightly. She cannot stop touching her elbows. The plumber mutters something about sealant. He moves quickly through Ms Emery's bathroom, hands feeling up the walls and probing into the hole. It is smaller now, barely big enough to accommodate his fingers. She wants to tell him it has changed, her whole arm fell through there, she could feel a space that widened, but the words don't come. He fills it with white paste from a tube, tells her not to get the area wet for two days. She wants to ask him to help her move the salt from the counter, as though his gloves and strength and presence will cleanse her kitchen and the flat will be whole again. She is silent and embarrassed.

Men start to knock on Tamsin's door. She attempts to brush them off kindly, but soon her rubbish is being taken away, her flat fixed up with the odd part here and improvement there. Then the women come too; she cannot remember opening the door to let them in. Her bed is made, the space under the kitchen counter pulses in shades of fresh paint. She has dreams of the women and men breaking in through her kitchen sink, through her walls, ordered as an invading army. She tries not sleeping, forcing her eyes open, hearing people move in their apartments above and below and around her. She wakes up with flecks of plaster under her nails. Outside, the concrete continues to soak up the sun and the building feels like it is expanding. When Tamsin returns from her shifts she thinks that there are more stairs to get back to her rooms, more floors squeezed into spaces that cannot logically exist.

A week later the first fat drops of water begin to fall. Tamsin is in bed clutching at her stomach, listening to the sounds of the block settling and moving. Windows are being thrown open to smell the washed air, somewhere someone is laughing. In Ms Emery's apartment four neighbours come around to see whether they can save her going out in the downpour, and after they have left she notices that the salt package has disappeared. From her window she sees them carrying it together, each using a hand to support the corners. The flakes spill out of the wet cardboard and start to dissolve, and Ms Emery sleeps soundly again.

That night Tamsin uses her hands to dig into the floorboards. The concrete and plaster seem soft like plasticine, and soon she has a chamber all to herself. She pulls the rug over the entrance and curls herself into the building. On waking she pulls the dry skin from her itching shoulders and eats it. She feels nourished and safe. The men start infiltrating her lair immediately, their heads elongating as she begins to disgorge eggs, translucent as uncooked rice. She runs through the tunnels under the walls, trying to reconcile her limbs with the six she thinks she has, and comes up against a plug of sealant. Ms Emery listens to the scrabbling in her bathroom and turns on the shower. Her flat is her integument.

Contributors

Guest Author

Wendy Erskine

Wendy Erskine's two short story collections, *Sweet Home* and *Dance Move* (Stinging Fly/Picador) were variously listed for The Edge Hill Prize, the Gordon Burn Prize and the Republic of Consciousness Prize. Stories from the collections were listed for The Sunday Times Audible Short Story Prize and the Irish Book Awards short story of the year. Sweet Home won the Butler Literary Prize. Dance Move was Book at Bedtime on BBC Radio 4. She edited *well I just kind of like it*, an anthology about art in the home and the home as art, for PVA Books. Other fiction and non-fiction has been published by Rough Trade Books, the Tangerine Press, Ration Books, Daunt Books, Faber, the Guardian and the Quietus, among others. In 2022, she was Seamus Heaney Fellow at Queen's University, Belfast and in 2023 was elected as a Fellow of the Royal Society of Literature. A frequent interviewer and broadcaster, she hosted a show on Soho Radio for Rough Trade Books until 2024. She is a head of department in a secondary school in Belfast. Her debut novel *The Benefactors* was published in June 2025.

Primary Authors

B.B. Fitton

B.B. Fitton is a caffeine fiend living in London. She has had fiction published by Litro and Open Pen and creative non-fiction published by New Statesman. Her writing has also appeared in The Big Issue magazine and she's been published by the Royal Society of the Arts. She studied English Literature and German at University College London and Freie Universitat, Berlin. She loves Camus and hates word counts. If she could live in a house built of Kafka novels, she would.

Jacob Parker

Jacob Parker lives in London and teaches in a sixth form college. His work has appeared in Open Pen, The London Magazine, Hobart, Structo, MIR Online, and others.

Josephine Bruni

After an education in Classics, I worked as a jester in Italy, writing imitation medieval poems and songs for a group of actors and musicians. Later I become an actress-puppeteer, writing scripts for award-winning shows. When I was forced into exile from Italy, for my political convictions during the Berlusconi years, I reached London with my two children who are now well settled. I work in a large church in the heart of Camden Town where I help people with serious addictions.

The novel I'm working on, *Saint Joan's Sword* recently won the HW. Fisher Scholarship with Curits Brown Creative.

Olivia Dunnett

Olivia Dunnett was born in London and completed her undergraduate degree in Philosophy at King's College. She went onto study creative and life writing at Goldsmiths University and was shortlisted for the Pat Kavanagh prize. She now lives in Bow and works as a features writer for a range of womens' magazines.

Ian M Macdonald

Based in North London, for the past nine years Ian M Macdonald has made a living (of sorts) working for the National Health Service. His stories – short works that are pre-occupied with the sick and the rude – have been published in Ambit Magazine and DASH Journal, and on websites such as Fictive Dream and STORGY. His morally dubious novella, Things We Get Away With, is available at a very reasonable price as an e-book.

Rob True

Rob True was born in 1971. Unable to read or write very well, he left school with no qualifications. His wife taught him how to use paragraphs and punctuation aged forty and he began writing stories. He's had stories published in various magazines, including Open Pen and Litro Magazine. His first book, Gospel of Aberration was published by Burning House Press. His second book, In the Shadow of the Phosphorous Dawn, was published by Influx Press.

Fernando Sdrigotti

Fernando Sdrigotti is an Argentine writer and cultural critic. He is the author of several books, including Shitstorm (Open Pen, 2018), Jolts (Influx Press, 2020), and We Are But Nothing (Rough Trade Books, 2023). He lives in London.

Ben Stone

Ben Stone studied art with Saburo Muraoka and Marina Abramovic and creative writing with Rohan Wilson. He exhibited with Chiharu Shiota in Japan and Germany and they nearly died one night lost on Korea's Mount Seoraksan. Ben's novels include *Sex and Death in Sigatoka*, *Natives*, *Monsters are Real*, and the forthcoming *Killer Keys* and *Little Big Dirty*. His new novel *Meat inc.* is due for release in 2025.

Bonny Brooks

Bonny Brooks' novelette Good Choices was published with Open Pen to acclaim from literary heavyweights like Lily Dunn, Andy West and Ray Robinson. Her fiction has won Arts and Humanities Research Council Awards and been shortlisted for prizes like Fish. She has appeared on the BBC World Service and her poetry has been broadcast on BBC Radio 4. Her journalism has appeared in The Independent, The Huffington Post and others. She was an IPS Research Fellow at the Library of Congress and her work has been published in Japanese.

Krystian Morgan

Krystian Morgan's fiction leans towards the dark and sardonic, but he's a fairly amiable fellow in real life. When not writing, he can be either found playing the guitar or fussing in the kitchen. He lives in a small cottage in Wales and is working on his first novel. www.krystianmorgan.com

James Hatton

James Hatton's short stories have been widely published and shortlisted for competitions. Since becoming a parent, he's been writing less but telling more stories, and he's excited about writing them down when he has time.

Louisa Adjoa Parker

Louisa Adjoa Parker is a writer and poet of English-Ghanaian heritage who lives in south west England. Her first poetry collections were published by Cinnamon Press, and her third, *How to Wear a Skin*, was published by Indigo Dreams. Her debut short story collection, Stay with me, was published in 2020 by Colenso Books. Her poetry pamphlet, *She Can Still Sing*, was published by Flipped Eye in June 2021, and she has a coastal memoir forthcoming with Little Toller Books.

Louisa's poetry and prose has been widely published. She has been highly commended by the Forward Prize; twice shortlisted by the Bridport Prize; and her grief poem, Kindness, was commended by the National Poetry Competition 2019. She has performed her work in the south west and beyond and has run many writing workshops.

Louisa has written extensively about ethnically diverse history and rural racism, and as well as writing, works as an Equality, Diversity and Inclusion consultant. She is a sought-after speaker and trainer on rural racism, black history, and mental health.

Sylvia Warren

Sylvia Warren is a writer and academic editor. Their fiction has been published in the Brick Lane Bookshop Short Story Anthology, Minor Literature[s], and Rituals & Declarations amongst others.

Microfiction Authors

Esther Cann

Esther lives in Suffolk and works in the charity sector on human rights and community projects. Her work has been published by Litro Online, MIR Online, Emerge Literary Journal and Open Pen. Her stories were also shortlisted for the Anton Chekhov Prize for Very Short Fiction, twice shortlisted for the Bridport Prize, and longlisted for the Mslexia Short Story Competition and Yeovil Literary Prize ('writing without restrictions'). She likes following wherever a project beckons, from mineralogy, geology and sound envelopes to spending time in hospital waiting rooms while perfectly healthy. Her work has received support from Arts Council England and Jerwood Arts.

Mileva Anastasiadou

Mileva Anastasiadou is a neurologist, from Athens, Greece and the author of 'We Fade With Time' by Alien Buddha Press. A Pushcart, Best of the Net, Best Microfiction and Best Small Fictions nominated writer, her work has been selected for the Best Microfiction anthology 2024 and Wigleaf Top 50 and can be found in many journals, such as the Chestnut Review, New World Writing, HAD, trampset, and others.

Katharine Orton

Katharine Orton is a children's author – her books include Nevertell, Glassheart and Mountainfell, which were published by Walker UK. Open Pen was one of the first magazines to ever print her writing. She lives in Bristol with her family and two feral cats.

Katie Harrison

From the metaverse to mugwort, Katie is a writer as at home in contemporary culture as she is digging in the mud. Her short stories have appeared in Open Pen, Byways, Shooter, and The Selkie. The houseplant book she ghostwrote even beat Alan Titchmarsh on Amazon. She lectures in Narrative & Voice at Central Saint Martins and was awarded the British Council's Nature Writing Scholarship. You can find her on Instagram @ katiesreadingroom or splashing in the Scottish sea.

Anita Goveas

Anita Goveas is British-Asian, based in London, and fueled by strong coffee and paneer jalfrezi. She was first published in the 2016 London Short Story Prize anthology, most recently in Flashback Fiction, Mojave Heart review, The Brown Orient, formercactus and Spelk. She tweets erratically @coffeeandpaneer.

Izzy Arcoleo

Isabelle Arcoleo is a copywriter (and writer-of-other-things) who recently moved from London to the French Midi-Pyrénées, where she spends a lot of time trying not to adopt more stray cats. Her short fiction has been published by Popshot Magazine and she's currently working on a novel, while seeking agent representation.

Holly Watson

Born and raised in Coventry, Holly's writing captures the essence of the people and places she encountered growing up in the city's suburbs. Now living in the North East of England, Holly balances writing with her role as a full-time carer for her daughter.

Her debut novelette, 'Never Seen The Sea,' is available in all good bookshops, and you can say Hello on X @coventryconch.

Geoffrey Heppenstall

Geoffrey Heptonstall's fourth collection of poetry, A Whispering, was published by Cyberwit June 2023. His first collection, The Rites of Paradise, received critical acclaim when first published in 2020. Sappho's Moon and The Wicken Bird followed. A novel, Heaven's Invention, was published by Black Wolf in 2016. The Queen of Alsatia, a novella, was published in Pennsylvania Literary Journal in 2023. A number of plays and monologues have been staged, broadcast and/or published. He is also a prolific short fiction writer, essayist and reviewer.

Alice Wooledge Salmon

Alice Wooledge Salmon is New York-born and long at home in London. Her essays and short stories have been published by PN Review, The Guardian, Stand, Tears in the Fence, The Frogmore Papers, Pen Pusher, Open Pen, In Vino Veritas from the Académie du Vin Library, and elsewhere.

Gerard Mckeown

Gerard McKeown has been shortlisted for The Bridport Prize and The Willesden Herald Award, and longlisted for The Irish Book Awards' Short Story of the Year and the BBC National Short Story Award. His work has been featured in a number of journals and anthologies, most recently Best Horror of the Year Volume 14 (edited by Ellen Datlow), and broadcast on BBC Radio 4.

Mazin Saleem

Mazin Saleem is the author of The Prick (Open Pen 2019) and The Pricklet (Open Pen 2020); his short fiction has been published at 3AM Magazine, The Mechanics Institute Review, The Mays and more; and he writes regularly on literature, films and art for

The Tribune, Strange Horizons and on his Substack, Artless, at https://mazinsaleem.substack.com.

Leo X Robertson

Leo X. Robertson is a Scottish writer and filmmaker, currently living in Stavanger, Norway. His stories have appeared in Best of British Science Fiction and Year's Best Hardcore Horror, among others. His films have premiered at festivals like Horrific Hope and Dead Northern, winning awards such as 'Best LGBTQ Film' and 'Best International Film.' Find him on Instagram @leoxrobertson or check out his website: leoxrobertson.wordpress.com.

Morgan Omotoye

Morgan wrote this bio while listening to the Inherent Vice soundtrack, not because he is a pretentious wank, rather he wants it understood, for posterity, his musical tastes are far superior to yours. Even though writing in the third person is a 'bump' and a 'gateway to Hell' according to Morgan's Dad, Morgan would still like you, the simple folk, to know his work has been published in the following august publications : Staple New Writing, Litro, Open Pen, The London Magazine. His essays on short stories (why they exist and why we should care about their existence) have been published in Thresholds. Morgan was shortlisted for The Threshold The International Short Story Features Competiton and has been dining out on this honour ever since. He interviewed Malachi McIntosh (gasp) for The Bookseller (double gasp). His Novelette, the genre busting, sexy as all get out, funny and incredibly moving and did I forget to say 'sexy,' Here is Where is published by the fine folks at Open Pen.

Having finished writing his bio for The Open Pen Anthology,

our illustrious, dashing writer-hero, wiped the sweat from his brow, stared vacantly into space, then put a full-stop to this sentence. Thought better of it, started a whole new sentence then remembered he had to get ready for work, but only after one more listen to 'Spooks,' track 5 on the Inherent Vice soundtrack. Tuuuuuune!